THE IMPORTANCE OF BEING AWKWARD

The Autobiography of Tam Dalyell

THE IMPORTANCE OF BEING AWKWARD

The Autobiography of Tam Dalyell

Tam Dalyell

BIRLINN

First published in 2011 by
Birlinn Limited
West Newington House
10 Newington Road
Edinburgh
EH9 1QS

www.birlinn.co.uk

ISBN: 978 1 84158 993 0
eBook ISBN: 978 0 85790 075 3

British Library Cataloguing-in-Publication Data
A catalogue record for this book is available from the British Library

Typeset by Iolaire Typesetting, Newtonmore
Printed and bound by MPG Books Limited

To the men and women of West Lothian – Labour, SNP, Conservative, Liberal, Communist – who, whatever their political opinions, were kind to me in all sorts of ways over 43 years as their representative in the House of Commons

Contents

List of Illustrations

Thomas Dalyell (1570–1642)

Tam Dalyell (1615–85)

Magdalene Dalyell, 'Lady of Binns' (1672–1732)

Sir John Graham Dalyell (1775–1851)

Aged two, being inspected by Colonel Piggott-Moody of the Royal Scots Greys

Aged four, pretending to make the porridge

Aged five with the Sheikh, head of the Khalifa family of Bahrain

With my mother and father on 1 September 1939

With Willie Martin of West Lothian County Roads department during the tarmaccing of The Binns drive in 1939

The ceremony at which the Binns was gifted to the National Trust for Scotland, April 1945

Fishing for sea-trout on Lower Kildonan Loch, Lochboisdale, August 1945

With friends from Tom Brocklebank's Eton House

As a member of a Centurion tank crew, in B.A.O.R.

With Bo'ness Academy Under-15 Squad, winner of the Scottish School Cup 1960

School camp at Aberfoyle, 1957

With pupils on the ship-school *Dunera*, preparing for a shore visit

Canvassing on my bike for the General Election of 1959

With Mrs Bessie Braddock, the redoubtable Liverpool MP, at the road sign which marks the entrance to Linlithgow

Acknowledgements

In 2006, West Lothian Council won the coveted title of UK Council of the Year. I was not in the least surprised; over four decades I wrote countless letters on behalf of constituents to their highly professional and ever helpful officials. I record my gratitude here to generations of Local Government officers.

For my first six weeks as an MP, I was under the impression I had to raise any problem a constituent brought to me with the relevant Junior Minister. Then the penny dropped. The Minister's office sought advice from their local office manager. Between July 1962 and March 2005 I went direct to office managers countless times, and I would like to thank them all for their unfailing co-operation and candour.

Without the care of the Richmond medical practice in Bo'ness, and the medical expertise of the staff of St John's Hospital, Livingston and the Royal Infirmary of Edinburgh, my wife, Kathleen, would not have been here to make her crucial contribution to the book, and I, at the age of 78, would not have had the energy to put pen to paper. I would like to express my gratitude to them all.

I would also like to thank friends and mentors, too innumerable to name, who, over a long public life, have educated and supported me. And, indeed, I owe thanks also to my enemies – also too numerous to mention by name – who have taught me much that I needed to learn.

The gift of our home, the House of the Binns, its collections and parkland, under the Country Scheme in 1944 could easily have caused friction between the National Trust for Scotland and the family. I would like to thank successive generations of those committed to the vision of the Trust within the organisation, who have worked in partnership with us, successfully, over two-thirds of a century, for their friendship and their tolerance of a controversial issues-politician, and all those who have worked and supported the family at The Binns.

Hugh Andrew, proprietor of Birlinn Ltd, conceived the book and its title. Andrew Simmons, also of Birlinn, guided the book through the editorial process and was a delight to work with. David Torrance, author of *The Scottish Secretaries* and biographer of Alex Salmond, made countless invaluable editorial suggestions. Patricia Marshall copy-edited the book with meticulous attention to detail. Kenny Redpath and Jan Rutherford of Birlinn performed vital duties. I would like to thank them all.

I would also like to thank my son, Gordon, and his wife, Dr Pamela Leslie, and our daughter, Moira, and husband, Ian Shearer, for their support in a myriad of different ways.

Finally, Kathleen knows more about the Dalyell family history than I do. As a member successively of the Historic Scotland Buildings Council, the Ancient Monuments Board, the Royal Fine Art Commission of Scotland and latterly as Chairman for five years of the Royal Commission on the Ancient and Historical Monuments of Scotland, she was uniquely placed to make a contribution of paramount importance – which she did. Not only did she type the whole script, but her skill as a worsdsmith secured many improvements. Quite simply, without her, *The Importance of Being Awkward* would never have seen the light of day.

TAM DALYELL
The House of the Binns
West Lothian
June 2011

Foreword

Even now, over six years since he left the House of Commons for the last time in April 2005 never to return, you have only to deploy one word – 'Tam' – within the walls of the Palace of Westminster and pretty well everyone knows instantly of whom you are speaking. He never held office, let alone sat in a Cabinet or led a political party, but Tam Dalyell is among a handful of individuals in post-war British parliamentary politics who possessed a tang and left a trace that is utterly distinctive. He is also greatly missed, and almost the first thought those who have their being at Westminster utter on hearing his name is that 'We'll never see the like of Tam again.'

We won't. Why? Partly because, as Tam admits inside these pages, the modern Labour Party would not let him anywhere near a loseable constituency, let alone a winnable seat. Even more to the point, the very special mix of compost that made Tam is no more. The rich ingredients of that ripest of composts are wonderfully displayed in this memoir. I didn't meet Tam until the mid 1970s, but I suspect that Napoleon's dictum – if you wish to understand a man or a woman think of the world as it was when they were 20 – applies powerfully to Tam (certainly by the time he became a schoolteacher in 1956 after Eton, National Service in Germany and King's College, Cambridge).

Tam is a highly intelligent man, but he has the quality of the natural autodidact – what Einstein called 'a holy curiosity'. He absorbed detail and possibility not just from the Grade A-listed minds who taught him at school and university but from nearly everyone and everything he encounters. And once on a case, he never lets go; a characteristic which inspires admiration and fury in abundance depending upon whether one is the beneficiary or the target. No small print in a government document is too tiny to see off the Dalyell curiosity – a gift he attributes to the training given him by one of his Cambridge mentors.

On occasion, he has been way ahead of the field. For example, the Butler Report into WMD and Iraq noted that 'During the 1990s, there were intermittent clues that A.Q. Khan was discussing the sale of nuclear technologies to countries of concern' coming the way of British Intelligence. Tam had been on the case since the last months of 1979, when the activities of Khan in the universities of Belgium and the Netherlands when he was still a research student, passed on to Tam by a scientific contact in the Low Countries, led him to warn in the House of Commons in December 1979 that this young man could turn out to be one of the most dangerous instruments of nuclear proliferation in history. So it proved; a remarkable piece of horizon-scanning by any standards.

A contemporary historian of British politics and government cannot have too many memoirs published – yet sometimes the cornucopia of near instant diaries and apologia becomes wearing, especially from those who are propelled by a belief that the world needed them when in office, and, even worse, that it still does once they've left. *The Importance of Being Awkward* is different. It's the record of a warm spirit, a quirky temperament and a great tenacity who was never in power but applied himself to the indispensable business of watching the mighty in their seats. The pages are the man. I'm so pleased he has put himself on paper. If he hadn't, it would have been impossible to explain Tam to generations to come.

LORD HENNESSY OF NYMPSFIELD, FBA
Attlee Professor of Contemporary British History
Queen Mary, University of London

CHAPTER ONE

Antecedents

MY MOTHER AND, to a lesser extent, my father were what the American sociologist David Riesman termed 'ancestor-directed persons'. And, as an only child of an only child, whose nearest relation was an American Senator from Missouri destined to become President of the United States, I cannot be but shaped by ancestors. They were present – they looked down at me from the walls of rooms in daily use and their portraits depicted serious people who had expectations of me. I suppose I was 'driven' by ancestors to be useful and not to let them down.

Perhaps the most prominent and too often portrayed as one of the villains of the turbulent history of Scotland was General Tam Dalyell (?1615–85). He was called many names, among the least unflattering were 'Black Tam' and, as Sir Walter Scott had him, 'The Bluidy Muscovite'. Although not exactly my role model, I admire him. This Dalyell was one of the few escapees from the Tower of London. He rose to command of the Tsar's armies at Smolensk. He resigned from the position of commander-in-chief of Charles II's forces in Scotland on a matter of principle – that his guarantee of mercy to women and children following the Covenanters, after the skirmish at Rullion Green in 1666, had been overruled by Lord Lauderdale, the political head in Scotland, and these unfortunates had been put to the sword.

Tam Dalyell's teenage education included participation in the Duke of Buckingham's abortive expedition to La Rochelle in the late 1620s. To reinforce his education and growing-up experience, his father sent him on a Grand Tour of Europe. He turned out to be no ruffian but cultured and with a knowledge of plants and horticulture. In the early 1630s, he became one of the 'blue-eyed boy ensigns' of Sir Thomas Wentworth, the Earl of Strafford, Charles I's powerful and competent Lord Lieutenant of Ireland, who was later sacrificed by his royal master and sent to the scaffold.

Back in the seventeenth century, his father, the aging Thomas and his wife, Janet, staying at the nearby Mannerstoun farmhouse, acted as their own clerk of works in the building of the House on Binns Hill that was later to take the name House of The Binns, incorporating sections of an early medieval tower house, in which Kathleen and I now live, and which was gifted to the National Trust for Scotland in 1944. By 1621, it was complete enough for Thomas and Janet to move in.

But the decade of the 1630s was not an easy one. They remained close to the House of Stuart and, in 1633, Charles I, on his visit to Scotland, was due to spend a night with them. A King's Room was prepared with intricate plaster ceilings depicting the Nine Worthies along with the emblems of the countries ruled over by the Stuarts – the thistle for Scotland; the rose for England; the harp for Ireland; and, because the Stuarts still styled themselves the Kings of France, the fleur-de-lis.

That Charles did not actually arrive at The Binns was due to the fact that his treasure ship was lost in a storm in the Forth on its way from Burntisland to Blackness. And he surmised that there was a likelihood of foul play if his death was rumoured in London. He made a six-day dash back to Greenwich to ensure that his Queen and young family were all right. But the Dalyells were increasingly dismayed by the rifts between monarch and people. Shortly after he returned from Ireland, Tam and his father signed the National Covenant of 1638, which was implicitly critical of Charles. But then, in 1639, came the Battle of Edgehill. It was make up your mind time. The Dalyells opted for the Royalist cause. In 1642, Thomas joined his beloved Janet, who had died in 1637.

We do not know the details of where young Tam was involved in the early years of the Civil War – probably he was at Naseby in 1645. 'After,' as my mother would put it to the raised eye-browed

visitors at The Binns, 'the King was murdered in 1649, Tam
Dalyell participated in the Battle of Worcester in 1651.' On the
occasion of the 350th anniversary of the battle, I was asked by the
Lord Mayor of Worcester to unveil the plaque to the Scots who
fell. We were given new information – namely that Tam Dalyell
had fought bravely, allowing the King to escape and hide up an
oak tree. We are inclined to think there is substance in this oral
history which would account for the warm nature of the letter
dated 30 December 1654 to Dalyell from the King, Charles II,
which we reproduce:

> Tom [sic] Dalyell, Though I need say nothing to you by this honest-
> bearer Cap. Mewes who can well tell you, all that I would have
> sayed, yett I am willing to give it you yonder by my owne hand, that
> I am very much pleased to heare how constant you are in your
> affection to me, and in your endeavors to advance my service: we
> have all a harde worke to do, yett I doubt not, god will carry us
> through it, and you can never doubt that I will forgett the good part
> you have acted, which trust me shall be well rewarded whenever it
> shall be in the power of,
>
> Your affectionate friend
> Charles R

Dalyell was captured. In 1962, on my second day in the House
of Commons, a huge colleague came and slapped me on the
shoulder: 'Mr Dalyell, I know all about you. Your ancestor was
captured and sent to Dudley Castle!' It was my first encounter with
the extraordinary George Wigg, the MP for Dudley and organiser-
in-chief of Harold Wilson's leadership campaign. Triggerer of
the Profumo Affair, he was sent off, in 1967, to be chairman of the
Horserace Betting Levy Board. Wigg was right. Dudley Castle
was, at that time, the biggest fortress in the Midlands. Tam Dalyell
was then transferred to the Tower of London.

In 1969, Bob Mellish, the government's Chief Whip and
dockers' MP for Bermondsey, which covered the Tower, arranged for some of his friends to go to dinner and take an evening

tour of the Tower. At one point, I slunk behind and said to our host, Lieutenant Colonel Sir Victor Turner, VC, 'I had an ancestor who escaped from here.' 'Mr Dalyell,' he said, 'when I saw your name on Mr Mellish's list, I anticipated that you might ask about your ancestor.' The lieutenant colonel governor then went to his desk, where a thin volume was flagged open with a piece of paper. He read out, 'Dalyell, Tam, 1652' and then, with something as near to a sneer as such an honourable and distinguished man could produce, looking down his pince-nez, added, 'Not one of our maximum security prisoners.'!

From the Tower, he landed up in Cologne, where Charles II was holding court in exile. The King gave him letters of recommendation to John II Casimir, the King of Poland, to his commander-in-chief, John Sobieski, and to the Russian Tsar, Alexei Mikhailovich Romanov, father of Peter the Great. He opted for the Russians.

In 1956, at the Lenin Library in Moscow, I traced him as having commanded a unit at Kaliningrad, as it was then called, now reverted to its ancient name of Tver. In Moscow, they were very helpful and friendly. A week later, in Leningrad, they were deeply suspicious and the Hermitage Museum authorities simply wanted to know whether I had any relations still alive in the Soviet Union and whether I was seeking to claim my ancient lands. General Tam, as was customary at the time, was paid for his services in kind and this included whole villages with their surrounding lands and the serfs who lived and worked there.

But we owe far much more detailed information to the work of our Russian friend Dmitry Fedosov, Senior Research Fellow at the Institute of General History at the Russian Academy of Sciences in Moscow, a scholar who knows more than anyone about the Scots and Russian connections. Dalyell served the Tsar Alexei, who preferred mercenaries to his unreliable and often disloyal boyar subjects, and rose to be commander of the Tsar's army, based at Smolensk, an important strategic city with a kremlin even larger than that in Moscow. Smolensk was vital as the gateway to Moscow, particularly when the enemy was the Poles.

After the Restoration of 1660, six years of correspondence between Charles I, recently restored, and the Tsar resulted in Dalyell being allowed to return to Scotland with twelve wagon loads of treasure. Actually, he was fortunate to get to Riga and escape by ship as Moscow had had a change of mind and was pursuing him to keep him in the Tsar's service.

I ought to relate a final tale, laced with fact, in relation to General Tam. There was a family legend that he had been playing cards with the Devil. Dalyell won; the Devil lost. The Devil was so angry that he picked up the card table and hurled it at Tam's head; it missed Dalyell's ample balding dome and went into the pond that National Trust visitors to The Binns pass on the west side up to the house. Fact one – this legend existed. Fact two – in the dry summer of 1878 when the estate workers were draining the pond to maintain the puddling, they came across a heavy object that they could not shift so, sending for help from round about, they eventually pulled out a table of Carrara marble – of Florentine workmanship I have seen in the Medici chapel – and one obviously inlaid with silver, long since gone. The question is – how did such an object find its way into a pond in Scotland?

In the late 1930s, my parents, concerned that I or some other five-year-old would pull it over ourselves, asked the local joiner, James Turnbull of Bonhard, to put the table on sold kitchen-table legs, discarding the original rickety ones. With his Old Testament beard, Turnbull told them that this would be one of his last jobs – one of his first had been in 1878, as a laddie, helping to pull the same table out of the pond.

My preferred explanation is that the table was hidden in a panic in shallow water during turbulent times. Other stories concern the Devil threatening to blow down The Binns house and walls, to be met by Dalyell's response, 'I will pin down my house with a turret at every corner.' A more likely explanation for The Binns' turrets is that General Tam was familiar with the architecture of Novgorod, Pskov, Riga and Tallinn and fancied a Russian Kremlin look for his own house.

It is perhaps understandable that the history of the Dalyell family should be dominated by General Tam Dalyell but he overshadows many other members of the family who are all equally significant, not least the women. Outstanding among the latter is his granddaughter, Magdalene, eldest child of his son and heir, Captain Thomas, who became the 1st Baronet, and his wife and first cousin Katherine Drummond of Riccarton. Magdalene is important as the first female heir of tailzie (a term in Scots law designating in an arbitrary fashion the right of succession) and through her heirs, combined with her strong character, ensured the Dalyell line should continue as vigorously as it did through the generations to the present day.

Born in 1673 and baptized at Abercorn in the same year, she was married at 14 to a near neighbour, James Menteith of Auldcathie Younger, whose father was heir male and representative of the family of Menteith, Ancient Earls of Menteith. She bore him 12 children, six sons and six daughters, and seems to have spent the major part of her married life as Lady Auldcathie being a good and busy wife and mother. During these years, she appears twice in the family papers – briefly but importantly. In 1682, in the General's bond and disposition of 3 August where, at the age of nine, she is named by the General, her grandfather, as heir of tailzie, failing heirs to her brothers. The succession is clearly set out by General Tam Dalyell.

This bond and disposition of the old General explicitly designating his female heirs and their right of inheritance after his male heirs seems unusual for the time but may be for a very human reason. Captain Thomas, the General's eldest son and heir, had gone to Russia with him. On his return to Scotland, he married his first cousin, Katherine Drummond, and together they had six children, four of whom survived. Gradually, he took over the running of The Binns Estate but the General found him increasingly unsatisfactory. The catalyst seems to have been his second marriage, after the death of his first wife, to a widow with a family of her own. The bond and disposition therefore bypassed the son and settled The Binns Estate on the eight-year-old grandson, the apple of the General's eye, and detailed the line of succession thereafter, first through the male then the female children of his son's first marriage, thus securing the bloodline and his grandchildren's birthright.

It was unfortunate that the grandson, Thomas, the 2nd Baronet, should prove feeble minded and become increasingly unstable – so much so that, in 1704, the second mention of Magdalene in the family papers comes when she and her husband were empowered by the Privy Council to take personal custody of her brother and keep him confined at The Binns. He died in 1719 willing his title and estate to his favoured younger sister, Janet, who had married Thomas Shairp of Houston. Thereafter, Alexander Guthrie, brother-in-law to Magdalene and her legal agent, acted as factor of The Binns Estate, appointing a Baron Baillie and a Baron Officer.

In about 1720/21, Magdalene and her husband moved from Auldcathie to The Binns, selling their old estate to the Earl of Hopetoun. This enabled them to increase their financial provision to their younger children, setting them up with apprenticeships or, in the case of their second son, funds to take with him to a new life in America. By this time, Magdalene was known as Lady Dalyell and her husband referred to as James Dalyell, formerly Menteith. The legal processes took about three years before Magdalene was designated heir and legally established her right with the Privy Council against the challenge by her nephew, Janet's son, Thomas Shairp.

But, by 1722, her position was clear and she had established her place as female heir of Tailzie. The General's bond and disposition of 1682 had prevailed. In 1723, Magdalene's eldest son James married Dame Helen Campbell with the consent of both his parents, though his father was becoming increasingly frail. By 1725, he had taken on the running of the estate and was established as Sir James Menteith Dalyell, 3rd Baronet (the younger children all retained their father's name of Menteith). Thomas, the second son, went off to Virginia in the early 1720s to seek his fortune in America.

There, he was joined by his mother, Magdalene, following the death of her husband, along with some of her younger children. She would have been in her late fifties when she crossed the

Atlantic. Thomas did well as a merchant in Virginia and, in 1734, he married Phyllis Gallop. Their daughter, also Magdalene, married into the Doniphan family. Magdalene Doniphan's daughter Elizabeth married into the Shipp family and her daughter, Emma Shipp, married William Truman, whose great-great-great-grandson was Harry Truman, 34th President of the United States of America. Over the years, the family had travelled ever westwards from Virginia to Kentucky to Missouri.

There must be many Scottish families where the eldest son stayed at home to continue the family line in Scotland and his younger brothers, seeking fame and fortune abroad, created their own family history. The Dalyells repeated the American experience in Australia but that's a story to be told elsewhere in this saga. The family links remain to this day between the Dalyells in Scotland and the Trumans, Shipps and the extended family of Sheppards (one of whom is currently Chief Justice of Indiana) in America. In 2004, Kathleen and I – as the only known European relatives – were invited to (and attended) Independence, Missouri, for the 120th anniversary of President Harry Truman's birth.

*

Sir Robert Dalyell, 4th Baronet, was born on 2 August 1726 and had no doubt of his future role in life from his earliest years. He and his siblings, children of the 3rd Baronet, Sir James Monteith Dalyell, were brought up and tutored at The Binns. He joined the army and, in 1745, as an ensign in General Collier's Regiment of the Scots Dutch Brigade, was based at the headquarters of the Dutch army near Breda in Holland. Succeeding his father in 1748, he continued his life in the army until the demands of The Binns Estate made it imperative to return to Scotland.

In March 1768, his cousin Thomas Shairp of Houston proposed him as a prospective MP and, to this end, he spent some time in London. But nothing seems to have come of this. For whatever reason, Sir Robert remained a bachelor until he was 49, eventually marrying Elizabeth Graham of Gartmore. A young beauty, she was the daughter of Nichol Graham of Gartmore, who was from a wealthy and respected family in the West of Scotland who had made their money in cotton and pimento in the West Indies and were the forebears of the colourful socialist, R. G. Cunninghame Graham, 'Don Roberto'. If they weren't involved in the slave trade, they certainly benefitted from it.

While Sir Robert was a bachelor, The Binns had been leased out to a series of tenants, most notably to the Dowager Countess of Traquair, seeking a roof of her own once her son and daughter-in-law moved into Traquair. The correspondence between these two, tenant and landlord, was acerbic – mainly complaints from the Dowager about the state of The Binns and the need for Sir Robert to repair windows and doors, to deal with draughts, etc. Sir Robert did very little so, on his marriage, a great deal needed to be done to satisfy, if not impress, his young bride and her rather grand family.

His changes to The Binns – continued by his son, Sir James, 5th Baronet – mark an important development in the architecture of the house. Thomas Dalyell's original home on the western slope of Binns Hill had been devised as the centre of a working estate tailored to his needs. It stood three storeys high, facing north to the River Forth, the Ochils and the high hills beyond, and south across the Lothians to the Pentlands, each room the width of the building with windows facing each other to give both views of the surrounding landscape. Two wings, two storeys high, extended south from the main building to house the servants and create a courtyard entrance. In Sir Robert's renovations, the original entrance laigh hall and dining room were combined into a large laigh hall on the north side and a new larger dining room and a morning room with higher ceilings and windows were added on the south on the site of the original cobbled entrance courtyard. The old entrance from the courtyard on the south side was moved to the north where it has remained since.

On the south side, the new rooms, light and airy, led out on to an upper terrace leading to a lower terrace, from which a woodland walk gently ambled down to a newly created walled garden. The parkland round the house was designed with great thought being given to tree planting and the setting of features in the landscape, like the Tower on Binns Hill. The old drive from the main road running straight north to the house was replaced by drives east and west through a landscape designed so that glimpses of the mountains, rivers, parkland and trees could be revealed as sudden delights before the arrival at the house (this 'designed landscape' was one of the features which later prompted the National Trust to ask for The Binns as their first property under the Country House Scheme).

Dying in 1791 and leaving a young family, it was Robert's oldest son, Sir James, 5th Baronet, who continued his father's work, most notably removing the charming dormer windows on the north side (those on the south can still be glimpsed) to make way for the crenellations in the Gothic style that was so popular in the early nineteenth century. Sir Walter Scott – the arch creator of this craze with his romances and poems – was a friend of the Dalyells and stayed at The Binns. It is clear that, from the time of his marriage, perhaps significantly due to the influence of his wife, Robert became deeply involved in not only his own affairs but also those of the Linlithgowshire community.

*

John Graham Dalyell was the second son of the 4th Baronet, Sir Robert Dalyell, born on my own birthday, 9 August, but 157 years earlier in 1775. He was the scholar of the family possibly due to circumstances as much as inclination. He had fallen, as a child, off a marble table at The Binns on to a stone floor and, as a result, was crippled for life. His brothers went into the army or navy, while he studied at the Universities of St Andrews and Edinburgh and, in 1797, became a member of the Faculty of Advocates. His health restricted his practice – mainly consultation work that he conducted from home – and he made it a point of principle not to ask for a fee from a widow, a relative or an orphan.

His scholarly interests soon turned his attention to the manuscript treasures of the Advocates' Library and extended over a wide field. His first book, *Fragments of Scottish History*, appeared in 1798 when he was only 23. He followed this with papers and books on the many subjects that interested him, including translations of works on natural history, Scottish poetry in the sixteenth century, a tome entitled *The Devil in Scotland* and several books on Scottish music. As Professor Sir Maurice Yonge, Regius Professor of Zoology at the University of Glasgow 1944–64, commented in his perceptive monograph, 'There were few avenues into which he did not penetrate in search of ultimate antiquarian ramifications.'

Edinburgh, during his time, was enjoying a golden age – the Scottish Enlightenment – with great intellectual activity and interest centred round the life of the New Town, the legal establishment and the university. Reading Lord Cockburn's *Memoirs* gives a flavour of the life of these years. We have a description of the relationship between John Graham Dalyell and his publisher Constable, whose son commented that he was a man devoted to antiquarian pursuits, an admirable classical scholar and a distinguished naturalist. His character was strictly honourable and, in spite of an irritable temper, he was not an unlovable man.

John Graham Dalyell was also a friend of Sir Walter Scott, who stayed with him at The Binns, but it was the field of natural history that interested him most and in which he became a leading light. Like Charles Darwin, whom John Graham Dalyell tutored, he went out with the Newhaven fishermen to collect specimens. His most famous curiosity was a sea anemone found on the shores of the Forth at North Berwick in August 1828 and called 'Grannie' on account of the number of offspring she produced. Knighted for his services to science and literature in 1836, he succeeded his brother James as 6th Baronet in 1841 and died 10 years later at his home, 14 Great King Street, Edinburgh.

*

My memory of my maternal grandfather, Sir James Bruce Willkie Dalyell, is of a benign elderly gentleman sitting in an armchair by a fire in the morning room at the House of The Binns, while my grandmother gingerly stuck bread on to a toasting fork. I was sent down every afternoon at 4.30 p.m. – teatime – to be seen by them.

I played with bricks and was read fairy stories by each of them in turn, before being packed off to bathe, eat a poached egg supper and bed an hour later.

He slipped away in the cold winter of 1935 and my mother, who adored her father, held him to be something of a role model. From January 1881 until July 1885, he had boarded at the Eton House of Arthur Ainger, much depicted in spy cartoons as one of the legendary Eton 'beaks'. My grandfather was then at Trinity College, Cambridge, from 1885 to 1887. His tutor was the mathematician and theologian Richard Appleton. As occurred, not infrequently in those days, he was summoned back home to look after the family estate, after sudden death and crisis, before he completed his law degree. About his time in Cambridge we know little, other than that, according to my mother, he thought the Great Court of Trinity was the most pleasing set of buildings in the world. It was his memories that propelled my parents to encourage me to try for Cambridge. Eton made the judgement, perceptively and rightly, that I would fit in better to King's rather than Trinity.

In the spring of 1900, his local Territorial Army Regiment, the 3rd Battalion King's Own Scottish Borderers, was ordered to embark on the RMS *Kildonan Castle*, bound for South Africa and the Boer War. My mother told me that, given his responsibilities at Foulden in Berwickshire as a landowner, he could have been excused the draft. But the social pressures were such that, as an able-bodied man of 33, he felt that he had no option but to go. Those who refused were known to have received white feathers from the ever-so-martially-inclined ladies of the Scottish Borders. (Years later, during the Falklands War, I was to receive a flurry of such white feathers from all over the country.)

From his letters, it appears he thought it was a bit of an adventure sailing 'with a good cabin shared with an officer friend on the port side of a ship of 10,000 tons, carrying 2,700 men with 115 officers, and good food, served at meals'. However, when the glad news, given to them by a passing ship in the Bay of Biscay, that Kruger and Steyn, the Boer leaders, had surrendered, turned out to be unfounded and later getting a signal from another ship on its way home to Britain that Mafeking was still under siege and that Field Marshal Roberts was stuck in Bloemfontein, my grandfather's ardour for conflict, if indeed it was ever there, cooled. It cooled even more when, after enduring horrible conditions at Koeningsdorf, he was confined to hospital in Kimberley with gastric fever/dysentery and a temperature rising to 103 degrees Fahrenheit.

His dissatisfaction with the competence of the generals grew and grew. He was appalled by the consequences for the Zulus, as he called the native South Africans, and developed a respect for the Boer farmers – as a countryman himself, he empathized with their problems. The final straw was when a proposal came from the military leadership that the Boers and their families should be herded into ships at Cape Town and dumped in Buenos Aires, so that they could farm the pampas.

James Bruce Wilkie was principled and stubborn. On his return from the war, he instigated enquiries into the reasons for the war and its conduct. He instinctively used his Eton and Trinity friendships to alert people of influence in London about the often-shameful conduct of the South African Campaign. But, specifically, he went to see his family's social friends in the Border country around his home at Foulden – Arthur Balfour at Whittinghame; Edward Grey (my mother's godfather), Foreign Secretary, at Fallodon; C. F. G. Masterman, Fellow of Christ's College, Cambridge, Parliamentary Secretary to the Board of Trade and well-known Cabinet Minister; Walter Long, President of the Board of Agriculture 1895–1900 and President of the Local Government Board 1900–1905; and Walter Runciman, President of the Board of Education, who was living in Northumberland – to bestow upon them unvarnished, first-hand information and to suggest an inquiry into the war.

They proved to be far more amenable to examination in public than Tony Blair and Gordon Brown were a century later in relation to Iraq. The result was a complete re-orientation of British colonial policy. In 1914 at the age of 47, my grandfather felt it his duty to go with his Territorial Army Regiment, the 3rd Battalion King's Own Scottish Borderers, when they were posted to the Mediterranean. He ended up in Gallipoli and was lucky to escape with his life following that murderous campaign. My mother and grandmother never forgave Winston Churchill for initiating such a daft escapade, which resulted in the deaths of so many British soldiers and, of course, the Australians and New Zealanders who had come to help from the Empire.

After Gallipoli, he went to serve in Cairo as part of the British presence in Egypt but he never entirely recuperated from his World War One experiences. On his return, not in particularly good health, he devoted much of his life to working on the family papers. Every Sunday afternoon, he had the assistance of the scholarly Rector of Linlithgow Academy, James Beveridge, in going through the documents that had been accumulated in the house over a period of 600 years. Their work was published in The Binns' Papers and is invaluable. 'Bev', as my family affectionately knew him, was special in that he was one of few people then, and even fewer now, who could read the ancient Scottish scripts. This came home to us when we had Professor Geoffrey Barrow, Sir William Fraser Professor of Scottish History and Palaeography in the University of Edinburgh, 1979–1992, browsing among our archives and he read out from a document of 1320 in beautifully scripted Latin, as if from an article in *The Times*.

*

My mother, Eleanor, was born in 1895, the only child of James Bruce Wilkie, and Mary Marjoribanks Askew Robertson of Pallinsburn in Northumberland. In later life, she used to reflect that the tension in her parents' marriage – never fatal and separation was not contemplated – derived from the fact that both Grandpa and Grandma thought they had 'married beneath them'. Actually, I suspect that the harmony of the early years was injured by absence at war in South Africa, 1899–1902, and the Dardanelles, Egypt and Cyprus, 1915–1919.

One of my childhood memories is sitting on a chair, watching my mother rummaging through her mother's clothes some days after she died. She came across a solid rubber object, some four inches long, with a blown up bubble of solid rubber at one end.

'What's that?' I wanted to know. She blushed slightly – she was generally oblivious to embarrassment – 'I will tell you one day!' 'But why can't you tell me now, Mummy?' I demanded. 'All right then, it is an artificial boy's organ, so that my Mummy could meet her sexual needs when Grandpa was away at war.'

It would not have occurred to my grandmother, or many of her class or generation, that they could have looked for solace else-where. Apart from other considerations, if discovered, it would have been seen as disloyalty to a serving officer. My grandmother came from 'trade', her grandfather and great uncles having been among Mr Gladstone's henchmen. Her Prime Minister, 'the Prime Minister' about whom she would talk to me as I toddled along when she fed her chickens in the morning or went through the pantomime of getting them into the hen-house at night so that the fox would not devour them, was not Stanley Baldwin, then in 10 Downing Street; nor her acquaintance, the Helensburgh Scot, Andrew Bonar-Law; and certainly not David Lloyd George (the only good thing about him as far as she was concerned was that somehow his name had been given to her favourite variety of raspberry plant); not Sir Henry Campbell-Bannerman, a family friend; not Arthur Balfour, her erstwhile neighbour from the Berwickshire/East Lothian Border; but Mr Gladstone. Mr Disraeli was also on her mind, but he was a scoundrel.

Five years before I was born, Grandma, as was her wont, was holding a bonfire on an autumn afternoon. A spark went into her hair and set it alight. Thereafter, she wore lace over her head to hide the scars. She was a skilled lace-maker and excellent needle-woman, doing beautiful embroidery work that we still have around the house – a now long-forgotten pastime in Britain, apart from talented enthusiasts, but then a skill all young ladies cultivated to a greater or lesser degree.

Child rearing was not my grandmother's scene. The only concession she made to me was to read the Scottykins stories about a little bear, from one of her two daily papers, the Glasgow *Bulletin*, long since defunct but a popular paper in the 1930s. She had not a clue how to change a little boy's pants when he had an 'accident'. Nappies were unknown to her and, it has to be said, to my mother. When my hands-on practical mother-in-law, Nancy Wheatley, said to my mother, 'But, Nora, have you never changed a nappy?', she was not astonished when my mother replied, 'Well, Nancy, no.' It was strange since she could skin and gut a rabbit or pluck a chicken and remove its entrails in double-quick time.

My mother was brought up at the family home, Foulden in Berwickshire, by a series of nannies, mostly unkind in her recollection, and kinder Fräuleins. My grandmother, pre-1914, thought the Germans more reliable than the French. As my mother was becoming lonely communing with her dolls, it was decided that, from the age of 9 until she was 17, she should be packed off, trunk and all, three times a year, to school at Lavanna, Wimbledon, where she recalled that she was happy.

There, teaching of maths and science was non-existent. The teaching of French, German and music, however, was excellent, which helped her in later life to become proficient in Arabic. The atmosphere was 'jolly hockey sticks' but not oppressively so. Among my mother's special friends and contemporaries was a girl bearing the name of Eleanora Guggenheim. Her family, who were to found the Guggenheim Museum in Bilbao and dispense much philanthropy round the world, would not allow Eleanora an extra penny above the spartan recommended pocket money. My mother went on at least two occasions to stay with Eleanora's family. It was an eye-opening experience for a young country girl from Berwickshire to see the wealth and sophistication of their lifestyle. But their sense of public obligation left its indelible mark on her. That she so willingly gave the House of The Binns to the National Trust for Scotland I suspect owes something to the Guggenheim experience and ethos.

Leaving Lavanna in 1912, there was no question of her going to university as she told me she wanted. My grandfather – and she was the apple of his eye, though not, she thought, the apple of her mother's eye – would not entertain the idea of her going to one of the female Cambridge Colleges, Girton and Newnham. In reality, they needed her at home to help with the 'flitting' from Berwickshire to the different world of West Lothian, when my grandfather inherited The Binns in 1913.

Heating had to be installed; electricity brought in; long-needed painting had to be supervised. Then came World War One. The Binns was handy for the Rosyth dockyard and was hastily leased out to a series of naval officers, while my grandfather went off to the war. My grandmother and her 19-year-old daughter went to stay with her brother, William Askew Robertson at his house, Castle Hills, near Berwick, a neo-Gothic structure (later a nursing home) which can be identified to this day from the train as it trundles at reduced speed over the Tweed Railway Bridge.

There they frantically knitted woollen socks for the troops and prepared sphagnum moss bandages. Like tens of thousands of other girls of her age my mother was distraught to lose a boyfriend – it pained her to talk about it – I think at the Somme in 1916. During the post-war years, after a brief sojourn at the Dairy School at Kilmarnock (which she loved as it taught her how to help sows farrow piglets – more her line than nappies), she was the dutiful daughter at home 'on the proverbial shelf', compounded by a generation of males having fallen in the Great War.

Then, in 1924, my father appeared, brought to lunch by Cousin Elma, Lady Seton, mother of Bruce Seton the actor, who enthralled early British television with his robust portrayal of Fabian of the Yard. The problem was that my father was due to return to his work in India and would not be home for another four years, so it was difficult for love at first sight to blossom.

It was all the more difficult because my maternal grandparents did not fancy their only child being hitched up to a man, however much they liked him, which they did, whose wife, the daughter of the Home Secretary of the Government of India, had left him and gone to Kenya to start a coffee plantation with his best friend.

My father's divorce, however, finally came through on the morning of their wedding day, 12 September 1928. After a honeymoon in Norway on which my father's younger brother Kenneth (future Lieutenant General, Master of Ordnance in India for the Fourteenth Army and, thereafter, Director of the British Council) accompanied them, they then were off to Mysore and later to Bangalore, where they were to be based and at that time a sleepy but pleasant town in the south of India. My parents would be astonished to contemplate the transformation of Bangalore into the hi-tech metropolis it has now become.

*

My father, Percy Gordon Loch, one of the Lochs of Drylaw, was on Government Service in India and the Near East from the age of 17. His father, William Loch, had been British Resident in Nepal (virtually Governor) between 1899 and 1902. He achieved lasting fame by having brought the water supply to the ancient city of Bhaktapur. One hundred years later, on an official Inter-Parliamentary Union visit to Nepal, I discovered that he had been bothered by one huge and pressing problem – the disappearance in the snows near Lhasa of the Quinquennial Delegation to Peking (eventually they were discovered alive).

William Loch's wife, Edith, was the daughter of Chief Justice Gibbs, who served as Vice-Chancellor of the University of Bombay. Alas, she died in childbirth having had five children in six years. William Loch married again – a nurse, Viva Orde-Wingate, who turned out to be a superb stepmother to the two remaining siblings, my father and his brother Kenneth, who became a Lieutenant General responsible for Ordnance in India and later Director of the British Council in London.

In 1901, my grandfather fell ill in Kathmandu and asked his boss, the Viceroy, Lord Curzon, if he could go home after three years in Nepal, on leave for medical attention. Curzon peremptorily refused. My grandfather asked again. The Viceroy again refused him. So, after a third refusal, my grandfather simply took himself back to England – where he died within a matter of weeks. This much-repeated episode in family history by my father had the effect of giving me an antipathy to callous authority.

Both the Lochs and the Gibbs had two or more centuries of ancestors who had served the East India Company and subsequently the British Raj. In childhood, my father would regale me with stories of the Delhi Durbar of 1911 at which he was present, as a junior official, and of his exploits in Gilgit, at the North-West Frontier, and subsequently in Mesopotamia.

It is not uncommon for idealistic young men entering the public service to have mentors, people whom they looked up to for the rest of their lives and from whom they learnt their craft. My father certainly had a mentor. At lunch and supper – never at breakfast – when he followed the old Scots custom of taking his porridge standing, bowl in hand in case of sudden marauders – he would regale me with stories about his mentor, Sir Percy Cox GCIE, a proconsul.

The system was that those who were successfully examined as potential entrants to the Indian Political Service at the administrative grade were obliged to serve two years as a subaltern in the British Army. My father did a year at RMA Sandhurst and passed out 29th in an intake of 700, which was deemed to be very good for a boy who was an orphan. He was posted to the Staffordshire Regiment – not that he had any connection with Staffordshire but because they happened to be doing a tour in Mesopotamia.

Partly because, on merit, he was in the Regimental gymnastics and boxing teams, my father established a good rapport with the lads from The Potteries. He became a lifelong, if absent, supporter of Stoke City FC and was wont to explain that this was on account of his 1907–09 experience with the County Regiment, rather than being dazzled by the magic of the young Stanley Matthews, as I was 30 years later. His first postings in the service of the (British) Government of India, which covered responsibility for Mesopotamia, were in Amara and Kut, later infamous for the massacre of the British garrison there in 1917.

Then, as military secretary to the legendary water engineer Sir William Willcocks, who was in charge of building the first dams on the Tigris, my father struck up a friendship with an archaeologist. This was Leonard Woolley, who was excavating Ur of the Chaldees. My father managed to siphon off some much needed money from public funds to help Woolley work on the ziggurat at Ur, regarded by Sir Henry Layard, the distinguished archaeologist, and others as the 'cradle of civilisation'.

When what he had done to make funds available to Woolley came to the ears of the military authorities – political officers were subject to Queen's Regulations – my father was told that a court-martial would probably follow, after the matter had been reported to the political resident in the Persian Gulf, Sir Percy Cox. To my father's great fortune, this Old Harrovian had developed an interest in archaeology while at school, and had become fascinated by, and something of a scholar of, the archaeology of Mesopotamia. Rather than endorsing the court-martial application, Cox decided that his initiative suggested that my father was the type of young officer whom he wanted for work in his private office.

My father later recounted his first meeting with Cox:

Loch: Sir, what do you want me to do for you?
Cox: Loch, you will do as my secretary tells you.

The secretary to whom Cox referred was his Oriental Secretary, Gertrude Bell – the extraordinary and highly controversial Boadicean – who is credited by some historians as having created the modern state of Iraq out of the old Ottoman Empire. My father had more sense than to demur. He was to get on well with Miss Bell and her milieu. Our house welcomed many Arabs and those connected with the Near East. This was the stable from which I came, in relation to the Iraq War.

My intense interest in Iraq and Afghanistan derives partly from my parents, both of whom were Arabic speakers and who spent the greater part of my father's working life in these countries. When I stood up in the House of Commons and asked Prime Minister Blair whether he knew of that Russian General who, on leaving Afghanistan, had sighed, 'Give me one Afghan on a donkey rather than four Russians in a tank', I had my father's memories in mind (I had asked him the same thing privately beforehand). As the only European going into the North-West Frontier border areas with a few Indian soldiers, my father told me that he would never dream of trying to do business with local elders of the tribes that ran that part of the world without arriving as a guest enquiring first about their families and their crops.

He was always very grateful for the medical help that had been given to my mother by Indians in Bangalore and subsequently in 1934 by Iraqi doctors and nurses when she was pregnant and desperately ill in Baghdad. My father saw clearly that the world, in which he and eight generations of his ancestors had worked, was coming to an end and specifically he advised me not to make my life in the East.

My mother enjoyed riding, the only way to exercise her Great Dane, Buon, whose whistle she kept in the hope that it would be buried with her. Alas, I forgot this had been her wish, expressed repeatedly throughout my childhood. In 1932, before taking up the prestigious post of Political Resident in Bahrain, they returned home on leave and had me, their first and only longed-for child after a number of miscarriages. My mother was 37 and my father 45.

I came into this world on 9 August 1932 at 13 Randolph Crescent, Edinburgh, now the French Institute. Number 13 was a nursing home run by two legendary Edinburgh matrons, Miss Butter and Miss Munro. In Bahrain, my parents were in their element. My father was the British Resident responsible for all matters affecting His Majesty's Government, including making arrangements for the visiting warships. Among the naval officers of the Indian Ocean Fleet who regularly stayed ashore with my parents was the World War I hero Admiral Sir Martin Dunbar-Naysmith VC, father of Kathleen's future esteemed colleague on the Historic Buildings Council, the distinguished architect, Sir James Dunbar-Nasmith.

Another was Tom Phillips, then captain of the cruiser *Aurora* but who would later, as Admiral in Charge of the Battle Group, go down in the *Prince of Wales* which was sunk by Japanese land-based aircraft off the coast of Malaya in 1942. My father worked well with the Sheikh's British adviser, Charles, later Sir Charles, Belgrave and the Khalifa family, who came to The Binns in 1937, while on the Sheikh's official visit to Britain.

My parents were invited to the state banquet at Whitehall in honour of the Sheikh. My mother found herself sitting next to a man to whom she took an instant distaste – the German Ambassador, Joachim von Ribbentrop, executed nine years later on the orders of the Court at Nuremburg for crimes against humanity. Discovering that my mother dwelt on the banks of the Firth of Forth, all he could talk about was the Forth Bridge and Rosyth. Was it co-incidence that the first German air raid on Britain by the Luftwaffe was on the Bridge on 15 October 1939?

*

The death of my mother's father in December 1935 resulted in death duties that required the sale of Mannerstoun House, where Thomas Dalyell had lived between 1612 and 1621, and Mannerstoun Farm land. My parents were confronted with an agonising decision – whether to retire from the Indian Political Service prematurely, when the statutory five-year period in Bahrain was due to come to an end, or accept the offer from the Viceroy and the India Office of the position of British Resident in Nepal, the post held by my grandfather, William Loch, between 1899 and 1901, and which my father had long coveted.

My father later told me that he saw war was inevitable and would have liked to have been in charge of Gurkha recruitment and training for the British Armed Forces. My mother was good at facing unpalatable facts and told him the brutal truth: 'If you go to Nepal, I'll come with you and either send six-year-old Tam to boarding school or take him with us. But, if you do accept, like your father, you will die in harness and I will be left in Kathmandu, probably finding it impossible to go home in the middle of a war.'

Aged 50 and having served in some of the hottest places on earth without the benefit of electrical cooling devices, my father was not a well man. Asked in hushed tones by friends, when he passed away in 1953, what were the causes of his death, my mother did not mention the pneumonia or other technicalities which were on the death certificate but would tell them, 'He died of the East.' In a sense, she was right.

The other consideration was to decide on the future of the ancestral home. They sensed that, if they did not come back, 320 years of association between house and family would be gone. To cement the link, my father changed his name by deed poll in 1937 from Loch to Dalyell. The Dalyell family is one of the few families in Scotland where, in default of male heirs, the title and estates can pass through and to female heirs. As such a female heir, my mother inherited on the death of her father in 1935.

In those days, it was rare for a man to assume his wife's family name. Furthermore, the Loch Family were rather hurt, not least because after years of letter writing from the remotest locations in India and Mesopotamia, my father had written a hefty volume, published and superbly produced by Constables of Edinburgh on the Loch Family going back to Norman times. It was the hugely complex saga of the change of name that brought him into contact with the Lord Lyon, King of Arms, the leonine and eccentric Sir Thomas Innes of Learney.

After only a few months, Innes invited my father to become Unicorn Pursuivant, de facto a junior Herald at the Lyon Court. This he did and he tried to master Heraldry for Beginners. On being told that my father was to be painted in a companion portrait to that of my mother, the Lord Lyon suggested to the artist, Stanley Cursiter, famous for his Orcadian seascapes, that Dalyell, as he had become, be painted in his Pursuivant's tabard. Cursiter jumped at the idea, with the results that can be seen in the portrait still hanging at The Binns. I have a childhood memory of hearing one end of a telephone conversation between two aging deaf old boys bellowing at each other, which went along the lines of: 'Hello, Lyon. Unicorn here.'

CHAPTER TWO

Childhood

MY FIRST ENCOUNTER with school was as one of four boys in the kindergarten of the then posh but now academically formidable St George's in Edinburgh. Now a famous girls' school, then it took boys. Only two memories survive. One was sitting in a classroom, amidst bolt-upright girls with immaculately groomed pigtails doing our little arithmetical sums and wanting to borrow a pencil sharpener from a 'nippy besom', who snapped that I could not have hers.

My second memory is of scrambling up a crab-apple tree to pinch one or two of the semi-ripe fruit and being sneaked upon for so doing by the gang of malign five-year-old girls, who were gleefully delighted when I received five gentle taps on the behind from the teacher. Half a century and more later when I was invited by the then Headmistress, Dr McClure, to deliver the speech at the annual St George's Old Girls' lunch, a stately Edinburgh lady blushingly owned up to being one of the mischievous tots who had been so thrilled to get a boy into trouble and see him – trousers kept on – chastised.

My posterior, relatively unscathed at St George's, did not fare so painlessly at my next educational port of call, the Edinburgh Academy House in Kinnear Road, known as Mackenzie House. It was ruled over by 'Beany' Reid, an excellent teacher of mathematics for clever 15–17 year olds in the upper echelons of the Academy, to whom a generation of Edinburgh boys owe their entrance to and glittering scientific degrees from Edinburgh, Cambridge and Oxford. Beany had been gassed in Flanders in

1917 and, in particular, had suffered shell shock. This made him allergic to unexpected noise. Woe betide any of us who made a noise in the dormitory – pyjamas down and whack-whack with the slipper on bare flesh. It was a sign of the times and the mores of the Raj and British India that, when I told my mother about my oh-so-sore buttocks, all she could do was laugh. Sympathy was there none. She and my father believed, as I myself have come rather belatedly to believe, that bouts of hardship can be a beneficial ingredient in the process of growing up.

*

During 1938 and the first eight months of 1939, our lives were taken up with organising the installation of a new electrical system to the House of The Binns. In charge of the team of four from a well-known Edinburgh electricians company, G. B. Smith Ltd, with headquarters off Queen Street, was Mr Steel, an extremely competent and conscientious installations engineer. He was prominent in the Edinburgh Communist Party and did not hide it. But he was extremely nice and kind to me, taking pains to explain to a child what he was doing with his electrical instruments, thus re-enforcing an opinion that all Communists must be charming people.

In the summer of 1938, the world-renowned Australian archaeologist Gordon Childe, with his bushy whiskers and antique sombrero hat, was a frequent visitor to The Binns. My mother and Childe were making arrangements that a young research student by the name of Stuart Piggott* should carry out his PhD thesis on Cairnpapple Hill, which was within sight of The Binns. Historic Scotland now recognises Cairnpapple as the most important Bronze Age site on the Scottish mainland and second only to Orkney in importance. Famously rude and difficult with adults, Childe would tell me entrancing stories about ancient peoples. He, like Mr Steel, did not hide his Communism under a bushel.

* Piggott later became the internationally known Professor of Archaeology at the University of Edinburgh.

Another pre-occupation at this time was to do the re-harling of the House of The Binns. Had it not been done in the nick of time – the job was completed in August 1939 – damp might have led to The Binns joining what the current Curator of the National Trust for Scotland, Ian Gow, called *The Lost Houses of Scotland* – the title of his scholarly book on the subject.

In late 1938, a year after her return from the East, my mother was asked to become County Commissioner of the Girl Guides and it was thought a bright idea that a seven-year-old boy and only child should be taken along to Guide camp.

The first thing that struck me was that the girls were so much more practical than I was! But they were nice to me – though not slow in telling me that their little brothers could beat me up in a fight on any afternoon. Actually, the fact that my mother was a popular County Commissioner, who frequently had parties of Guides at The Binns, helped to remove many of the hesitations that the women members of the 167-strong selection meeting for me as a parliamentary candidate might have had about taking on an Old Etonian.

Then, on 3 September 1939, 'the balloon went up' as my parents put it. The outbreak of war shattered the orderly routine of Edinburgh Academy Preparatory School as the Luftwaffe was likely to blitzkrieg Edinburgh. The alarm was such that the six-to-eight-year-olds were dispatched with three Academy teachers, the no-nonsense dames Miss Haggart, Miss Goldie and Miss Mitchell, to a farm, Tulloch Gribbin, near Grantown-on-Spey. The smell of the gas lamps lingers with me, as does the memory of walks and occasional treasure hunts in the rugged land – the treasure was rare blocks of chocolate, usually concealed down rabbit holes or in the forks of ancient trees.

These lady teachers gave us a sounder grounding, I suspect, than was the lot of most evacuated kids. Alas, my time at the school came to an end when I suddenly got searing pains in the tummy. It was my appendix and the situation was urgent, the local surgeons having gone off to the British Expeditionary Force (BEF) in France. What to do? My mother was out of contact. Mercifully, the local vet was available and willing to deal with my perforated organ. Had the vet not taken rapid and decisive action, and the teachers accepted responsibility, there would surely have been no me to tell this tale.

At the start of the war, my father, then aged 52, volunteered within hours of the declaration of hostilities and became, along with the sculptor Charles d'Orville Pilkington Jackson, and Major Ned Fiddes, retired of the Sudan Civil Service, one of three liaison officers between the Royal Artillery who manned the anti-aircraft guns, and the RAF based at Turnhouse Airport. My father happened to be on duty both during the first German air raid on Britain – that on the Forth Bridge and Rosyth in October 1939 – and on the day Rudolf Hess made his extraordinary foray, landing on the Duke of Hamilton's estate.

At the same time, he formed the Bo'ness branch of the Local Defence Volunteers (LDV), which metamorphosed into the Home Guard. Since a lot of the volunteers would turn up at our house, I became integrated into the myriad networks of the West Lothian community to an extent that I might not otherwise have done. A lad whose regular apparel was a red Dalyell tartan kilt and sweater was ken-speckled and I became accepted – though I was coy about explaining why they did not see me for 35 weeks in the year because I was away at something called 'boarding school'.

One of the prominent members of the LDV was Robert Milne, rector of Linlithgow Academy, friend of my father and Alex Salmond's maternal grandfather.

There were two reasons why I was dispatched by myself at the age of seven on the Edinburgh–Carlisle train and then on to Whitehaven with a label round my neck, bearing the address of Harecroft Hall, a small 40-boy prep school near Gosforth, in Cumberland. My father was doing eight-hour shifts as a liaison officer and Harecroft – which had been recommended by the mother of the future UK Lord of Appeal, Lord Jauncey, the chairman of the Chinook inquiry in 2002 – was the one preparatory school they knew of that continued to teach seven-year-olds to ride. My parents thought teaching me to saddle up, ride and sweep out and clean stables at an early age would be useful if I were to become a cavalry officer.

Harecroft had two huge pluses. Gosforth was near what we then knew as Drigg, 'Workplace of the atomics', which became Calder Hall, which in turn became Sellafield. It was convenient for some scientists, who had been required to uproot to Cumberland, to send their boys to nearby Harecroft. The result was that I was taught alongside some very clever boys. They were also very friendly boys. There was no whiff of bullying; the teasing I had was good-natured. I was the only Scots lad in the school. My nickname became 'Zero–Eight' – the score by which England beat Scotland at Maine Road, Manchester in October 1943. Huddled round a wireless, my friends and I had listened to the excited tones of Raymond Glendinning, a peerless commentator.

Many afternoons were spent in the fields surrounding the school in the autumn doing our bit for the war effort by tattie howking – picking up and bagging potatoes. Even more important was the gathering of fields of carrots – the sandy soil of the area was ideal for the vegetables, which went away in lorry loads as far as London. Imaginatively, each boy was allocated a tiny allotment in the old kitchen garden. Mine was next to that of an older boy, whose patch was immaculate and highly organised, and he taught me, as a seven-year-old, how to propagate radishes. His name was that of my lifelong friend, Dr Nigel Hepper, who gained the reputation as Assistant Keeper of the Herbarium at Kew, as being the greatest expert in Europe on the plants of Africa.

I could hardly have been more fortunate in having Miss Reeman, a kindly Durham lady from an ecclesiastical family, as matron and three male teachers, which was unusual in wartime. Another plus was that four of my teachers were outstandingly good and others competent, in the coming and going of wartime. The Headmaster, Thomas McClelland, had been declared unfit for war service but had a degree in Greats from Oxford and taught Latin and maths rigorously, resulting in scholarships for his pupils to top public schools and great grammar schools such as Leeds. I owe the fact that later, in my first 'half' (term) at Eton, I won the School Fourth Form Latin Prose Prize to his grounding. J. Aylesbury Keyes, who every Sunday went off to St James's Church,

Whitehaven, was McClelland's assistant head. A diminutive, Oriental-looking man, he was a brilliant teacher of English, history, geography, bridge and chess.

Years later, when I invited Keyes to lunch in the Members' Dining Room at the House of Commons, he appeared in the shortest of shorts – he was against long trousers – with the result that the Westminster dress code required that I take him into the cafeteria and, even then, there were raised eyebrows from parliamentary colleagues. If ever a teacher enjoyed being awkward, it was J. Aylesbury Keyes. But his pupils owe him a lot.

Then, until he was called up for war service in India, there was the wonderfully interesting, then Communist Party member, and later successful children's author, Geoffrey Trease. When, some 40 years later, Kathleen and I went to call on him at his home in Malvern, he said how lucky we were to be brought up in the Northern Lakes, and to go bike riding up Wasdale, under the shadow of Wastwater Screes, Great Gable and Scafell Pike.

The last but not least of this quartet was Miss 'Bendy' Kendall. She taught French – with a Cumbrian accent – and riding – where she was some disciplinarian. On one occasion, etched into my memory, she had yelled at me not to irritate the mouth of her personal horse, Desire, by holding the reins too tight. When I continued out of trepidation, since Desire was many hands high, Miss Kendall had me dismount, take down my jodhpurs and underpants and touch my toes. She had no qualms about applying four strokes of her horsewhip to my naked buttocks and then told me that it served me right for hurting her horse and I should ask myself what Desire felt like with me nagging the reins. When, eventually in the following holidays, I told my mother, her reaction was to laugh and tell me that she would have done exactly as Miss Kendall had done – though she might have dispensed six of the best not four. The state of my posterior was of lesser concern than the welfare of the mare.

Nor did I evince a scintilla of sympathy from my father, who found out (I wasn't going to vouchsafe the information) that my friends and I were frequently spanked by the headmaster, not only for talking in dormitory, but for school work which he deemed careless or sloppy. My father's attitude was that the slipper or, occasionally, the cane would do you no harm and, anyhow, it would be preparation for inevitable tanning at public school and would teach me not to blub when being punished. Deep down, my father thought it was important to face adversity with equanimity. Uneasy though we may be in this age of child abuse, my father's were the mores of the Raj and Anglo-India 70 years ago. It may seem odd but I very much liked the headmaster, who administered strap and cane but who also showed great interest in us and wrote detailed and perceptive reports to our parents. I not only respected but also adored my then 55-year-old dad. No hard feelings.

My only disagreeable memory of Harecroft was having an argument with one of those Lake District walls of solid stone, when my brakes failed on one of our ten-mile bike rides. The wall was okay but two of my front teeth were knocked out. For the next 70 years, I have imposed on dentists!

*

My father, like many Scots who had spent their working lives in the East, was passionate about kilts, the pipes and all that pertained to Scotland. It was on this account that he arranged that I should have lessons on the chanter in Edinburgh Castle from the personal attention of Pipe Major William Ross, perhaps the greatest pipe major of his generation.

At the age of 11, I was sent into Edinburgh on the train and, from Waverley, climbed up the steep hill to the Castle where I had been dispatched with a note to Pipe Major Ross who was expecting me, which ensured I got past the sentry, who directed me to the room of this bucolic genius. I remember his huge purple nose, probably due to his exertions on the pipes and a good dram to whet his whistle. Pipe Major Ross was arguably the greatest teacher of piping of the century. However, it became quickly obvious that I was squandering the great man's time and my father's guineas. To my father, he just shook his head. I fared little better by having tuition in Highland dancing from Mr McLennan, who tutored in the art of dancing in his spacious room in Shandwick Place, Edinburgh. This can have been of no surprise to my headmaster at Harecroft who reported that, 'He has little sense of rhythm, no ear, no muscular control and very little music in him. But is of the definite opinion that he should study Beethoven.'

Throughout the war my mother and father made a habit of offering hospitality and opening their home to Australian and New Zealand aircrew from 12,000 miles away. Every one of them was really nice to me as a 9-to-12-year-old child. They would tell me in detail about their cricketing heroes – Bill O'Reilly and Clarrie Grimmett, demon spin bowlers; batsmen, Bill Ponsford and Stan McCabe; and, above all, a young man from the Outback, Donald Bradman. My first encounter with death was when, tearfully, my mother told me that one of her favourite guests, Flight Lieutenant Easterbrook, had gone missing, presumed dead, over Germany.

My mother was acutely conscious of her patriotic duty. She kept and looked after some 40 pigs. Her boar – a rough and clumsy old customer we called Cork since we bought him from Willie Connor, who hailed from Southern Ireland – gave me my first lessons in sex when he mounted the sows. As an eight-year-old, I yelled at my mother that Cork was doing a terrible thing and attacking Beatrice, an elderly large white sow. She calmly told me not to fuss because Beatrice was enjoying it and, in ten weeks' time, she would be having 'little ones'. Sure enough, two-and-a-half months later, eight little piglets arrived and, six months later, I shed tears as they went off to the bacon place – i.e. the abattoir.

But my mother's most significant contribution to the war effort was as Chairman (she would have been offended by the description 'Chairperson') of the Soldiers, Sailors and Airmen's Families Association (SSAFA). One of her roles was to perform the desperately difficult task of going to a house and breaking the news to a distraught family that a father, brother or son had been seriously wounded, listed missing or killed in action. On occasions, my father was out on duty and there was no one to look after me at The Binns so I would accompany her and wait in the car. Sharing the grief of the family, she would usually return in tears. This imbued in me an understanding that war could be a terrible business for families caught up in the loss of loved ones. Twenty years later, one delegate to the 1962 parliamentary selection conference in West Lothian confided that she had voted for my candidature on the basis that my mother had broken the news of her young uncle's death with the Fifth Army in North Africa with great kindness and compassion and had followed up organising support for the family.

*

In July 1944, a letter, which was to have huge consequences for the Dalyell family, arrived. The sender asked for it to be destroyed after it had been read. It came from my parents' solicitor, Professor (later Sir) Ernest Wedderburn of Shepherd & Wedderburn. He was also Professor of Conveyancing in the Faculty of Law at the University of Edinburgh and he asked if my parents would be prepared to meet him, on a very delicate matter. Wedderburn was a member of the Scottish National Trust's Council and he wanted them to come for a lunch meeting with him and Sir Iain Colquhoun of Luss, who was President of the Scottish National Trust, Sir John Stirling Maxwell of Pollock, Colonel Teddy (later Sir Edward) Stevenson, the Trust's Honorary Secretary, and Arthur Russell of the law firm Strathearn & Blair, their Treasurer. My parents guessed that this invitation meant only one thing – the embryonic National Trust would like to have the House of The Binns. Sitting round the table at Shepherd & Wedderburn's boardroom at 16 Charlotte Square, overlooking the green space and trees so familiar to Edinburgh residents and enjoyed by visitors to the Edinburgh Book Festival, a proposal was put to my parents on which, as my father would put it, 'they had to chew the cud of reflection'. The Scottish National Trust had acquired properties of outstanding landscape such as Glencoe but had not acquired any country houses at a time when the English Trust were doing so to ensure their survival in a period when many of them were struggling.

But beginning to look forward to their position after victory in the war – now looking increasingly likely – the Scottish Trust were concerned about the number of important houses being 'lost' or simply blown up in Scotland. They noted how the English National Trust had developed a 'Country House Scheme', under which the donor family could remain in their home with the proviso that it be opened to the public under the National Trust banner. Was there any chance that Eleanor Dalyell would consider giving the House of The Binns as the first, ipso facto, experimental property to the National Trust for Scotland?

There were four basic reasons why the Trust's first approach should have been to the Dalyells. First, The Binns was only 15 miles away from their headquarters in Edinburgh; secondly, the early seventeenth-century property was in fairly good condition, far better than many of the same period; thirdly, knowing my parents well, Ernest Wedderburn surmised that they would not ask for payment and might, indeed (as they did), offer the Trust an endowment as well as the house, parkland and contents. The fourth reason was that there were few foreseeable complications in relation to the collateral claims on the property. It had been the experience of the English Trust that, in acquiring properties, they had had to deal with claims from brothers, cousins, aunts, uncles, nieces or nephews of donors who were aggrieved that their birthright and consequent claims had been forfeited against their will.

In the case of the House of The Binns, I was an only child of an only child and our nearest relatives were in the United States. The man with the best claim had been chosen by Franklin Roosevelt as his running mate and, from April 1945 when the news of President Roosevelt's death came through from Palm Springs, Georgia, Harry Truman, for it was he, was focused on what he should say to Marshal Stalin and General Douglas MacArthur, rather than fussing about some claim of doubtful validity to an obscure property in Scotland.

My parents were thoughtful about involving me, explaining to a 12-year-old what handing the property to the National Trust might mean for him. They pointed out that, if I opted to follow my father in going into public service abroad or enlisted in the Armed Forces, financially and physically (logistically) it would be impossible to maintain the House of The Binns in likely post-war circumstances. They also felt that, in a very real sense, the house did not just belong to the Dalyell family, but to Scotland's history. When Kathleen congratulated her mother-in-law on 'carrying out a very socialist act', she was met with a twinkle and the reply, 'Not exactly what I had in mind, my dear!'

My parents did insist that my name and signature should be on the formal charter handing over the property with One Penny Blench Money inlaid in the document to the Trust. I have always been grateful to them for their foresight, as they thereby established my position as a donor. They took the trouble to send the charter to Harecroft Hall, my prep school, where, for the first and only time, the headmaster allowed a boy the use of his fountain pen. Vividly I recollect the occasion, penning my signature at the very desk under which, the day before, I had had to bend down and take six of the best for some misdemeanour or other. In those days, it was all part of the routine!

In April 1946, when hostilities had ceased, the transfer was formally celebrated. My parents suggested, and the Trust eagerly agreed to, a Sasine Ceremony, by which a clod of earth was handed by me, as heir presumptive and donor along with my mother, to the vice-president of the Trust, the Earl of Wemyss, shortly to become president but then standing in for the extremely ill president, Sir Iain Colquhoun of Luss. My father was dead keen on what he believed was the ancient Scottish way of transferring property and made a point of asking John Carruthers Little, president of the Amalgamated Engineering Union and a conviction socialist, when visiting The Binns as a member of the committee under Sir Ernest Gowers, which included Professor Anthony Blunt and Sir John Imrie, whether families remaining in houses which had been donated to the National Trust was acceptable to him; his answer was an unequivocal 'yes'. (Years later, the erudite St Andrews historian Ronnie Cant was to tell us gently that my father's beliefs were misconstrued – it was an Anglo-Saxon ceremony!)

The year we opened to the public – 1946 – was to be a steep learning curve. We had no notion as to how many visitors there would be or, indeed, whether there would be any at all, who would part with their two-shilling entrance fee. One problem was who would show them round the house on a guided tour. My parents decided that the ideal guide would be an ex-Scots Grey, demobilised from the forces. They thought they had come to an arrangement with a Squadron Sergeant Major, who had fought from Palestine in 1937 to the Elbe 1945, but the National Trust thought that, with his medals and waxed moustache, he would terrify visitors.

Maybe they were right to be shy of him, and decline to employ him, but I admired him for insisting that he should wear his array of medals. So, at short notice, there being no ex-Grey, The Binns had to make do with an ex-sergeant of the Scots Guards. He was to be called a Baron Officer, going back to the family's entitlement to hold a Baron's Court at The Binns. A Binns Officer's Baton was provided, which he wielded with great pride as he conducted his parties round the house.

The Scots Guard Sergeant was succeeded by an RAF Mess Sergeant and he by another Scots Guard, whose family, probably unbeknown to him, purloined some artefacts which had been given to the Trust as 'plenishings' along with the house. When my father died in 1953, my mother, alone in the house as I was at university, decided that she would rather have seasonal students. The first of these students was the son, then at Edinburgh University, of the Minister of St Michael's in Linlithgow and a distinguished future Moderator, the Rev. David Steel. The guide was therefore the future leader of the Liberal Party, the first Presiding Officer of the Scottish Parliament and much else, Lord Steel of Aikwood.

David became a great favourite of my mother's and was extremely kind to her. He accepted the wearing of the specially measured black uniform with its silver buttons with aplomb but understandably forgot to take the baton with him when showing parties of visitors round the house. The baton was 'de trop' to a younger generation and remains on show beneath my father's portrait. David later told me that showing three separate groups of strangers round a National Trust house each summer afternoon was an enormously confidence-building experience in public speaking. I myself went through the same experience, when I used to get back from Bo'ness Academy, where I was teaching, to take the 5 p.m. bus tour round the house and, one time into my bedroom – a public room – with, on this occasion, the bed unmade! That particular group were tickled pink and said that they much preferred a lived-in house to a museum showpiece. The National Trust for Scotland then acquired another 'small beer' property, as their factor of the day put it, Leith Hall in Aberdeenshire, before taking on the Marquis of Ailsa's spectacular Culzean Castle on the Ayrshire Coast.

The Trust's original Honorary Secretary, Colonel Sir Edward Stevenson, was succeeded by a paid Secretary, the youngish Jo Grimond. Culzean presented financial problems for the Trust, unlike The Binns, where my father had given a substantial proportion of his life savings to top up my mother's original endowment. Culzean was hopelessly underfunded. My parents were dismayed. My father, a man of both circumspection and of charitable disposition, hit the nail on the head about Grimond: 'The blighter is using the National Trust and is simply interested in becoming MP for Orkney and Shetland.' An ambition he achieved in 1950.

What dismayed me when I first heard it was the fact that Jo Grimond, on leaving the Trust, which he did after a comparatively short period, left a memorandum for his successor, a young Kelso solicitor with a good war record called Jamie, later Sir Jamie, Stormonth Darling, saying that, in his opinion, the National Trust for Scotland would inevitably have to be wound up.

In all the years in which we were parliamentary colleagues, Grimond would never talk to me about the National Trust for Scotland. I can only think he was embarrassed to do so although, as a fellow member of the Ancient Monuments Board, my wife had the highest regard and deep affection for his wife, Laura Grimond.

*

My parents' relationship was warm and affectionate. They made it a rule not on any account to squabble and not to criticise one another. I expect that my meticulously organised father was often exasperated, silently, by my mother's untidiness but he was adept at suppressing his feelings. Differences of opinion, if they existed, did not surface in my presence – except once.

In the early summer of 1949, the programme for the Edinburgh International Festival arrived. In the previous couple of years, we had hugely enjoyed the great orchestras – the Vienna Philharmonic, under Bruno Walter, playing Mahler's 'Das Lied von der Erde' with Kathleen Ferrier and, the following year, the Amsterdam Concertgebouw, under Eduard van Beinum. But the great orchestra programmed for Edinburgh's Usher Hall in 1949 was the Berlin Philharmonic under the conductor Wilhelm Furtwängler.

My father, a pre-war Wagner enthusiast, was all for buying tickets. My mother was against. Furtwängler had repeatedly played for Hitler between 1933 and 1943. My father pointed out, it now seems accurately, that Furtwängler had assisted many Jewish musicians to leave the Third Reich. My mother doubted the denazification process and quoted the cliché of the time: 'Wagner's music makes a man want to invade Poland!' My father prevailed by saying that, if their Jewish friend Rudolf Bing, the first director of the Festival, could stomach inviting Furtwängler, she should bury her objections and go. However, the argument was fortunately to resolve itself. There was a timely change of plan: clearly, Bing had been taken aback by the widespread sharing of my mother's view and tactfully withdrew the invitation to Maestro Furtwängler and substituted Sir John Barbirolli to conduct the first of the two Berlin Philharmonic Concerts and Eugene Goossens, the second. We went to both and it was magical.

During my childhood, my father's love of rod and line fishing took us to the anglers'-orientated hotel of Finlay Mackenzie in Lochboisdale, South Uist, for an annual holiday in August. When the midges – and anyone who has ventured to the Western Isles in late summer knows what formidable opponents the midges can be – made angling impossible, we went off on a picnic to the *machair*. This is an almost unique shore-scape, 70 per cent of the world's *machair* being on the west coast of North and South Uist. It revealed a farming situation, in harmony with the wildlife of the shore.

I used to watch these hardy men, and even hardier local women, cutting off seaweed, partly for fertilizer, partly to sell as raw material for alginates, but never being greedy and taking too much. 'It will be back in the same quantities in three years' time,' one explained. Odd things lodged in my childhood mind – the beautiful, ever-so clean-skinned potatoes; the shallow ploughing; the care they took not to destroy the wild flowers; and the bees producing delicious honey in high summer, before they were 'sent to the heather' in September. It was watching the bees on the *machair* that determined me to be a beekeeper.

*

It was to follow my grandfather that my mother insisted that I go to Eton rather than to my father's old school at Cheltenham or my own choice, at the time, of Repton or Oundle. I arrived at Eton for the summer 'half' – the Etonian lingo for 'term' – in May 1945, the week of Victory in Europe, and was to spend five happy and formative years there. As the only boy from Harecroft ever to go to Eton – my contemporaries mostly went on to Leeds Grammar School, Oundle, Repton or Sedbergh – this was a bit of a shock to the boys coming regularly from schools such as Ludgrove and Summer Fields, who rather took such success for granted.

Mine had been very much a last-minute place. My father had somehow procured an interview with R. T. Assheton (RTA), whose span of house-mastering was due to run for several years. He seemed taken with the serious little boy in a kilt who could fill in an unexpected vacancy in his house of 45 boys at Jourdelay's Place. RTA, first cousin of the then Chairman of the Conservative Party, Ralph Assheton, was, alas, rapidly overwhelmed by cancer and had to give up being a housemaster. He was an excellent teacher of chemistry, in a school where many of the 'beaks' – Etonian lingo for masters – were formidable classical scholars but past retiring age. Alas, he was to die of a ferocious cancer in his early fifties and his house passed to Tom Brocklebank. A diamond sculls oarsman and a member of one of the 1930s' expeditions to Mount Everest, Brocklebank had an insecurity and volatility which was rooted in the fact that he had been declared unfit owing to a heart condition, attributed to rowing, for war service. He was hugely sensitive to his contemporary colleagues returning with their DSOs and MCs from military service and the natural authority that they exercised. If you had gone from El Alamein to the Elbe, via Monte Cassino or Normandy, the slightest indiscipline from 13–18-year-olds could be met robustly.

A quarter of a century after I had left his house, I invited Tom Brocklebank and his ever-charming and good-natured wife, Jane, to dinner in the Strangers' Dining Room of the House of Commons. I also invited others who had been in his house: Nicholas Ridley, enemy of Ted Heath and later Mrs Thatcher's favourite Cabinet Colleague; Michael McNair Wilson, MP for Newbury; Winston Churchill, MP for Manchester Stretford; and the Earl of Coventry.

'Why is it,' purred Brocklebank, 'that there are more Members at Westminster from my house than from any other Eton house?'

'Tom, do you really want to know the truth?' I responded.

Perhaps unwisely he said that he did.

'Well, Tom, you were so difficult, so unreliable, so fickle, sometimes so downright malign, that you prepared us for the vicissitudes of public life!'

Nick Ridley instantly chimed in with, 'I agree with Tam.'

I fear Brocklebank was hurt but his wife nodded and laughed. I learned from Brocklebank that, to be awkward effectively, one had to cope with awkward and unkind people. But I was touched, years later, when he poured out his soul to me about his shortcomings and unhappiness as a housemaster. He said school teaching was a happy and productive occupation for those under 35 but, over 40, he thought it ceased to suit him and the school found him less suitable.

I got on much better with my superb maths teachers: the gammy-legged war hero Cecil Chamier; the algebraically elegant J. S. Herbert; and the severe Thomas Hutcheson Smythe. As an inky small boy, I fancied myself in the school Chess Cup, the biggest piece of silverware to be placed on the table of an Eton house – there were cups for everything, double skulls, under-15 cricket, nine boxing weights, rifle shooting and much more.

Silver was displayed on the table at every meal in the house – the symbols of achievement were ever present to spur us on. In the Chess Cup third round, I was drawn against a boy, P. Swinnerton-Dyer. When I went to his house for the match, by chance I bumped into the housemaster, the witty G. W. 'Wigley' Nickson, friend of R. A. Butler and father of the future CBI President, Lord David Nickson.

'Boy, you know that lock-up [curfew to be back in our own house] is in half an hour,' he told me. 'You'd better go back.' As I turned to go, to the giggles of my friends in Nickson's house, including the future Mr Justice Blofeld, Nickson said, 'Who is he to play?'

'Swinnerton-Dyer, sir,' I replied.

'Come back,' G. W. N. called to me. 'In that case, I suspect it may not last very long. You'd better go to his room and play!'

I did. It didn't. Sir Peter Swinnerton-Dyer, Dean of Trinity, Cambridge, Professor of Mathematics, Chairman of the University Grants Committee was then 17 years of age. It encapsulates the Eton style that, two days later when passing Mr Nickson in the street, he simply smiled at me – he had discovered my name – and said, 'Dalyell, thought so!' and proceeded on his way. One learned at Eton to eschew loquacity. The loquacious, as Neil Kinnock was to find when he fluffed the chance to get rid of Mrs Thatcher in the Westland Debate, can never be effectively awkward.

From John (A. J.) Marsden, I learned German and a lot about Germany. I also learned not to make silly, ill-informed criticisms of people. Marsden took half a dozen of us to the 2nd Test Match at Lords on the day that Sydney Barnes, opening for Australia, made 146, and there were substantial innings from Arthur Morris and Donald Bradman. I opined that the great England medium-paced bowler, Alec Bedser, was 'no good'. Marsden tore a strip off me and put this absurd utterance in my end of term report. Being silly does not chime with being awkward.

When my wife and I were on a visit to the College Political Society in 1990 and staying the night in Provost's Lodgings with Lord Martin Charteris, we went to call on the 91-year-old John Marsden at his home in Windsor. In his loo was the Croix de Guerre, awarded by the French for conspicuous bravery. He told us that it had been the consensus that those fortunate enough to get a place at Eton owed a debt of service, in whatever capacity, to Britain.

My second headmaster was the immensely impressive figure of Robert Birley, fresh from heading the Education Department of the Allied Control Commission in Germany, after the war. He had been chosen for this post by the Americans and the White House after being proposed by Clement Attlee. Previously a Fellow in Modern History at Balliol College, Oxford, and head-master of Charterhouse, he was well known after he left Eton for his part in initiating the significant 'Königswinter' conferences on Anglo-German relations, and for having become a Professor in South Africa, working with mainly black students.

It was a privilege to be in the class of 16/17 year olds to which once a week Birley himself came into the fifteenth-century, oak-benched and -desked classroom to teach us Dante's *Inferno* and *Paradiso*. It was because he taught us that he deputed the late Alec Metaxa CBE and I to conduct some of his European guests round the school, including, on one occasion, General de Lattre de Tassigny, French Commander in Algeria, and, on another, a lady who had been a wartime Burgomeister of a great German City.

When I asked her politely, 'Wie ist die schönste stadt Deutch-lands?', she replied with one word: 'Praha.' Much put out, as this was the capital of Czechoslovakia, I told Birley the following day what had happened. 'Sir, I could not believe my ears when she said Prague.' Birley smiled indulgently and laconically observed, 'Dalyell, you've learned something.' I had – denazification was not a simple matter.

When I wrote to his widow on Sir Robert's death, Eleanor Birley replied with a letter I treasure: 'Robert always took a special lifelong interest in the "Eton deviants".' Fortunate was I to have a headmaster who approved of and encouraged pupils in awkward tendencies. My first headmaster – or 'Head Man' to use the peculiar Eton lingo – had been Claude Aurelius Elliott with whom I had but one contact when he presented me, in the formal elegance of the MacNaughton Library, with an expensive production of Cicero's works, for having won the Fourth Form School Latin Prose Prize – the result of Tom McLelland's excellent teaching at Harecroft. In later life, an elderly Elliot lamented to me that a headmaster at Eton in his day had no power. Eton was run by the barons – by which he meant the housemasters. As Eric Anderson and Adam Nicolson say in their excellent book, *About Eton*:

> You only become aware of the Head Master . . . when bad behaviour leads you to 'The Bill' . . . or when good word has sent you up for reward. It is the Housemaster who deals with your parents; he consults them about you and your choice of A levels and of university; he is the one who becomes concerned if you are not doing well enough academically and who investigates your misdemeanours . . . The first Housemasters were entrepreneurs who built or bought their own Houses, admitted their own boys and collected their own fees. There were barons of whom the Head Master had to be wary. (pp. 162–63)

I returned to Eton again in June 2010 to make a lunchtime speech to leavers of 60 years before – a daunting experience for an ex-Labour MP addressing a flotilla of City heavyweights, captains of industry, diplomats and others who had been my contemporaries at school all those years earlier. Among them were the former Conservative Chief Whip, Tim Renton, who had been a key figure in ditching Margaret Thatcher, and my lifelong chum Tim Sainsbury, co-secretary with me of the Eton College Junior Archaeological Society, purveyor of groceries to the Queen and the nation and a former Tory minister for trade. The then headmaster, Tony Little, told me that the barons system no longer held sway and, as headmaster, he could go into boys' houses, which had previously been forbidden to head-masters.

I never knew until later in life how many of the Eton masters, or 'beaks' as they used to be called, voted Labour in 1945. What I do remember is being ordered by my housemaster to go to a political meeting in Slough at which the local MP, Fenner Brockway, whom I later knew as a parliamentary colleague and icon of anti-colonialism and civil liberties, was to speak.

Furthermore, it was at the Eton College Political Society that I first heard Leonard J. (as he then called himself) Callaghan, who told us there was nothing dishonourable in being an ambitious politician. Ian Mikardo, later Chairman of the British Labour Party (and Chairman of the Parliamentary Labour Party, whom I served as an executive member), Arthur Deakin, General Secretary of the then huge Transport and General Workers' Union, and many others also addressed the Society.

Eton, during the years 1945 to 1950, believed in pummelling what John Stuart Mill described as 'the deep slumber of a decided opinion'. My wife says I do indeed pummel others' deep slumber but do nothing about my own. My 'modern tutor', under the Eton system in my last two years, was René Peyrefitte, who had come to the school from the University of Montpelier and was to leave after a few years to become a professor at the Sorbonne. Years later I met him in Paris and he told me that he found Eton a place 'absolument extraordinaire' and, of course, it would have seemed totally strange to a French socialist intellectual.

The Head of Languages, later to be Lower Master at Eton and Headmaster of Charterhouse, was Adam Oliver van Oss. He entranced us by teaching with the aid of the short stories of Guy de Maupassant. However, I remember him for something else. In my report, handwritten and sent to my parents, he ended up by writing, 'I wish Dalyell, sitting at the back of my class, would not yawn so much.' My father was incandescent. Why should he scrape together the school fees only to find that I yawned? I pleaded with him to believe that it was not I who yawned.

At the beginning of the next term, I politely tried to remonstrate with van Oss saying that it was not I but the boy in the next desk, Charlie Morrison, later MP for Devizes, who was the yawning miscreant. Van Oss brushed me aside, saying, 'Dalyell, that will teach you that life is unfair,' and passed on. Life being unfair is a lesson that, in one form or another, every Etonian learned to their great advantage.

At Eton, I was gently teased but not bullied. My immediate contemporaries were Simon Loder, Jim MacDonald-Buchanan, son of the classic race-winning mother, the formidable Hon. Mrs MacDonald-Buchanan of Cottesbrooke Hall, and Michael Talbot-Ponsonby, from the epicentre of fox hunting society. Perhaps we had little in common but they tolerated me and, later in life, Michael became a friend.

Other particular friends were Ian Pugh, an 'outsider' like me in Eton terms, from Wales, who joined the RAF for his National Service and died in an air crash, still only a teenager, which was my first brush with the sadness of contemporary death, and Frederick Nicolle, who was intent on becoming a medical student. He later blossomed into a distinguished pioneer of cosmetic surgery.

Other boys in my life were my fag masters, Paul Graham-Watson and Nicholas Ridley. Fagging, long since abolished, was a system whereby a 16–18-year-old among the half dozen senior boys in the house – a member of 'library' – would be allocated one or two boys in the Lower School to run errands, clean shoes and perform any menial task within reason. Paul Graham-Watson was a scholar martinet who, in 1948, was to go to Malaya on National Service with the Scots Guards and be slaughtered, along with his platoon, after what, I am told, was an impetuous decision to disobey orders. Nicholas Ridley's mind was focused on two things: gaining entrance to Balliol College, Oxford, where he later gained first-class honours in engineering, and his painting. My own fag was a sullen little boy called Jacob Rothschild, who was allocated to me by my housemaster on the grounds that I was the senior boy most likely to cope with a difficult 13-year-old. I know I failed. Subsequently we became friends and he chairman of the Board of the Trustees of the National Gallery and then Chairman of the National Heritage Memorial Fund, administering the Heritage Lottery Fund between 1995 and 1998.

Only once in 43 years as a Member of Parliament was I chided by any colleague in the Parliamentary Labour Party as either one of two Old Etonians, or the only Old Etonian, in their ranks. Not as the reader might think by Dennis Skinner, not by John Prescott and certainly not by that formidable champion of the working class of yesteryear Ellis Smith from Stoke on Trent but by the patrician James Callaghan, whom I had first heard address the College Political Society two decades before.

The circumstances were instructive. In 1966, I was the elected Chairman of the Parliamentary Labour Party Backbench Education Committee. After Callaghan had come to the PLP as Chancellor of the Exchequer to explain the traumatic dent in the Labour government's spending plans announced on the fateful date of 20 July 1966, he summoned me: 'I heard you say that one of the savings should be the cutting back of the school leaving age proposals from 16 to 15. I am angry. You have had the very best of educations at Eton and King's College Cambridge. I know what it is like later in life to have been required to leave school early and forfeit any prospect of higher or further education. It certainly does not lie in your mouth to suggest that our plans for raising the school leaving age should be postponed. Etonians should know better.'

It was of little avail when I tried to appease him by saying that my view emanated from personal experience at Bo'ness Academy when I had to teach a class of boy and girl leavers, some of whom left at Christmas, others at Easter and the rump at the summer, all depending on which month of the year their birthday fell. All I was suggesting was that pupils would be required to complete their education, leaving en bloc.

Of course, there was great curiosity among my parliamentary colleagues about Eton and my reply was always the same: 'I was a very fortunate boy to be superbly taught and to have such a stimulating environment where one was treated for the most part not as a school boy but as an undergraduate. Eton gave me, like many others, the confidence to be awkward.'

CHAPTER THREE

Maturing

THE ROLE OF National Service in determining the character and attitudes of politicians, who spent their years between the ages of 18 and 20 in the forces, is an interesting, and individually complex subject. My friend and contemporary George Younger told me that he had been 'made' by his experience with the Argyll and Sutherland Highlanders in Korea, in particular on the night when his platoon appeared to be surrounded by North Korean and Chinese troops – something that was confirmed in David Torrance's authoritative biography of George. Another Defence Secretary, Tom King, told me he felt the same way about his National Service as a Somerset Light Infantry officer seconded to the King's African Rifles to combat Mau Mau in Kenya.

My experience was altogether different but no less formative. Both my father and mother were very tolerant and did not pressurise me to shine at school. But I sensed that they were desperately keen not that I should be a regular soldier but that I should do my National Service as an officer in the Scots Greys. So, having opted for the Armoured Corps, comprised of Cavalry Regiments and the eight Royal Tank Regiments, I duly arrived at the Nissen huts of Catterick Camp on 19 October 1950 to join the Basic Training Regiment, at that time the 17th/21st Lancers, the 'Skull and Crossbones Boys', whose regimental day was Balaclava Day! Their officers, sergeants and corporals were men of high quality, who were well equipped to give the basic training before we went off to our chosen regiment.

At first, all went well. I was selected as a potential officer, after eight weeks of basic training. Like others under the watchful eyes of Captain Ives and Sergeant Sargent, I was made to crawl through drainpipes in January on the North Yorkshire Moors. I duly passed the dreaded War Office Selection Board and off I went to Mons Officer Cadet School at Aldershot, where I sailed through the first six generalised weeks with a respectable grade of +30.

Because my name began with D and there were no As, Bs or Cs, I was the first 'Cadet Troop Leader' in 'G' Squadron, the specialist training course for those going into the Royal Tank Regiment or the Cavalry Regiments. I made a hash of it; the shortcomings were mine. Worse still, the Royal Tank Regiment (RTR) captain in immediate charge of us, who did not care for the cavalry attitudes very much, got it into his head that I was 'playing on my name' as descendant of the founder of the Scots Greys to get through. Honestly, it was not true but I later realised why he could be forgiven for jumping to this conclusion. Unbeknown to me, Brigadier George Todd, the Colonel of the Greys who had interviewed me at Catterick, had inserted into the military record 'Dalyell of The Binns'. So it was small wonder that I was treated with some hostility by those immediately in a position to determine whether I should be commissioned.

I had a bad performance during the 'trek' exercise on Salisbury Plain, during with I contrived to 'mislay' an armoured car – that is, as Cadet Troop Leader, I had not the slightest notion where it had got to. Later, I discovered that those of my fellow cadets in charge of the said armoured car were having a sly kip in the vehicle and were being thoroughly unhelpful. It taught me that so much depends on the decency and goodwill of those with whom, albeit fleetingly, one has to work. Being returned to Unit and sacked as a potential officer – although it was kindly done by Major Edward Crankshaw of the Cherry Pickers, 11th Hussars, and Captain Peter Duckworth of the 5th Royal Inniskilling Dragoon Guards, later to become a lifelong friend – was a sore blow at the time.

For a brief period, I was sent to the Queen's Bays at Fall-ingbostel near Hanover and was allocated to a troop where 'Van' (Robert Vanderburg), the sergeant, spoke fluent German and took those of us who were interested to the Hanover State Opera. The corporal, Jim Bundy, also became a lifelong friend. I was lucky. The troop was detailed to work alongside Heinz, a displaced East German, who was eking out a living by preparing maps of the areas to which we were to take our tanks on exercises. Heinz had been a German tank commander at the Battle of Kursk (the largest tank battle ever fought) and made a great impression on me by describing his truly terrible experiences in the Russian winters of 1942 and 1943.

To please my parents, I had reiterated my desire to go to the Scots Greys and this was arranged easily, since the two regimental colonels, Humphrey Weld of the Bays and Douglas Stewart of the Greys, were both famous riders (Stewart was later a gold medallist at the Helsinki Olympic Games in 1952) and friends. Thus I found myself installed in the superbly efficient SS Barracks in Luneburg – which had showers, hot water and easily cleaned four-soldier barrack rooms – as 22424588 Trooper Dalyell in a regiment which had been founded by an ancestor of the same name – and, moreover, everybody knew it had been founded by General Tam Dalyell since a knowledge of regimental history was instilled into every recruit to the regiment.

On day two, I was summoned to the colonel, who was direct: 'You have chosen to come to us. We are pleased to have a descendant of our founder but you may have problems and, if it becomes too awkward for us or for you, I will send you back to the Queen's Bays.' Again I was extremely lucky. Officers, NCOs and fellow troopers far from making my life hell – and they might well have done – were thoroughly decent. It helped that I could speak German, which enabled me to winkle eggs out of farmers for a few Pfennigs when we were on exercises and then provide a good line in bacon and eggs by the side of the tank. I reckoned that, by the time I was demobbed, I knew every square kilometre of Luneburge Heide (Luneburg Heath) – the British Army of the Rhine (BAOR) training area.

Once, I did land myself in potentially serious trouble. Because I could speak German, my friends in 'A' Squadron thought I was ideally placed to flog their cigarettes for Deutschmarks. I became bolder and more careless and was eventually caught with a huge caseload of cigarettes by the Military Police in the optimum market venue – the Reeperbahn or red-light district of Hamburg, which they were patrolling for other reasons. I have to thank my lucky stars that the Acting Regimental Sergeant Major, 'Tiger' Shaw, then RQMS, later Major, got hold of the Military Police and told them, 'Tam Dalyell has been an extremely silly ass in getting caught but he is *my* silly ass and I will deal with him.'

I got fourteen days' 'Jankers' (detention in barracks with extra guard duties, etc.) but, if the Military Police had had their way, I would have been sent to Bielefeld, the Military Detention Centre for Rhine Army, and lumbered with a criminal record. And had I had a criminal record, I could not have become a parliamentary candidate for Labour in Roxburgh, Selkirk and Peebles eight years later. Looking back, what could have been a disaster turned out extremely fortunately for me.

At weekends a small group of us, if not fulfilling our weekly turn of guard duty, would take advantage of cheap rail travel. Luneburg to Munich and back was 12 Deutschmarks and 20 Pfennigs – the equivalent of three quarters of a pound of coffee from my loving parents. We went all over Germany, including to Aachen, Augsburg, Bad Reichenhall, Berchtesgaden, Bremen, Bremerhaven (to see the U-boat pens), Essen, Flensburg, Fulda, Garnisch-Partenkirchen, Goslar, Heidelberg, Koblenz, Köln, Lübeck, Mainz, Munich, Nuremberg, Stuttgart, Ulm – and also to Copenhagen.

Over 60 years, I have maintained warm relations with the regiment, who made me an Honorary Officer in 1997. I wrote for the *Independent* the obituaries of Colonel Douglas Stewart, 'Tiger' Shaw and a number of others from my time with the regiment, now the Royal Scots Dragoon Guards. But, as Aidan Sprot, a squadron leader during my National Service (and Willie White-law's brother-in-law), later himself Colonel of the Regiment, put it kindly to my biographer, Russell Galbraith: 'Unlike his fierce ancestor, Tam Dalyell was not cut out to be a soldier.' Fair comment!

*

It was a poignant moment that I will never forget and one which, at the time, felt acutely embarrassing. It was my last day in the army at Bovington Camp in Dorset. I was being demobbed from National Service, handing in my kitbag (but allowed to keep my army boots) alongside a friend of mine. We had been in the same squadron of the Scots Greys. He had been a better tank wireless operator than me. He was certainly smarter on parade than I had been.

He said to me gently and without any outward sign of rancour, 'Tam, you don't know how jealous I am. Here you are going to Cambridge next week and here am I going back to Lancashire to resume serving behind the counter in a hardware store. But good luck. Keep in touch.' I did until he died young in a road accident not, I gathered from a report of the inquest, of his making.

I also knew that I had been doubly fortunate since I was told that I had just scraped into King's College in the entrance exams of that time. I suspect that what swayed the decision in my favour had been two lucky interviews. The first was with Donald Beves, an elderly bachelor don whose pride and joy was his collection of French porcelain, in which I expressed an interest and knowledge – based on Sevres pieces and other artefacts at The Binns. The second interview was with the senior tutor, Patrick Wilkinson, with whom I 'clicked' but who was adamant that the offer of a place depended on my doing my National Service first.

It was a strange experience rumbling around Luneburg Heath in a tank and ten days later, sitting at dinner in Hall, as a freshman at King's College Cambridge. The first night I went back to my room in the hostelry at 7 Peas Hill, run by a Mrs Palmer on behalf of the college, wondering what on earth I was doing in Cambridge. In Hall, I had sat down among a group of undergraduates I did not know. They were not unfriendly but their conversation was glittering. Conversationally, I wore hob-nailed boots.

Two South Africans in particular rocked my confidence as to whether I could survive in such company. One was Arthur Jenkins, who was to get a Starred First in History and later became a lecturer at Trinity College, Dublin, before moving in semi-retirement to Cambridge and to a charming farm called Cenna near Pienza, where Kathleen and I stayed with him and his wife, Rosemary, for a week. The second was the ebullient Sydney Brenner, who was to be a Copley medallist and Nobel Prize winner, with whom I remained in contact even after he moved from the Laboratory of Molecular Biology in Hills Road, Cambridge, to the West Coast of the United States. After some weeks, I discovered that not all students in Cambridge were the equal of Jenkins and Brenner.

Although my entrance exam was based on languages and maths, the College recommended that I read history. It was an indication of the care taken by King's in those days that, in the Rhine Army, I had received a long, handwritten letter from Christopher Morris, Director of Studies in History, recommending a substantial list of books I should read 'in the spare time, which I know many National Servicemen will find'.

They were mainly classics, such as Motley's *Rise of the Dutch Republic*, and various works of F. W. Maitland. For three years Morris was to show a keen personal interest in my academic progress. As a teacher, he was a wonderful devil's advocate, especially in the essays he liked to set on Hooker, Hobbs, Locke, Montesquieu and Rousseau. I wrote an affectionate obituary of him for the *Independent* and another for his ever-hospitable wife, Helen, who every weekend had undergraduates to her house at 5 Merton Street, for drinks. Indeed, my memories of the Cambridge dons with whom I came into contact remain fresh after six decades.

My second first-term supervisor was John Saltmarsh. With his sideburn whiskers and scholarly demeanour, he simply *was* the early medieval world with a razor-sharp mind. To be taken round the roof of King's College Chapel was to discover that he was acquainted with the fifteenth-century architects and their master masons personally. Though Saltmarsh was never to publish any book or manuscript of note, his 9 a.m. lectures, three times a week, packed the large theatre in Mill Lane. Nowadays, I doubt if he could keep a post in a university.

In those days, Cambridge valued inspirational teachers who saw no reason to compete in print. After four weeks, Morris decided that I was robust enough – my friend and contemporary Neal Ascherson was another – to go to Noel Annan for supervision. The future Provost of King's, Provost of University College London, Chairman of the Royal Commission on Broadcasting, and prominent Member of the House of Lords, was a formidable young don, already with a well-received book on Leslie Stephen under his belt.

In my second supervision, Annan asked me, 'Tam, what class do you think you are?' I said that I supposed I came from 'the Scottish lairdry'. 'Oh, yes,' said Annan, 'I know exactly what you mean – "not quite county".' Throughout my parliamentary life, until he died, I would go to see him in UCL and later in the Lords. He was not pleased with me over the Falklands: 'Oh Tam, you do not understand the fog of war.'

I also owed a lot to Arthur Hibbert, Fellow of King's and an economic historian who never produced anything after he was awarded his Fellowship but was a superb teacher of the art of deploying historians' arguments. These days Hibbert would not last and history teaching would be the poorer for it. Finally, one of the King's historians then was the young Communist Marxist intellectual Eric Hobsbawm. I marvelled at the care and constructive help he was prepared to devote to an Old Etonian. I reproduce one of the most treasured letters I have ever received:

Dear Tam

I am sorry to see that you have decided to retire from the House. I can understand why you might want to, especially in the present situation, but with your going something important will be lost both to Parliament and the Labour Party. I can see nobody like you to follow as someone who justifies the function of the independent back-bencher, nor anyone who will serve the Labour Party in Parliament with such total disregard for the possible rewards of a political career. You have deserved well of politics, perhaps just because your behaviour has been so consistently unlike that of 'the politician'. You have deserved better of the Labour Party than it merits, particularly today.

I have admired what you have done in and outside Parliament with your characteristic mixture of intelligence, integrity, stubborn pursuit and Lothian pawkiness. I dare say you will be getting a fair number of regretful notes on your retirement, but I hope you don't mind one from someone who has known you since we both met in King's a half century or so ago. Throughout that long period nothing that you have done has been boring and most of it has been worthwhile. Congratulations.

If you maintain a foothold in London, let's keep in touch. It is not very likely that I shall find myself in Scotland much.

With all good wishes for a long future

Yours ever

Eric

In the History Faculty at Cambridge in my time there was a galaxy of remarkable lecturers, whose sessions I regularly attended. Four Professorial Fellows of Peterhouse each made a lasting impact. Herbert Butterfield, author of *George III, Lord North and the People*, was a purveyor of controversial argument but with a wonderful overview of world history. Denis Brogan had an encyclopaedic knowledge of both French and American History. I once asked Brogan, when he came to tea with a group of my undergraduate friends, 'How do you know so much about America?' The reply came back, 'By sleeping with women in the 48 states of the United States.' 'Which state did you miss?'

I asked. 'I didn't get to Idaho!' (The 50th, Hawaii, had not then been accepted as a state.)

Then there was Michael Postan, Professor of Economic History and a Ukrainian by birth, who revealed in his lectures that, between 1905 and 1914, Tsarist Russia made remarkable economic progress. And Dom David Knowles, Benedictine monk and Regius Professor of Medieval History, enthralled undergraduates with his exposition of the thoughts of St Augustine, St Thomas Aquinas and others among the scholars of the Middle Ages.

From Peterhouse, too, came Brian Wormald, a lugubrious lecturer of enormous erudition, whose course covered the period from 1639 to 1660 in Britain – by the time we came to only two weeks to go before the Tripos examination, Wormald was still reflecting on the events of the spring and autumn of 1642 – and Denis Mack-Smith, with his exciting exposition of the Italian irredentist campaign and the Risorgimento.

From Trinity came Peter Laslett, a pioneer of social history, and the unique Walter Ullmann, a Viennese lawyer who fled the Anschluss and made himself a world authority on the history of Canon Law. Douglas Hurd was to say that he was privileged to have been supervised by so great a scholar.

Otto Smail of Sidney Sussex, meanwhile, lectured brilliantly on the Crusades, dispassionately analysing Saladin's point of view, while his colleague, David Thomson, later Master of Sidney, dealt with the events leading up to, and then the unwinding of, the French Revolution.

Two lecturers, as yet un-knighted, (Sir) Geoffrey Elton of Clare and (Sir) Jack Plumb of Christ's were great orators. Elton was the first to espouse the cause of Thomas Cromwell as the founder of the Civil Service, while Plumb was marvellous on eighteenth-century corruption, examining the roles of the Duke of Newcastle and other patrons and of sinecure holders such as 'Taster of the King's Wine in Dublin'. But even Elton and Plumb would have to give way in the oratorical championships to Harry Hinsley, Historian of Intelligence and later Master of St John's. During the Falklands War, I would go to see Hinsley, like the Oracle of

Delphi, in the sepulchral Master's Lodge in St John's. Hinsley
had various views but was basically critical of the Fleet, about
which he knew a lot, being dispatched on such a mission for what
he believed were mainly political purposes

I owe a lot to two other St John's historians – Edward Miller,
the authority on Henry III, the Law Giver, and Frank Thistle-
thwaite, historian of the United States and latterly of his own
county of Lancashire. When Kathleen and I went to see him in
Cambridge when he was crippled and over 90, he was justly
proud of having been the founding Vice-Chancellor of the
University of East Anglia. There were others, starting out in
their distinguished careers: Christopher Brooke, son of Zachary
Brooke (Zachary Brooke and Charles Previte-Orton were
dubbed 'the twins of the footnotes'), and his Gonville and Caius
senior colleague, Philip Grierson, the most erudite numismatist
(student of coinage) in the world.

*

As a 21st-birthday present in 1953, my imaginative parents
(inspired by Magdalene Dalyell's adventurous experience in
going to the New World) gave me a trip across the Atlantic in
a Donaldson Line tub, the 11,000-tonne *Lismoria*, and a third-class
ticket on the Canadian Pacific Railway from Montreal to Vancouver with a return by Canadian National Railway. I could stay
for a few days on Vancouver Island with the family of their
friends from Arabia, Sir Stewart and Lady Pears. It was up to me
(apart from anything else dollars being severely restricted) to find
myself a job.

I thought I had been very clever. I had arranged to be
employed as a lucratively paid labourer at the huge aluminium
plant at Kitimat on the British Columbia coast. Alas, a fortnight
before I arrived, there had been a strike; one of the terms of the
settlement of the strike was that there should no more employment of 'limey' students. I was seriously short of cash, a novel
experience which was good for me. But I found a job, picking
loganberries for 15 hours a day to make a (foul) product called
Logana wine. One night the Pears family and their brother-in-

law, Herb Barton, invited General Perks, later the Canadian defence minister and a commander for the Royal Canadian Navy, and his wife to dinner. These modest men brought home to me what few of my generation fully realised – the extent of Canadian sacrifice in two World Wars from Flanders, Passchendaele and the Somme to the Dieppe Raid in 1943 and beyond to Normandy and the Rhine Crossing. Did I know, he asked, that 68,000 Canadians had died in World War I?

Having left the security of the Pears' home, I went to Vancouver and stayed in the cheapest hostel in town. My fellow dormitory inmates were mostly Canadians of Japanese origin, many of whom had had a hard time, having been interned until 1946. It was the first time I had been confronted with problems of race and ethnic minorities, whose cause was so effectively championed by Ben Whitaker, the only other Old Etonian Member of the Parliamentary Labour Party in the years 1966–70 and, thereafter, as a member of the United Nations Human Rights Committee from 1975 to 1988.

Looking back, I guess the seed was sown for my support of the Chagossians and other displaced peoples during conversations in those Vancouver dormitories.

I had earned enough – just – in dollars to travel by Greyhound bus from Vancouver to Boise, Idaho, and then Salt Lake City. After marvelling at the achievements of the Mormons, one lad, whom I met casually viewing a Mormon Temple, I suspect with an eye to recruiting me to his faith, said, 'I'll take you to experience a dip in the Salt Lake. I've got a second pair of bathing trunks.' Off we went. It was a new sensation floating easily on the water. We then went to the showers, where there was no distinction between male and female. Most of the locals had no hang-ups about being seen in the nude by the other sex. Being a prudish European, I washed, or attempted to wash, myself with my bathing trunks on. I did not manage to do the crevices and the private parts properly. How I suffered due to the salt for the next two days. It spoilt an otherwise exhilarating visit to a lodge in the Grand Canyon and viewing of the magical changing colours. Years later, on visits to Israel and subsequently to Jordan, given the memories of the Salt Lake itch, nothing would induce me to paddle in the Dead Sea.

Then it was on to Glendale, California, to stay three nights with my mother's school friend Vi Gordon and her Ohio-born blue-collar husband, Jo Foster. Reluctantly they had voted for 'Ike' Eisenhower the previous November and harped on that Senator Robert A. Taft of Ohio would have been an altogether better president and believed that Franklin Roosevelt had been the devil incarnate and that Harry Truman was not much better. I found out that America was a very different place to Britain and that California was a very different place to Washington and the East Coast. On my last evening with them, Vi told me that the idea of a 'special relationship' with Britain, the country where she had grown up, was a delusion. Jo put it more forthrightly: 'Hogwash.' Jo Foster's gruff voice remained with me all my life: 'I was brought up as a supporter of Warren Gamaliel Harding [corrupt Ohio senator and president of the United States from 1921 to 1923]. I'll tell you, Tamus [as he insisted on calling me], America will do what suits America. There ain't any room for East Coast do-gooders like Woodrow Wilson.'

If only British leaders had been willing to accept Jo's sentiments. Part of the trouble is that British prime ministers were dazzled by the panoply of power in Washington. For example, one evening in 1965, Dick Crossman, at that stage Minister of Housing, came back to 9 Vincent Square, where I stayed with him during the week, late at night after Harold Wilson had returned to report to Cabinet on a visit to Washington. 'The trouble is,' he told me, 'that little Harold just adores having "Hail to the Chief" played in his honour on the White House lawn.' Though I do have to say in fairness to Harold that he resisted the huge pressure from Lyndon Johnson to enter the Vietnam War. Similarly, how Mrs Thatcher lapped up having her picture taken being driven round by Ronald Reagan in his buggy!

My actual twenty-first birthday was spent among the great redwoods in a log cabin in Oregon. This was the first occasion on which I had heard the name of a Scot, rightly famous in the

United States, John Muir, founder of the wonderful American National Parks that set the model for similar preserves worldwide. On the return journey, I stopped off at Calgary to accept an invitation to speak about General Tam at the monthly dinner of the Calgary St Andrew's Society. This was my first encounter with the Scottish Diaspora. My host had a huge milk and dairy products business and described himself as a 'monarch' of butter in Alberta, which other members confirmed he was. Calgary, at that time, seemed to be run by men of Scottish and Ukrainian descent. Many of those present were engineers, working on the amazing riches of the Athabasca tar sands.

Canada entered my blood and it was partly on account of this experience in my first long vacation from university that I chose 'The emergence of Self-Government in Canada between 1837 and 1852' as my specialist subject in Part I of the Cambridge History Tripos. The lecturer to the small group – attendance was obligatory – was Professor E. E. Rich, Professor of Commonwealth History and later Master of St Catherine's College. Rich was a scholar of great precision who also made us think about the motives, explicit and hidden, behind the original texts which we were obliged to study. Were the Earl of Durham, of the Durham Report, or the Earl of Elgin being devious when they signed particular papers? Was such and such being done because of difficulties with French Canada?

What Rich's special subject did for me above all was to provide an insatiable curiosity about the wording of government papers and statements. I did not smell a conspiracy theory in all documents or, indeed, in the majority of them but Professor Rich taught us to be discerningly suspicious and to scrutinise the small print. I applied much of what Rich taught me to the Iraq Dossier, my first reading of which is encapsulated in Peter Brookes' cartoon reproduced in the plate section.

*

One of the strengths of the Oxbridge Colleges is that undergraduates can mix with contemporaries and not only contemporaries but other dons in the College, if only by sitting next to them at breakfast, lunch or dinner in Hall, where there was no understandable apartheid between dons and students after the formalities of the intoning of grace.

One of the regulars at breakfast in Hall I remember was Professor (later Sir) Frank Adcock, Vice-Provost, editor of the *Cambridge Ancient History*. By reputation, he was one of the best decipherers of U-boat messages reaching Bletchley Park, as he had, before World War I, been a pupil/graduate student in Berlin of Wilamowitz-Moellendorff. The Senior Tutor, Patrick Wilkinson, himself author of a book on Horace, described him as the 'Greatest Scholar of the Age – any age'.

He referred to himself as nothing but Adcock – so it was not 'I think' but 'Adcock thinks'. He used to bring *The Times* with him to breakfast and commentate to any of us who would care to listen. On one occasion, I was transfixed. An undergraduate arrived with a copy of *The Times* and sat down next to Adcock with a plate of bacon. Opening his paper, he proceeded to give a commentary on the various items of interest. Adcock's bald dome steamed with rage and his face went almost purple. But he restrained himself, with obvious difficulty, from saying anything. The name of the undergraduate was John Barton, celebrated the world over four decades later as Director of the Royal Shakespeare Company.

Equally punctual for 8 a.m. breakfast in Hall was Philip Radcliffe, Director of Studies in Music. He was remembered fondly by a pupil of a later generation, Dr Oona Ivory, former Chairman of Scottish Ballet and Governor of the Royal Scottish Academy of Music, as an inspiring teacher of musical theory. In October, Radcliffe would ask me what opera I had seen or orchestra I had heard at that year's Edinburgh Festival and proceed to hum arias and tunes. He was a friend to many undergraduates who did not read music but who were to maintain and develop a lifelong interest.

Then there was the stern and usually unforthcoming figure of Richard (R. F.) Kahn, Professor of Economics and famous as the PhD student of Maynard Keynes, who had done the detailed work on the multiplier effect, which contributed crucially to

Keynes's *General Theory*. Science at breakfast was represented by the young Hal Dixon, destined to serve the College for 40 years as a tutor in biochemistry and in many other important responsibilities that contributed towards making King's what it was; and Kenneth Harrison, whose idleness in the lab, I was told by Sir Alec Todd (later Lord Todd of Trumpington), drove his colleagues to despair. Harrison, however, made a considerable contribution to the life of the College, not least because he was acknowledged as the leading European authority on medieval stained glass.

But King's made up for any shortcomings in biochemistry with a young radical Research Council postgraduate. His name was Dr Fred Sanger – now OM CH, Copley medallist and winner of not one but two Nobel Prizes. It was to be eight years after winning his first prize that he won his second, having published nothing of significance in all that time. The value of thinking time! I do wonder whether the pressure nowadays on academics to publish – and lose their job if they fail to publish – is sensible.

The Senior Tutor, Patrick Wilkinson, complained to the best man at our wedding, Dr James Cargill-Thompson, then Lay Dean of the College, that Sanger did not pull his weight in the running of the College. Years later, Sanger told me, in the company of the Argentinean César Milstein, also a recipient of a Nobel Prize for his work on monoclonal antibodies, that he would have done anything that the College asked him, within reason, but he dreaded becoming bogged down in administration. Milstein, who came to lunch at the Commons with me in 1983 to discuss the aftermath of the Falklands War, which had pained him terribly, told me he turned down many offers of a professorship on the grounds that the responsibilities would have made it impossible for him to do original work.

Sanger had a room on 'A' Staircase, where in my third year (1954–55), I had been allocated a beautiful room overlooking the Chapel, once the abode of Maynard Keynes before he married the ballerina Lydia Lopokova. The condition imposed on me by Patrick Wilkinson, the Senior Tutor, was that I pop my head round the doors of his elderly bachelors, one on the ground floor, the other on the first floor, to see that they were all right last thing at night. They were E. M. Forster, author of *A Passage to India* and one of the iconic writers of the twentieth century, and Arthur Pigou, Emeritus Professor of Economics. Occasionally, Pigou invited me in to give him a game of chess, if his regular opponent had failed to turn up. His adversary and friend was Paul Adrien Maurice Dirac, one of the great mathematicians of the age. I never so much as drew a game with Pigou.

Membership of the Ten Club, a College Play Recording Society, allowed me minor participation in the evenings with the literary scholar and theatre director G. H. W. Rylands (known as 'Dadie'), who had lived in the same rooms for more than half a century and had entranced generations of undergraduates. He was the sworn enemy of F. R. Leavis of Downing and his wife, Queenie D. Leavis, both of whom were English literary critics and essayists.

Lunch in Hall brought undergraduates into contact with dons who had families but needed a quick bite to eat in the middle of the day. George Salt FRS was a world authority in entomology and preached the importance of insects in the firmament. Edward Shire, Director of Studies in Physics, asked some of the non-scientists to visit him in the Cavendish Laboratory, where he worked. David Stockdale, Director of Studies in Chemistry, with farming connections in Dumfriesshire, befriended me as a fellow Scot. A looming presence was the choirmaster, Boris Ord, who gained international fame through the televised Christmas Eve programme, *Carols from King's*. Lawyers there were none. Sir John Sheppard, elected Provost in 1933 and holding the post for more than a quarter of a century, did not think law suitable as a Cambridge University subject!

But one chance juxtaposition at a lunch in Hall was to influence my life. Harry Johnson, a Canadian and young Fellow in Economics, later Professor *seriatim* at the University of Manchester, the London School of Economics and invited by Milton Friedman to be his colleague at the University of Chicago, asked me what I intended to do. 'To go to Moray House Training College to qualify as a teacher in Scotland,' I replied.

To this, Johnson said, 'You have got a good degree in history but you are still one of those sloppy-minded historians.'

'What can I do about it?' I asked.

'You could read economics.'

'Who would teach me?'

'I will.'

And Harry Johnson did. Such an extension would not have been possible these days. Part II of the Cambridge Tripos was very demanding. We used to be supervised in pairs. Normally, I went with the Hon. Christopher Maclaren, who had transferred from engineering and who later became Director of the South Bank Polytechnic. His sister, Anne Maclaren, an animal geneticist, was to become one of the first women officers of the Royal Society.

No divisions in politics in which I participated were as cantankerous as those in the Cambridge University Economic Faculty of 1955/56. On the one side were the traditional economists such as: Sir Denis Robertson, the charming gentleman who ran the Political Economy Club, which met after dinner in his rooms at Trinity Great Court and who was so admired by my grandfather; C. W. Guillebaud of St John's and Stanley Dennison of Caius, both of whom had headed important government committees on the coal industry; Dr Prest of Christ's, an authority on public finance; Peter Bauer, pioneer of the economics of international development; Professor E. A. G. (Austin) Robinson, editor of the *Cambridge Economic Journal*, reinforced by the free-marketeers, Harry Johnson himself and a visiting American professor by the name of Milton Friedman. Ranged on the other side – the radical left – were Austin Robinson's estranged wife, Joan, Richard Kahn, Nicky Kaldor and Robin Marris. The clash of ideas was thrilling for undergraduates and lucky were we to be forged in such a cauldron. It was the year in which Joan Robinson, who had written one of the seminal books of the 1930s, *The Economics of Imperfect Competition*, was putting the final touches to her magnum opus, *The Accumulation of Capital*.

In the early summer of 1956, I was sent to her for four supervisions. These took place when she, still in her sari, emerged from a hut in the bottom of her garden on Adams Road. She was a friend of Zhou Enlai, the first Premier of the People's Republic of China, and became vehemently opposed to the Vietnam War. When I did not, in 1967, vote for a critical motion in the Commons, Joan said she would never speak to me again. Two years later, I could point to the remarkable fact that Harold Wilson had resisted the blandishments of Lyndon Johnson to send a 'battalion of bag-pipers' as a token of British support for the Americans to Vietnam, albeit thanks to the advice of Sir Maurice Oldfield, who had been the head of MI6 Station in Indo-China, and of continual and vociferous pressure from a group of left-wing MPs in the Commons, of which (I am ashamed to say) I was not one.

My regular supervisors were Harry Johnson and Nicky Kaldor. Kaldor had an extraordinarily fertile mind, and was to combine this with great tact as a Treasury adviser to the Labour Government of 1964–70. He repeatedly told me that it was after our lunch *à deux* in the Commons, having heard me pour my heart out about 6.5 per cent unemployment in West Lothian, that he devised the Regional Employment Premium (REP). REP had the advantage of simplicity and served the purpose in alleviating unemployment in many parts of the United Kingdom.

If I have dwelt at length on my College and academic life in Cambridge it is because they were crucially formative years. Politically, I became Chairman of the University Conservative Association (but joined the Labour Club in my last year) and Vice-President of the Cambridge Union Society.

On reflection, I deserved to become one of the first Vice-Presidents rather than be elected President. Quite simply I made more bad speeches than good. And, the Liberal Richard Moore (father of Charles Moore, in his time, editor of the *Spectator*, the *Sunday Telegraph* and the *Daily Telegraph*), who beat me in the autumn of 1954, was a far better student orator.

Despite that I did not spend, thankfully, much time politicking, although I did make many student friends, many of whom, regardless of party allegiance, proved to be lifelong. Inevitably and justifiably, I am often asked, 'What made a person of your background switch from Tory to Labour?' The answer can be encapsulated in two words – Suez and unemployment. Fifty-five years later, it is not easy to convey the emotions set alight by the Anglo-French-Israeli action to thwart President Nasser over the Suez Canal. In my gut, I felt that what Anthony Eden was doing was wrong. So did my Arabic-speaking mother, who had no time for Eden anyway, since she and my father had seen him at close quarters during India Office occasions.

It may seem odd, in the light of the statistics in later years, that unemployment of six per cent should have been such an element in my conversion. But it was. My university supervisors, Nicholas Kaldor and Joan Robinson, and also student contemporaries such as Sam Brittan and Walter Eltis, later to be a *Financial Times* guru and Oxford don respectively, convinced me of the merits of a planned economy. Above all, a young student at Trinity stayed with me at The Binns for three weeks over the Christmas and New Year of 1955/56, when it was not worth his while to go back to Calcutta and return in early January. He was very persuasive on the merits of centralised planning of the economy. The student's name was Amartya Sen, later to be Professor at Harvard, Master of Trinity and a Nobel Prize winner in economics.

I confess that there was also a rather different consideration. Ever since hearing Fenner Brockway, Arthur Deakin, Ian Mikardo and, indeed, Leonard James Callaghan at Eton, I had socialist sympathies. Yet, I thought that, if I joined the Labour Club at Cambridge, many of my contemporaries would ascribe it to 'sour grapes' at not becoming an officer during National Service. I should not have let it bother me – but it did.

*

A childhood desire to go where General Tam had been came to fruition when, in 1956, I was awarded a Rupert Brooke Scholarship by King's College for travel, which paved the way for my being included in the first National Union of Students (NUS) delegation to the Soviet Union. We travelled from London, hopping perilously from Northolt Airport to Frankfurt, on to

Warsaw and a final stage from Vilnius to Moscow. Landing in the Lithuanian capital at an ungodly hour, we passed a huge white marble bust of Stalin on our way to an office to sort out the interminable documentation required in those days for entry into the Soviet Union. Three weeks later, on our return journey, lo and behold, Stalin was gone. It was the time of the momentous Twentieth Party Congress, during which Khrushchev denounced Stalin, who had died three years earlier.

Years later, I was told the following story by Douglas Jay, Harold Wilson's President of the Board of Trade and the MP for Battersea. Towards the end of the third hour of his five-hour speech, Khrushchev was interrupted. A little man at the back of the huge hall could not contain himself any longer. He stood up and shouted out, 'And when Stalin was doing all these awful things which you describe, what were you doing?' He was pointing at Khrushchev himself and then at the assembled grandees on the platform – Malenkov, Voroshilov, Mikoyan, Suslov, Kaganovich and Molotov – the men who had run Russia for the previous quarter of a century along with Stalin. Khrushchev paused and said, 'Would the comrade who shouted at me please stand up?' Five seconds went by, 10 seconds went by, 20 seconds, 45 seconds. There was deathly silence and no one stood up. Then Khrushchev beamed and said, 'Comrade, that was what we were doing during the Stalin years.'

From Moscow, the NUS Delegation went to Kiev, the capital of the Ukraine, a city which in the year AD 1000, according to my Cambridge lecturer Professor Michael Postan, who was himself of Ukrainian extraction, was the most advanced metropolis in the whole world (only historians of Cordoba in Spain might dispute this). My memory of Kiev was not so much its iconic site – the beautiful and half-destroyed monastery of Lavra – but of the collective farm in the rich and fertile land of the Ukraine to which we were taken. They told us about all the statistics of the two crops of wheat in the year that they were able to grow and their milk yields from the huge black and white local breeds.

I mentioned to the manager that I was a beekeeper. Immediately he sent for the collective farm's master of bees. A giant of a man arrived in a singlet with remarkably hairy arms and legs as well as a luxuriant black beard. The manager was delighted to please the beekeeper and the beekeeper was even more delighted to meet the guests from Britain. He swept me into his jeep-like vehicle to go and see his hives. The bees were obviously used to him, not that they could sting him through his hairy protection, but they were altogether less pleased to see a young alien Scotsman in a kilt with plenty of unhairy surfaces. I was stung in my private parts where it hurt most and had to spend the night in a Kiev hospital, where I remember the Uzbek nurse who expertly plucked out, with complete sangfroid, the stings from down under. Although she could speak not a word of English and, as I gathered, very little Russian, it emerged that her father, who lived near the ancient city of Bokhara, kept bees and she was familiar with what had to be done – probably the reason that she was instructed by the hospital authorities to deal with me. Ever since, I have been well disposed to Uzbeks.

From the Ukraine, we went to the Crimea where we visited the Young Pioneers' camp at Artek. With their red scarves round their necks and their immaculately clean skirts and shorts, an indelible impression was made of a society different from ours but which had its merits. From Simferopol, the capital of the Crimea, we took the train on the long 36-hour journey to Leningrad. Here the monastery was terribly destroyed and it brought home the devastation of the siege of Leningrad during World War II, when the city held out against the Germans' relentless bombardment by land and air for 872 days.

Much later, when I was chairman of the Parliamentary Labour Party foreign affairs group, we had as a speaker Professor Olkonikov, an editor of a Leningrad newspaper who, with his family, had lived through the siege. My colleagues and I were struck by the way in which he described how they would set out full place settings, with cutlery, plates and glasses, and then proceed to eat rats or whatever they could get hold of. He said, 'Keeping up standards helped see us through this traumatic period.' Of course, we were taken, not only to the Hermitage, whose treasures are so well known now but to us was a revelation, but also to the Yusupov Palace, home of the assassin of Rasputin, and the Stroganov Palace, with its beautiful marble staircase, then being used as a teachers' training centre.

I left Cambridge in 1956 having made the most of every minute of my time there, deeply aware of my good fortune in participating in the life of a superbly stimulating college and emerging with a 2:1.

CHAPTER FOUR

Work

Within a week of leaving Cambridge I was pitched into my career as a teacher. Andrew Ewing, then number three in the official hierarchy of the West Lothian Education Authority, whom I hoped would be my future employers, had taken me aside in Easter 1956 and told me that it would (a) be good for me as a potential teacher and (b) earn more 'Brownie points' with those allocating teaching posts, if I were to offer to help out at the school camps run by West Lothian Council. I volunteered. Fifty-five years later, I reckon that the four weeks spent at Abingdon on the Clyde and at Dounan's Camp, Aberfoyle, were dispro-portionately important in my life.

The experience gave me a breezy confidence in handling young teenagers, with the realisation that my Etonian vowels and cut-glass accent were not necessarily an impediment in relating to youngsters from a very different background. It helped that I was a no-nonsense and effective whistle-blowing games referee, who was clearly in charge and was fit enough to lead the early-morning runs up the hill behind the camp at Aberfoyle. But above all, school camp was the foundation of my excellent relations with a cross-section of West Lothian schoolteachers. Unquestionably, had I not been at ease with them and, more importantly, they with me, I would not have been even con-sidered as a parliamentary candidate in 1962.

West Lothian is a community where reputation is transmitted in detail on the grapevine. At camp, I formed an admiration for the qualities and dedication of the overwhelming majority of the teachers of that generation. In particular, I was impressed by the pupil skills of primary school headmasters, who had not been to university, had done but one year's teacher training course but who had served in the forces for six years. Lifelong friendships were formed playing Monopoly late into the night, after the kids were, hopefully, asleep.

At Abingdon, however, I had one of the very worst moments of my life. I had taken a group of boys, all of whom assured me they could swim, to a pool in the Clyde. One boy misled me. Out of the corner of my eye I noticed him, coming up for the third time, after which he would have drowned and I would have been held responsible. This time he survived. Alas, two years later, the same boy – his name was Ian – was to drown in the Bathgate Public Baths.

Throughout my period of teacher training, I was supremely lucky in encountering men – they happened to be all men – who would determine my professional future. Peter Sommerville, son and grandson of Fauldhouse coalminers, was headmaster of South Queensferry Junior Secondary School, where I did my first month's teaching practice before going to the Training College at Moray House. He observed me and concluded privately to me, 'You're fine with the boys but your background could give you real problems with the lassies. Take my advice. Treat 'em rough from the beginning.' I did – by formally calling them 'Miss' followed by their surname – but it was not easy at first. Fifteen-year-old girls, about to get jobs in Distillers' Whisky Bottling Plant at South Queensferry, had things other than history or mathematics on their post-pubescent minds!

My day-to-day mentor at South Queensferry where, on account of teacher shortage and sickness, I was thrown in at the deep end to take classes on my own, was the teacher of technical subjects next door, Alex Mitchell, a member of the Labour Party, who became a lifelong friend. Both Sommerville and Mitchell were to spread the word among their Labour Party friends, six years later, to the effect that 'Tam Dalyell is okay'. At Moray House, I was allocated to the course for 1st Class and 2:1 Honours Graduates. My director of studies, an Englishman and amateur archaeologist called Alan Rae, accompanied by his pocket-battle-ship of a wife, Vi, would take us on 'his dig' at Cramond. It was an educational experience and I learned a lot about archaeological methods.

Unlike some of my friends and contemporary honours gradu-ates from the Universities of Edinburgh, Glasgow and St Andrews, I took my teacher training very seriously, feeling somewhat vulnerable as a Cambridge graduate in the unfamiliar Scottish educational system. The Professor of Education, John Pilley, a distinguished philosopher and disciple of Alfred North Whitehead, from the University of Edinburgh, took worthwhile, if sometimes abstruse seminars, for the Diploma in Education. But the person who rendered me the greatest kindness was the scholarly Director of Moray House, Dr W. B. Inglis. Seeing me in my snow-clad wellington boots in the freezing January of 1957, he beckoned me to his office. 'I know you have to travel 15 miles each day by bus, and I learn you are certain to be awarded your Parchment [licence to teach]. I have on my desk, out of the blue, an invitation to send a student for the month of February to the Salzburg Seminar in American Studies. Would you like to go?' he asked me.

I jumped at the invitation. And those four weeks in the Schloss Leopoldskron reinforced my National Service pro-European prejudices. Cooped up in a dormitory in the magnificent apart-ment built by Ludwig the Mad of Bavaria and used by Max Reinhardt's mistress as her boudoir, my particular friends were Andreas Meyer-Landrut, my table tennis partner and later to be the West German Ambassador to China, and Mario Bassano, later of the Milan newspaper *Corriere della Sera*. Sleeping in the next bed, Mario would practise his English on me into the small hours. When I expressed surprise that his grandfather was Dean of the Communist Party in the Italian Senate, and his great-uncle was a Cardinal, his reply was: 'We are nice people in Italy!' Until they died, I kept up with the American faculty directors, Dexter Perkins of Harvard, Dr and Mrs Ross of the University of Denver, Colorado, and Chandler Morse, Professor of Economic Theory at the University of Cornell. Much benefit accrues to a politician who keeps such friendships in good repair.

I was lucky also in the teaching practice assignments I was given at Moray House. At Tynecastle Secondary School the headmaster, Dr John Kay, assigned me to a young teacher, Douglas Currie, who was to be a lifelong friend. At Boroughmuir, the great headmaster Robert Carswell put me into the hands of Urban Harris, an impressively effective head of the history department. At Heriot's the fierce headmaster, William McLachlan Dewar, assigned me to Willie Gould, an imaginative head of department, and Paddy O'Malley, later promoted to the Oratory School in London where, as an MP, I used to go and speak to his pupils. Years later I thanked Mr Dewar and asked him why he had taken so much trouble to see us students about our progress and reports. 'A headmaster has no higher duty than to guide these young men and women who are entering what I regard as my noble profession,' was his memorable reply. The ultimate accolade came in the form of one of the pupils, 14-year-old Terry Nealon, later a Hong Kong businessman, telling his mother, Councillor Mrs Rina Nealon, the powerful chairman of the City of Edinburgh Health Committee, that 'Mr Dalyell has a posh voice, but a with-it sense of humour – and is a well-informed Jambo'. (A Jambo is a supporter of Heart of Midlothian Football Club.)

I was lucky above all to get a teaching post in the secondary school of my choice, Bo'ness Academy, just four miles from The Binns. Retrospectively after 50 years and more, many of my former pupils, still living and working in Bo'ness at the point of reaching pensionable age, reckon that I was an excellent teacher. At a time of chronic shortage of maths teachers, because I had an economics degree, I was called upon to take the maths classes which, actually, I enjoyed more than teaching history.

In 1961 discipline was nothing like the problem which prevails in many schools in 2011. Belting on the hand was the accepted form of punishment. My belt remained in the drawer for weeks at a time. On one occasion, I was provoked by twins in my form class playing up and making life hell for a newly arrived temporary female teacher. I belted the boys. 'We'll get our dad up here to sort you out,' they screeched. The following week, I said to them, 'Billy and Jimmy, you told me that your dad would come to school to see me!' The twins, to their credit, gave a broad, wry smile. 'When we told our dad, he made us take our trousers down and it was far harder, sir, than what you handed out to us!' Such automatic support from a parent – in this case a coalminer – for a teacher is rarer these days. Years later in the Commons, I bit my tongue and voted with the herd of anti-corporal-punishment-in-schools brigade, led by my friend Dennis Canavan, then an MP, who, as a first-class maths teacher in Stirling, had been far handier with his belt than ever I was.

My memories of Bo'ness Academy are extremely happy. My colleagues on the staff were without exception cordially well disposed. I had the strong impression that art, biology, chemistry, drama and technical drawing were better taught than the same subjects at Eton. In the early 1960s, health and safety regulations were less 'developed'. Many of my pupils, 50 years later, have treasured memories of cycle rides to the Kincardine Power Station and of visits down the coalmine and to local factories. A few pupils volunteered to help me with my bees and, on one occasion, we angered them and got badly stung. I dread to think what trouble a teacher would incur these days for landing a 13-year-old with a dozen beestings. I phoned Mrs Stevenson, whose son David had been the main target of the bees' wrath, who said, 'Please invite David to help with your bees next weekend. He wants to come and I want him to go.'

Perhaps the most memorable of my expeditions was with two janitors, Sandy King and Jock Mackie – wise teachers make friends with the janitors – taking 144 boys in three bus-loads to the European Cup Final for a 7.30 p.m. kick-off on the evening of 18 May 1960 at Hampden Park. It was the legendary occasion when the Real Madrid forward line, Kopa of France, del Sol of Spain, di Stefano of Argentina, Puskas of Hungary and Gento of Spain, wove their magic and put seven goals past the Eintracht Frankfurt defence. After the match one boy, Tarry McAdam, got separated from our group in a trouble-free crowd of 133,000. Eventually, having found him, I was returning the last boy to his parents at Newton Village at 2 a.m. An angry 6-foot-4 father came to the door – furious not with me but with himself for giving his ticket for the game to a friend and watching it instead on television. It encapsulates the loyalty of often cheekily down-to-earth Bo'ness teenagers that not a single one of the 144 pupils failed to turn up on time for school the following morning.

*

In any person's life it is strange how determining points of that life can be triggered by the most unlikely of beginnings. On one summer evening, after I had returned to The Binns exhausted by one of my few 'bad days' – discipline-wise – with Class 3F of 15-year olds at Bo'ness Academy, I looked out of the window and saw a ship, which I conjectured was the one I had read about in that day's paper on its last voyage bound for the breakers' yard. What a pity, it occurred to me, that such a ship could not be used to take frustrated teenagers to experience life outside their familiar surroundings.

Timing is everything. It so happened that I had been chosen as one of the West Lothian delegates to the annual conference of the Educational Institute of Scotland (EIS), held at the Assembly Hall of the Church of Scotland in Edinburgh. I submitted a motion, in a personal capacity, but not on behalf of my branch of the EIS, advocating the use of ships for educational purposes. Normally such a motion would have fallen off the end of a busy day's agenda. However, previous business for the afternoon took less time than was anticipated and I was given a hearing.

Since, as soon as my motion was published, I had taken the trouble to go to see two of the most powerful and influential ladies in the EIS at that time, Miss Pearl Kettles and Miss Helen Hyndman Dewar, they spread the word that Tam Dalyell's motion should not be rejected out of hand but should 'lie on the table'. Importantly, through Miss Kettles and Miss Dewar, I gained the goodwill of the EIS president, Edward Britton, deputy rector of that academically rigorous school, Hamilton Academy, and of the general secretary, William Campbell, and his deputy and successor, Gilbert Bryden.

This non-rejection by the EIS gave me the confidence to speak on the subject at the Scottish Labour Party conference. Shortly after I had done, so the secretary of the Scottish Labour Party, Will Marshall, a wily ex-miner from Fife, beckoned me over and said, 'I don't want to pour cold water on your contribution this morning but, take my advice – if you are going to try and land the Party with such a policy, you must flesh out your ideas. Why not put them in book form?'

I replied, 'Yes but who would publish such a book?'

Marshall said he had a friend who ran the Civic Press in Glasgow – basically printers – who had published occasional tracts. They undertook to print 1,000 copies of the book, and try to distribute them at modest cost to myself.

So, I hurriedly wrote my first of nine books, *The Case for Ship Schools*. Frankly, it was a naive and somewhat immature polemic in floating the concept of educational cruising and sold some 200 copies. Then I had a huge stroke of luck. The publishers had sent a review copy to the *Manchester Guardian*. The then young editor, Alastair Hetherington, whose father, Sir Hector Hetherington, Vice-Chancellor of the University of Glasgow, had been a friend of my parents, instead of consigning it to his wastepaper basket, flung *The Case for Ship Schools* to his most junior reviewer. His most junior reviewer and occasional leader writer was one Brian Redhead. Now, I had been a member of the Cambridge Union committee in the summer of 1954 when Brian Redhead was president and we had become great friends. Handed the book, Redhead wrote an over-generous fourth leader, in which he opined that Tam Dalyell 'should be given his head' and that educational cruising should be considered as one among a number of projects to stimulate non-academic pupils. Redhead, of course, was to move from the *Manchester Guardian* to the BBC, where he became a much-admired presenter of the *Today* programme, famous for his concerns for 'friends of the M6', along which he regularly travelled to and fro to his hometown of Macclesfield.

I repeat, timing is everything in life and I again had a stroke of good fortune. Redhead's leader was spotted in the *Manchester Guardian* by Sir Colin Anderson, a director of Peninsular and

Orient (P&O) and a great power in British shipping, who brought it to the attention of his brother, Sir Donald Anderson, chairman and managing director of P&O. P&O was the parent company of BI, the British India Steam Navigation Company. BI had a problem at that precise moment. The 12,000-ton *Dunera* had been built specifically as a troop ship to take British servicemen to Mombasa and Singapore. With improvements in air travel, which the War Office deemed more efficient and cost effective, the government told BI that they were breaking their charter contract with them but the Treasury would give BI £5 million in compensation. Now the Anderson brothers, with all the attitudes of their age, associated with Eton and Trinity College, Oxford, disdained being mere 'accountants' and regarded themselves as 'shipping persons'. They were looking for ways to let their troop ship live the normal lifespan of such a vessel and avoid laying off British Merchant Marine officers and the faithful Goanese crew. So, they instructed the chairman of BI, Kenneth Campbell, and his senior manager, John Sharpe, to see me.

We clicked. A meeting was arranged at Southampton on board *Dunera*, to which a number of directors of education and head-masters were invited. I was invited as one of a number of speakers, each allowed five minutes. I spoke to my carefully rehearsed points for 4 minutes and 50 seconds. Two of the other speakers rambled on for a quarter of an hour beyond their allotted time. This may seem a trivial point to record after half a century but my sticking to time had a momentous consequence. The captain of the *Dunera*, a Devon seadog, soon to be Commodore of the Fleet, Ben Rogers, told me years later that he had said to Sir Colin Anderson and Kenneth Campbell, chairmen of BI, 'I'll willingly have that young man on my ship – he will do as he is told.' Rightly BI, when they finalised their decision to prepare the *Dunera* for experimental educational cruising, appointed a senior London headmaster, Clive Harston, a man I came to like very much, as director of studies, and I was offered the job of his deputy.

Acceptance meant that I had to ask West Lothian Education Committee about their attitude to my rather precipitously leaving their employment. The chairman, David Drysdale, a coalminer from Whitburn, his director of education, James Taylor, and his deputy, Andrew Ewing, soon to leave to become Chief Education Officer of the London Burgh of Hounslow, were marvellous. They suggested a two-year leave of absence, with the guarantee of a teaching post in West Lothian when I returned and no loss of seniority when I applied for promoted posts in their schools. Furthermore, they cast a benevolent eye on my successful efforts to organise a party of pupils from West Lothian. Drysdale, who later was to come with his wife and the county convener, Peter Walker, and his wife, as guests of BI on the *Dunera*, to witness what it was like, took the attitude that 'nothing is too good for the children of coalminers – let them see the world'.

The first two voyages out of Greenock in April 1961 cost the parents £17 per child. After the pioneering cruises proved successful, the rate went up to £34 – still excellent value for 13 days at sea – including four or five land visits. Costs were containable since *Dunera* could take 830 pupils in the 35 dormitories, designed as accommodation for other ranks. The officers and warrant officers had tight cabin accommodation, which BI upgraded to accommodate teacher/party leaders, observer dignitaries who were guests of the company, the occasional journalist and some paying passengers.

I was very much in BI's good books. As soon as they appointed me as deputy director of studies, I used the ten days' autumn break from school, when the pupils went 'tattie howking' (lifting potatoes from the fields) to leg it round council education officers, to drum up support. Again, I was lucky. Because they knew what had happened in the EIS, many were prepared to see me personally, along with three dynamic employees of BI, Tony Moores, Peter Motion and John Rees, who had been seconded by Campbell and Sharpe to work full-time, marketing the project.

Five directors from major authorities turned up trumps: Andrew Cameron of Dunbartonshire; Hugh Fairley of Renfrewshire; Tom Henderson of Midlothian; Douglas Mackintosh of Fife; and Dr George Reith of the City of Edinburgh. James Wallace came himself, as deputy director of education in Ayrshire, supervising a contingent of nearly 200 pupils. The first voyage took us to Corunna, Gibraltar and Lisbon. The second sailed out of Greenock and returned to Leith so that *Dunera* was well-positioned for the third voyage, out of the Tyne, which took us to Bergen, Oslo, Copenhagen, Hamburg and Amsterdam.

Part of my remit was to do slide presentations three times a day, to more than 280 pupils per sitting, about what they would see next day. The evening before we were to disembark in Bergen, I showed Grieg's house and played a little of his music on a gramophone; before Oslo, with the help of slides, I explained about the Viking Ship Museum and the statues in the Vigeland Park; and before Amsterdam, I covered places their party leaders could take pupils, such as the Church of Our Lord in the Attic and the Rijksmuseum. Having an explanation of Rembrandt's *The Night Watch* or of *The Anatomist* stimulated their interest, especially when they saw the actual painting the following day.

It was on the *Dunera* that I visited Russia for a second time in 1962, taking the Bo'ness Academy cup-winning football team with reinforcements from the Scottish Schoolboys' International Side. We played a match at the Kirov Workers' Stadium before, astonishingly, a crowd of 12,000 people. The Leningraders seemed overjoyed to have this contact with the West and the hard-fought match ended in a 2–2 draw. The boys were told all about Kirov, the popular party boss in Leningrad in the early 1930s – so popular that he was eliminated by Stalin.

It was also my central responsibility to ensure that teacher/party leaders got some work out of pupils in the form of writing up their logbooks properly and producing essays about what they had seen on the previous day ashore. I tried, usually but not always successfully, to ensure that at least a sample of work done was submitted to chief education officers as feedback was very important if future voyages were to be well supported. Besides, since for 37 weeks in the year cruises were in term-time, there was a moral obligation and, indeed, a legal obligation, to prove that 13 days on the *Dunera* was not simply a jolly.

As my 18 months working on the *Dunera* went by, my high regard for my teaching colleagues grew and grew. All right, most of them hugely enjoyed going abroad and eating delicious

Goanese curries on board ship. But very, very few came along for
the ride. Most were immensely conscientious and worked very
hard to ensure their pupils got the maximum benefit out of this
unusual opportunity and relate their schoolwork to the experience. Overwhelmingly, especially in term time, they were from
secondary modern schools (in Scotland, junior secondary
schools).

Benefiting from the kindly and encouraging advice from a
number of educationalists, such as Alec (later Sir Alec) Clegg of
the West Riding of Yorkshire and Edgar Heelas, a chief schools'
inspector in the city of Birmingham, who came as the company's
guests, I became a vastly improved teacher. They did me the
courtesy of coming to my pre-port presentations and putting me
through a post-mortem over dinner. Years later, when I visited
his home in Birmingham, Heelas (who was, by then, nearly 90)
told me that he reported to his boss, Sir Lionel Russell, chief
education officer of Birmingham, that the *Dunera* was the best
value for money of any of the many educational initiatives taken
for the benefit of secondary modern pupils. My parliamentary
colleague Jeff Rooker, MP for Perry Barr, confirmed that
Heelas's judgements were highly respected by Birmingham
councillors, of which he was then a group member, and MPs.

I was also directly responsible to the captain – rightly, he was
the ultimate boss in all matters on board his ship – for discipline.
I cannot pretend this was an onerous responsibility, since party
leaders had myriad methods of dealing with their own pupils. On
the fifth educational cruise, after two from the Clyde and two
from the Tyne, *Dunera* sailed from Tilbury. I stood at the top of
the gangway anticipating trouble, as streams of 14- and 15-year-
old girls in their high heels, miniskirts and unusual hairdos
scrambled aboard. As one who had been accustomed to the
relatively douce girls of Scotland, with similarly familiar pupils
from Northumberland, I thought, 'What have we here?'

I need not have worried. Their teachers were wholly in control,
led by a huge bear of a hairy-armed man, the headmaster Alf
Roberts. One night, there was some trouble, which matron
reported to me, in one of the East Ham girls' dormitories. I told

Alf Roberts. After his second course at dinner, he said, 'Excuse me.' A quarter of an hour later, he returned for the third course. 'I've sorted that out,' he said before tucking into his pudding

'How did you do it?' I asked.

'Spanked the lot!' he replied, matter-of-factly, in a cockney accent as broad as that of any of his pupils.

'You did what, Alf?' I said incredulously.

'Spanked the lot,' he reiterated, munching away at the cheese.

I was somewhat taken aback.

The following morning I recounted what had happened, somewhat gingerly, to William Openshaw, the distinguished director of education for West Ham, who was travelling as a guest of BI. The response was blunt: 'Tam, don't you on any account try to interfere in what Alf Roberts does with his own pupils!' Later in the day I saw Alf Roberts playing deck quoits with the girls, all as happy as Larry.

A third of a century later, in May 1994, I was canvassing for Stephen Timms, Labour candidate in the Newham North East constituency, later to be a Treasury minister, at the by-election following the death of Ron Leighton. I knocked at a door and an ample East-End matron answered. She looked at me and said, 'I've seen you somewhere before.'

'On the telly?' I suggested.

'Ah,' she said, 'and weren't you on the *Dunera*?'

I nodded. 'Did you go?'

'Yes, smashing.'

'Who was your party leader?'

'Alfie Roberts.'

I decided to remind her of the dormitory episode.

'Yes,' she volunteered with a laugh. 'I was one of those spanked. The slipper hurt my buttocks but it was a fair cop.' Such were the mores of the East End.

The only recurrent disciplinary difficulty was youngsters being a bit high on the first night or two at sea. Many pupils had never been away from their parents before in their lives. I confess I prayed for a good force-9 gale. Nothing else was so effective a disciplining procedure as universal seasickness. All right, it did produce a stench. But it also brought home the power of the sea, which was one of the reasons for educational cruising in the first place.

If the water was calm, my method was to go into the most obstreperous boys' dormitory, accompanied by Mr Hughes or Mr O'Gorman, ship's officers in their full Merchant Marine attire, and order them out of their hammocks, tell them to get dressed, go into a classroom on the upper deck and write out *Dunera*'s fire regulations. Much later, in my last two years as an MP, men in the London Tube eyed me. 'Mr Dalyell?' one asked. I nodded. I had been on *Sky News* that morning and, indeed, week after week, twice a week, going into the studio at 4 Millbank where Peter Spencer, the early morning duty reporter of *Sky News*, and Peter Murphy, of ITN News, were only too glad to have an MP physically in the studio before 7 a.m.

I supposed the men in the Underground would comment on my politically current pearls of wisdom. Not one bit of it. Twice they said, 'So you were the bastard that made me write out the ship's fire regulations!' And three times, 'So you were the geezer who made me write out the *Dunera*'s fire regulations in the middle of the night!' On each occasion, it was followed by a laugh which cleared my conscience that they had been nursing this particular grievance for 40 years.

Perhaps on account of my own background, as at Bo'ness Academy, I found the 14-plus girls more difficult to teach than boys. On *Dunera* the girls' dormitories were a no-go area as far as I was concerned and I was reduced to asking Matron to go in to stop the cackle, while I bellowed at them through the door. Matron, a very sensible lady, was highly qualified medically but not as a teacher. The female party leaders did not care for having their evening meal in the ship's restaurant interrupted by being summoned to sort out their charges. My own routine was to have breakfast and lunch in the dining room, so I could get to know the party leaders, and take the evening meal with the youngsters in the cafeteria so I was free to go round at the point of maximum commotion.

In my judgement, the most valuable part of the *Dunera*

experience was communal life on board, coupled with rudimentary instruction in navigation involving visits to the bridge of the ship. I was delighted years later when, on a political visit to Dundee, a pupil who had been at Harris Academy told me that he had first seen the point of mathematics at school when he stood on the bridge with the rest of his class on the *Dunera*. He told me that he was a very average pupil but had since become an engineer travelling the world.

Among the most productive party leaders were teachers who, 20 years before, had been in the navy during the War. One such was my lifelong friend Lionel Joseph, from the Sondes Place Secondary Modern School in Dorking. Having served as a young naval officer on HMS *Eskimo* and HMS *Tartan*, Joseph did superb work, briefing pupils on the working of the ship from engine room to the communications operation. Interestingly he, along with his equally committed and talented wife, Joyce, conducted a study of how many of his pupils, now approaching pensionable age, have fared in later life. Joseph's findings are a remarkable testimony to the lasting value of the educational cruising experience.

The success was such that *Dunera* was replicated by her sister ship *Devonia* under the command, in the first instance, of Captain Ivan Bowerman, who had been second-in-command on *Dunera*. Following them were the 18,000-tonne *Nevasa* and the 14,000-tonne *Uganda*, which was commandeered by Mrs Thatcher as a hospital ship in 1982 for her Falkland War. Battered by South Atlantic weather, *Uganda* was not to be re-converted to educational cruising. But, between 1962 and 1982, more than a million schoolchildren were given an experience which they would not otherwise have enjoyed.

When Kathleen and I visited Ben Rogers in his Newton Abbot home during his retirement, he said that, as commodore of the BI fleet, *Dunera* had been the highlight of his 42 years with the company. My relations with him were excellent – on the understanding that whatever the captain wanted was a command. Only once was I summoned to his cabin for a rebuke for 'gossiping' on the ship's Tannoy, which he found intolerable, particularly in the afternoon, when many sailors take a rest.

There were many highlights. In midwinter BI flew pupils to Venice and from there *Dunera* sailed to Dubrovnik, Piraeus and Corfu. I had no greater pleasure than taking the academically gifted pupils, sometimes precocious boys of the High School of Glasgow and Eastwood Academy, round the Acropolis and, on the second day, paying our respects to the Oracle at Delphi.

There were hairy moments too. In the early months of 1961, I was exceedingly nervous, as was the BI management, that something could go drastically awry. On our second visit to Copenhagen, *Dunera* was docked near the famous Little Mermaid on the Langelinie. The shore visit seemed to have been a success as I counted the parties back at the top of the gangway. Then two elderly lady leaders returned, breathless and distraught. Three of their young girls had got separated from their group in the Tivoli Gardens. Had they returned to the ship? No, they had not. *Dunera* was due to sail. Captain Rogers was fretting and tetchy. The port charges for extra time spent alongside were about the highest in Europe. Just as I was about to despair a huge Cadillac drove up, with the Stars and Stripes fluttering from the bonnet. Out stepped the three girls. They had had the sense to knock on the door of the United States Embassy. The Ambassador had asked his personal chauffeur to convey them back to the ship. Never was I so relieved.

There was relief also when, after a call at the port of Naples, all the teenage girls returned, having enjoyed themselves 'fraternising' with the young of the city. For many, getting to know the locals was a more attractive use of time ashore than wandering round the marvels of Pompeii and Herculaneum. On several occasions the *Dunera* and her sister ship *Devonia* were hired on charter by the National Trust for Scotland to cruise to Fair Isle, Shetland, St Kilda and the Western Isles. I maintained my modest, tiny cabin, while the Trust's President, the Earl of Wemyss, willingly slept in a dormitory with the NTS members. It was an unforgettable and huge success.

CHAPTER FIVE

Parliament: the 1960s

I've got a real P.P.S. who acts as my Private Secretary. He not only cooks my breakfast at 9 Vincent Square, he's a confidante, a Sancho Panza, listening to his Don Quixote talking, talking, talking, saying everything aloud in his presence and knowing nothing will be passed on. He also does a great deal of contact work in his smoking-room and makes notes of all my conversations and reminds me of the promises I've made. So he really is doing the work of a civil servant now.

Richard Crossman's diary, 29 December 1967

To him society should be purposeful as well as classless. Politics are to ensure that people get value for money and a better deal. Tam is against any government that squanders Britain's fiscal and manpower resources on defence indefensibles, when so many other ways exist of being socialist, scientific, humane and wise . . . His parliamentary role is self-imposed. It is to keep Labour on the right lines on the big issues – science, technology, education, sport. These are his chosen specialities, charting their deeps for MPs with less aptitude or time to be so well informed on them. Tam has the intellect as well as the instinctive arrogance needed for the task. It means he goes straight to the experts, asking tirelessly and becoming expert himself.

Robert Brown in the *Guardian*, 3 September 1968

The circumstances of why I became a parliamentary candidate in 1958 were bizarre. John P. Mackintosh, then history lecturer at the University of Edinburgh and one of the most compelling orators of the day, had been adopted as candidate for Berwick and East Lothian. He said, 'Do me a favour. If you're free on Sunday afternoon in two weeks' time, go down to Galashiels and make the leet for candidates for Roxburgh, Selkirk and Peebles respectable. You won't be selected.'

I was free so I went and was invited to lunch with Jack Donaldson, Galashiels party chairman, and Andrew Turnbull, party secretary for Hawick.

'Where is Sinclair Shaw?' I asked over the soup. Mackintosh had told me that this prominent QC would be selected.

'Sinclair has called off; he has a long, lucrative case, and has told us he doesn't have time to be a candidate.'

'And your second string, Bob McGowan?'

'He's been appointed Professor of Philosophy at the University of Brisbane.'

'And Laurie Morrison, your previous [1955] candidate?'

'He doesn't want to run again!'

'And our friend from TSSA [Transport Salaried Staff Association] from St Boswells?'

'His wife has put her foot down!'

They then broke the news to me that I was to be the sole candidate.

In the ensuing selection conference at the Elwyn Co-operative restaurant, I gave my view on Gaitskell's policy document, 'Industry and Society' and was candid about myself, as I did not want them to think later that they had bought a pig in a poke. After I had duly performed, I was sent out of the room. Watt Cranston, CLP chairman and Hawick dustman, summoned me in after 45 seconds and declared, 'You'll do!'

My determination to raise issues of science in the House of Commons, if I were ever to get there, was kindled on a wet August afternoon in the Peeblesshire village of Carlops in 1958. I was canvassing, going round the village on my bicycle, knocking on doors to say, 'Could I introduce myself as the Labour candidate for Roxburgh, Selkirk and Peebles constituency, in a General Election which is certain to take place in the next 15 months?' Then it started to rain cats and dogs, as it does so often in the lee of the Pentland Hills.

So was I glad when, at a detached cottage door, a frail old man asked me to come in out of the wet and have a cup of tea. He ambled off into the kitchen to put the kettle on, leaving me in his front room. Politely I stood looking at the pictures on the wall. A photograph caught my eye and transfixed me. There was my host some 30 years younger but definitely him, standing at the edge of the second row. Seated in the front row was the unmistakable Moses-like figure of the convener of the Solvay Conference held in 1927 in Brussels, Paul Langevin. He was flanked by Madame Marie Curie, Niels Bohr, Albert Einstein, Max von Laue, Max Planck and Ernest Rutherford. Standing alongside my host were Enrico Fermi, Otto Hahn, Werner Heisenberg, Wolfgang Pauli and, I thought, Theodore von Karman, the father of Hungarian physics.

In a flash, I realised this must be the home of C. T. R. Wilson, whose work with the cloud chamber and the tracing of particles significantly helped to usher in the atomic age and earned him a Nobel Prize. The elderly gentleman shuffled back with the tea and was surprised and delighted that I had recognised the photograph and its significance. We talked about his time at Sidney Sussex College, Cambridge, and his relations with those in the photograph. 'Yes, I admired them all,' he told me, 'and liked them all other than one – Werner Heisenberg, of whom I was not in the least surprised when I was told he had co-operated with the Nazis. Thank goodness Mrs Bohr stamped her foot and told Niels that, on no account was her husband to give crucial information to Heisenberg, who had come to visit him in Copenhagen at the beginning of World War II.'

I was entranced. As I bid farewell (he was to pass away a few months later) he asked me, 'If you should be elected to the House of Commons – and it will not be for Peeblesshire – would you take an interest in helping to promote good science?' I promised that I would and kept my promise.

My candidacy in Roxburgh, Selkirk and Peebles was valuable in one important respect. Had I not stood, I am convinced the West Lothian Labour Party would not have looked at me as a possible candidate in the 1962 by-election. My predecessor, John

Taylor, had been MP for 11 years and had risen to be Deputy Chief Whip. The Whips' office had the choice of trips abroad and John exercised his right to go on an official visit to Tanganyika, as Tanzania then was. He returned with pleurisy, complicated by an unidentified tropical disease, and withered away.

My selection as his successor was completely different from my experience in 1958. By then, I had caught the bug and wanted to be a Member of Parliament. In Roxburgh, Selkirk and Peebles, there had been 16 in the room. In West Lothian, 162 duly accredited delegates packed into the hall in Armadale. I often made bad speeches in those days but, on this occasion, I made a good one, saying that the price of coal was the price of pneumoconiosis and I was a believer in nuclear power. I was plain lucky as to the order in which the five other candidates were eliminated. Had the 63-year-old candidate Dan Kellachan gone out on the fourth ballot, the AEU candidate would almost certainly have beaten me. As it was, he failed to edge ahead of the NUM candidate by a number of votes that could be counted on the fingers of one hand. And I'm pretty certain of something else. In no other circumstances would I have been selected as a Labour candidate in a winnable seat.

I was a most unlikely Labour candidate. I was from the lairdry. I lived in a house which my butter merchant, axle-grease trading ancestor Thomas Dalyell had built between 1612 and 1630 and which was the first house to be asked for by, and given to, the National Trust for Scotland. I was an Old Etonian, with a cut-glass accent to match. And, in February 1962, when the Selection Conference took place, at 29 years of age, I was very, very young to be sent to Westminster for those days. *Time and Chance* was the ever-so-apt title of James Callaghan's autobiography and both combined to give me the opportunity to serve the people of Linlithgowshire, as it used to be, and Linlithgow, as it was to become again in the 1983 General Election, for 43 years.

A week after I was chosen as candidate, the constituency party received a visit from the National Agent at Labour Party head-quarters, (later Dame) Sarah Barker. In her direct Yorkshire way, referring to my youth, she told me, 'You are a very lucky young man. If you behave properly and do the job seriously, you'll become Father of the House of Commons one day.' At the time, I simply could not bring myself to believe that I would last so long.

During the by-election, I spoke at 49 evening meetings buttressed by Scottish Labour MPs. As a matter of policy, no Labour 'high heid yin' from south of the border was invited. During the day, I went to factory and foundry meetings and also meetings at pitheads. Those were the days when employers thought it their duty to invite all candidates to speak on the premises. At every available moment, morning and afternoon, I went from door to door introducing myself – there is no substitute for shoe leather during an election campaign. It all paid off in the result:

Dalyell, T. (Labour)	21,266
Wolfe, W.C. (SNP)	9,750
Stewart, I. (Con)	4,784
Bryce, D. (Liberal)	4,537
Swan, Mrs I. (Communist)	1,511

It was only years later that I appreciated the impact of my by-election on the course of British politics. On offering Enoch Powell a polite personal apology in the Commons corridor for interrupting one of his declamations in full flow – he was a great Commons orator – with a point of order, he replied, 'How can I be vexed with you? You got me into the Cabinet.'

'*I* got you into the Cabinet?' I asked. 'How?'

He explained it was quite simple. The Tories – already concerned by a stunning Liberal victory in the Orpington by-election of March 1962 – had polled just 4,784 votes in West Lothian two months later, having won more than 18,000 votes in the General Election three years previously. Their deposit had been lost and Macmillan's reaction was to sack half of his Cabinet – 'the wrong half' as Harold Wilson memorably put it.

Among the casualties, to his ill-concealed public consternation, was Dr Charles Hill, also a well-known wartime and post-war 'radio doctor' and Macmillan's public relations minister as Chancellor of the Duchy of Lancaster. A Cabinet berth became available in the Health Department and Enoch Powell was the beneficiary. This version of events was confirmed to me when I subsequently found myself sitting next to Selwyn Lloyd, then Leader of the House, at a dinner. As we sat down, Selwyn Lloyd opened the conversation by saying, 'You're the young man who got me sacked!'

'Sacked?' I replied. 'What as?'

'As the Chancellor of the Exchequer.' He explained that the West Lothian by-election result had been the final straw that triggered what was to become known as 'the Night of the Long Knives' in July 1962. As Jeremy Thorpe, the future Liberal leader, memorably remarked, 'Greater love hath no man than this, that he should lay down his friends for his life.'

But the West Lothian by-election was also significant for something else – that the Scottish National Party (SNP) gained 9,750 votes, coming a creditable second to my 21,266. Subsequently, the SNP were to run me even closer. William Wolfe (the SNP's candidate in 1962 and party leader from 1969 to 1979) and I shared a spot in the *Guinness Book of Records* – never had the same two parliamentary candidates contested seven consecutive parliamentary elections.

In the last six months of 1962, my initiation period in the House of Commons, I was often asked what had surprised me most about becoming a Member of Parliament. As the weeks went by, my answer became ever more repetitive: 'The difference between the public persona – through newspapers, radio and television [not as important at that time] – and the persona at close quarters.' Not that the media was always wrong, simply that many of those who carried weight and made a difference in parliament were by no means necessarily the same men and women who attracted widespread public recognition.

Within weeks of taking our seats in June 1962, Dr Jeremy Bray, a scientist who had won the Middlesbrough by-election a few weeks before mine in West Lothian, and I were peppering the parliamentary order papers with pertinent questions on scientific issues. Soon, I was summoned to the office of Hugh Gaitskell, the Leader of the Opposition, who wanted to put me in touch with a group of left-wing scientists, of whom the most eminent – and most left-wing – was the brilliant Professor John Desmond Bernal.

I did not know Gaitskell well, having met him only twice – once when I sat next to him at the Cambridge Union and a second time when, following the West Lothian by-election, I was required to go to his room for a semi-formal welcome. Gaitskell said to me, 'The only thing I know about you is that you were taught by my friend Nicky Kaldor. Who else taught you?'

I said that I had been supervised not only by Nicky but by Harry Johnson and Joan Robinson.

Then came a litmus test question: 'How did you get on with Joan?'

I decided that candour was the best course. 'She could be a really excellent supervisor,' I replied, 'but she terrified the life out of me when I was a very tough fourth-year undergraduate.'

Gaitskell smiled and simply said, 'That makes two of us. She still terrifies me.' He then explained that his Chief Economic Adviser would be her estranged husband, Professor E. A. G. (Austin) Robinson. I believe that, if Austin Robinson rather than Tommy Balogh had been the economic guru of the Labour government, then economic policy and certainly relations with the Treasury would have gone infinitely better than they turned out to be in the volatile economic period of 1964–67. In the event, Gaitskell died and Wilson preferred his friend Balogh to Robinson.

As I went out of the room, Gaitskell had an afterthought: 'Just one word of advice from an Old Wykehamist to an Old Etonian. For heaven's sake never try to hide from the Parliamentary Labour Party your background. Provided you don't pretend to be what you are not, your parliamentary colleagues will happily accept you for what you are!'

Six months later Gaitskell was dead, a contributory factor being that he had returned to work from an illness before his doctors thought wise. Speculating on the 'if only' associated with premature death is not useful. Who knows whether he would have made a great prime minister?

With the benefit of half a century's hindsight, my first few months in parliament were verging on the catastrophic in terms

of all-important relations with my Labour parliamentary colleagues. On the day of the announcement of the by-election result,
Charles Douglas-Home, then a rather junior reporter at the
Scottish Daily Express, later to be editor of *The Times*, asked me if I
was 'going to raise hell in London about Scottish unemployment'
to which I recollect responding with a 'yes'. Quasi-legitimately,
the then widely read Beaverbrook newspaper screeched screeds
of headlines about 'Dalyell – the Hell-Raiser!'

The implication was that some 40 Scottish Labour MPs had
not been doing enough to highlight the unemployment problem.
The reality was that Labour MPs from Scotland, with no home to
go to from Mondays to Wednesdays, had kept the Commons up
into the small hours, using every procedural device to highlight
the problem. It was only human that they did not appreciate a
young by-election victor insinuating that they were not doing
their job properly.

Many MPs jumped to the conclusion that I was a 'pain in the
neck'. My friends in the Parliamentary Labour Party (PLP) had to
concede that I was an 'awkward blighter', though 'blighter' might
not have been the exact word that they all chose. My trouble was
that Labour colleagues sensed – and rightly so, I fear – that I
would be difficult or awkward, not only to political opponents but
to my own party. First impressions take a long time to evaporate.
Indeed, if ever. One episode in particular enhanced the perception that I was difficult although that turned out to be fully
justified. What silly me at the time did not realise until years later
is that, in British politics, one is usually forgiven for being wrong.
Being proved right on the other hand is a sure way of raising
hackles and often of making enemies.

The background was that I played early morning squash with
Bill Whitlock, an ex-paratrooper and Nottingham MP. In the
shower, he told me he was coming off the Public Accounts
Committee (PAC), on appointment as an opposition whip,
and would I like it if he recommended me to the chairman,
Harold Wilson, as a likely MP to fill his place. I agreed and
Wilson agreed. So I found myself at the age of 30, alongside
senior MPs like Cledwyn Hughes, later a Cabinet minister and

chairman of the PLP, cross-questioning permanent secretaries and industrial heavyweights such as Sir John Cockcroft of the Atomic Energy Commission, Lord Christopher Hinton of Bankside, the engineer and chairman of the Central Electricity Board, and Lord Alfred Robens, chairman of the National Coal Board, and a galaxy of permanent secretaries. Supported by the 500 or so staff of the National Audit Office, the PAC, more than 100 years old, then as now, was the most effective of the Commons Select Committees.

Now, it often happens that an MP's campaign is germinated by a constituent's visit. Within weeks of my being elected, I had a visit to my home from two senior executives of the then prominent building firm Harrison's, Alec Gillies and Alec Mulholland. 'Why was it,' they asked, 'that the biggest building contract, hitherto awarded by Livingston New Town Development Corporation, should have gone to a firm, a tiny firm by the name of Pert's from the Montrose area, almost a hundred miles away, rather than to one of the substantial building contractors around the Firth of Forth?'

They smelled a proverbial rat and so did I. I wrote a polite letter of enquiry to the general manager of the Development Corporation, Brigadier Arthur Purches. In a delayed response, I received a terse brush-off letter from an underling. Contracts were none of an MP's business! Gillies and Mulholland were dissatisfied. So I tried again. The reply, again tardy, verged on the downright rude. So, after months, Harrison's suggested that I might frame a Parliamentary Question (PQ). It occurred to me that, rather than ask a desultory PQ, I would paddle along to see Harold Wilson's successor as PAC chairman, Douglas Houghton, later Lord Houghton of Sowerby, famous as a host of the popular radio program 'Can I Help You?' and senior Cabinet minister in the Labour government. Only years later was I to discover that my righteous awkwardness as a member of the PAC was to render me less *papabile* as a possible junior minister. Naively, I believed in those days that non-partisan scrutiny by a member of a Select Committee would be applauded by his senior party colleagues. Not one bit of it. Understandably, they would be

nervous about taking on an awkward cuss in their ministerial
team.

Houghton responded positively to my tentative suggestion that
the Pert's of Livingston constituency problem might be a suitable
peg on which the PAC should look at the Scottish Office. A blunt,
peppery Yorkshireman, married to Vera Houghton, the formidable abortion law reformer, Houghton could be as awkward as
any man – I confess he became a bit of a role model for me as he
had been in the 1930s for the young James Callaghan, his deputy
general secretary at the Inland Revenue Staff Association.

Houghton summoned the Scottish Office. Cue consternation
in Edinburgh. Instead of a PQ and tossing off an answer to a
rookie MP, the self-regarding mandarins of the Scottish Office
were required to get the night sleeper from Edinburgh to
London, along with the chairman of the Development Corporation, the large-scale farmer and business man Sir David Lowe
and his general manager, Brigadier Arthur Purches. They were
far from amused by the detailed questions with which the
National Audit Office had armed the MPs. They were even less
amused when the PAC report forced them to remove Lowe from
the chairmanship. The National Audit Office had exposed the
deeply unsatisfactory nature of the contract.

The episode taught me what an MP could achieve by persistence and using the grey cells. I attribute my uneasy relations with
Willie Ross, when he became Secretary of State for Scotland –
relations had been warm between 1962 and 1964 in opposition –
to a poisoning of the well by certain senior civil servants, in
particular Sir Douglas Haddow, an able mathematician and
permanent secretary at the Scottish Office, who could not forgive
me for humiliating him, other Scottish Office civil servants and
the Livingston New Town Development Corporation and showing them up under the spotlight of the National Audit Office to
have been remiss and, indeed, culpable in their handling of the
first major contract for the biggest Scottish New Town.

If I established myself, as I did, as an extremely effective member of the PAC, it was largely due to the personal interest and,
yes, capacity as a tutor, shown towards me by the Comptroller

and Auditor General, the erudite and ever-so sharp Sir Edmund Compton. After Harold Wilson's last meeting as PAC chairman, I asked him if he had any advice for me as a new MP and an even newer member of the PAC. 'Yes,' he replied, 'for the first six months, do as Edmund Compton tells you. After that, be your own man but warn the chairman of any controversial line of questioning of permanent secretaries on which you wish to embark.'

I followed his advice. Consequently, I had an excellent rapport with Wilson's successor as chairman, Douglas Houghton, who gave me my head and benignly stopped me in my tracks if he thought I was going up an irrelevant alley. To be effectively awkward on most committees, but particularly on the PAC, one must have the goodwill of the chairman. For a century, the PAC wisdom was that the chair should be occupied by the senior opposition MP. So when, in October 1964, Houghton became Lord President of the Council in the incoming Labour government, he was succeeded by John Boyd-Carpenter, the outgoing Conservative Minister of Pensions and Chief Secretary to the Treasury.

Appalled at the huge inroads made into the budget proposals of the new Labour government by what I saw as a profligate Ministry of Defence, of whose policies I was critical, I went to see Boyd-Carpenter in his PAC chairman's room. Would it not be a good idea if the PAC were to ask the Comptroller and Auditor General to investigate the deal between the Ministry of Defence and the firm of Ferranti in the development of the Bloodhound missile system? Boyd-Carpenter assented. He was not averse to embarrassing the Labour government.

Actually, I am not at all proud of being awkward on this occasion. I thought I had done a great job at the time, asking piercing questions, following up a tip I had had about Bloodhound from a constituent who was one of their employees in Edinburgh. The PAC hearings revealed that, on the Bloodhound contract, Ferranti had made unacceptably excessive profits at the expense of the taxpayer. Substantial sums were then recouped by the Treasury. I was the beneficiary of some applause in the press and more applause from Labour colleagues, who were unhappy about the level of defence spending inherited by the Labour government. At the time, to many people it appeared that, by being awkward, I had done a service to a government beset by financial pressures. What I did, in retrospect, was not clever, either from my own point of view or, more importantly, from the point of view of the long-term interests of the country. Personally, I had made a nuisance of myself to the Defence Secretary, Denis Healey, who, before real friendship blossomed, was to regard me as in the tradition of Henry Labouchère or, less politely, a 'pain-in-the-arse gadfly'.

In 2006, when Healey came to see me at The Binns, he said, 'My wife Edna reflected to me that, on every issue on which you and Tam have disagreed, Tam was right and you, Denis, were wrong!' But, on Bloodhound, my awkwardness came at a price. I had not properly understood that 'frontiers of knowledge' defence contracts are subject to financial 'swings and roundabouts'. A firm makes a whacking great profit on one project and heavy losses on another. Years later, I was shamefaced when separately, in a mood of sorrow rather than anger, both Bill Gregson, a senior executive of Ferranti, and Basil de Ferranti, who had been one of Harold MacMillan's blue-eyed ministers, explained to me that I had injured the research programme and put them at a disadvantage in relation to American competition. Alas, too often, these are unintended consequences of being awkward.

*

In February 1963, Harold Wilson pipped George Brown and James Callaghan to become leader of the Labour Party. I was one of five out of some 45 Scots MPs to, as Jimmy Boyle, my agent at the 1962 by-election, put it, 'back the right horse', incurring the wrath and withdrawal of patronage by George Brown.

Wilson appointed his friend and fellow member of Labour's National Executive Committee, Dick Crossman, to be Shadow Secretary of State for Education and Science. Crossman had fallen out with Hugh Gaitskell, whom he had asked to be godfather to his son but with whom he subsequently ceased to be close. I shall always believe that the root of the tension was that Crossman had been head boy at Winchester and Gaitskell, two years his junior, had been a less than prominent member of the school. When I went to see Isaiah Berlin, Crossman's successor as philosophy don at New College, Oxford, and Mrs Mary Bennett, daughter of H. A. L. Fisher, when researching my book *Dick Crossman: A Portrait*, written at the request of George Weidenfeld, they both confirmed this impression. But, as Crossman put it, without malice, 'In politics, while there is death, there is hope!' He became a member of the Shadow Cabinet, looked around for a young MP as an aide and alighted on me (after the General Election of 1964 I continued as his Parliamentary Private Secretary, or PPS). Whether it was altogether wise for an Old Wykehamist to choose one of the two Old Etonians in the PLP at the time – the other was the fox-hunting Reggie Paget – was a matter for comment. It was held against Crossman that, in his much-read column in the *Daily Mirror*, he had written that there were only four trade union-sponsored MPs who were fit to hold senior ministerial office and had been silly enough to name them.

In his new post, Crossman had devised a scheme whereby the Labour Party would host 34 scientist/politician conferences in different parts of Britain, for the most part based in universities, but beginning with a two-day exchange of ideas at the Bonnington Hotel, Southampton Row, over a Saturday and Sunday. Since it was thought that there would be a Labour government with a substantial majority in a 1964 General Election and the scientific community did not see great hope that the government of Sir Alec Douglas-Home would do much for them, there was a hugely encouraging participation.

Along came politically uncommitted heavyweights, Sir Robert Robinson and Sir Howard Florey among them. At 19, Patrick Blackett had been in charge of a gun battery at the Battle of Jutland and now, actively committed to the Labour cause, he was one of the main speakers. He already had his Nobel Prize for physics and was later to decline Harold Wilson's pressing offer to be his minister for science, preferring instead to become rector of Imperial College, London, and president of the Royal Society. There were also young scientists, among them Steven Rose, later a professor at the Open University and well-known participant in the BBC's *Moral Maze*, who, at that time, was described by Crossman as the 'cleverest and most dangerous young man in England'.

It was the Bonnington conference which furnished the background for Harold Wilson's much remembered speech at the 1963 Labour Party conference in Scarborough, which encapsulated 'the white heat of the technological revolution' and pledged that science was to be harnessed to help resolve the country's economic problems and make Britain great again. This did not seem fanciful since the Courtaulds boss Sir Frank Kearton and other captains of industry attended the conference and endorsed the policy. Other young scientists, Brian Flowers, later an SDP peer, and Captain Robert Maxwell, of whom more anon, had produced the most politically practical paper on the modernisation of British industry and the ways in which science could be harnessed.

Almost every weekend, from the late summer of 1963 until May 1964, there were Two-Way Traffic in Ideas (TWTs as we used to call them). Kathleen undertook the lion's share of the work in sending out the invitations, and organising speakers and venues. It was one of the disappointments of my life that Crossman was never in a position to implement as a senior minister the proposals that had emanated from the work of these conferences. That he did not do so was for the silliest and most gratuitously unnecessary of reasons.

On a hot early evening in June 1964, a delegation of about half a dozen people from the nursery branch of the National Union of Teachers (NUT) came to see Crossman and squeezed into the pokey room which had been allocated to him as a Shadow Cabinet minister in the House. He had had an exhausting day and offered them gin and tonic. The ladies, a little shocked, declined. Could they have a cup of tea? But we had no tea and no available soft drinks, let alone milk. It was a bad start, not improved by the fact that the Shadow Secretary of State nevertheless poured himself out a gin and tonic – I declined as I'm allergic to gin.

Well, it was indeed a bad start and it got worse when the leader of the delegation embarked on a long-winded groan about the perceived iniquities of local authorities and, in particular, Labour-controlled education authorities. Crossman's patience threshold was pretty low at the best of times and he could not or did not conceal his irritation by looking out of the window when the NUT Leader was in full flow. She rebuked him and he became cringe-makingly rude. The delegation broke off abruptly as a Division Bell went and, by the time we returned from voting, the NUT nursery delegation had left.

I was told later by the general secretary, Sir Ronald Gould, that he and the president of the NUT would not have made an undue fuss but the representative at the meeting of the North East of England was mightily offended by Crossman's boorishness and bad manners. She complained bitterly to the NUT-sponsored MPs for her area and in particular to Ted Short, then Deputy Chief Whip, and to Ernie Popplewell, a National Union of Railwaymen (NUR) veteran whom it was unwise to upset. They went to Harold Wilson and said, 'We cannot possibly have Dick responsible for education.'

Reluctantly, as he told me years later after Crossman's death, Wilson decided that the antagonism of Short, Popplewell and a whole cohort of former MPs deeply involved in education was not worth the candle so, at the last moment, he swapped the portfolios of Crossman and Michael Stewart, who had done four years' assiduous work on housing and local government problems in preparation for office. The ostensible reason – the one put out to the press – was different and stated that, with a slender majority of five seats and the prospect of a second General Election, it was better to have the dynamic Crossman in housing where an impact could begin to be made before going to the polls. I thought this was a pretty spurious reason but that was the excuse.

Michael Stewart, meanwhile, was a person with a Rolls-Royce mind and a first in Greats at Oxford. But 'Black Michael', as he was known, had no intention, as the incoming Secretary of State for Education and Science, to follow up the work of the TWTs.

The result was that many of those who had been excited to be involved and had hoped that their relationship with the Labour Party, nurtured in opposition, would continue in government became disillusioned. Worse was to come. As the first minister for science, Wilson appointed someone who at best had been on the periphery of the TWTs – C. P. Snow had a reputation as a novelist for dealing with problems of science and the arts but he had no standing among serious scientists.

For the Department of Education, Wilson did choose someone as minister of state who had been pivotal in the TWTs – Vivian Bowden, Vice-Chancellor of University of Manchester Institute of Science and Technology (UMIST), who was ennobled as Lord Bowden of Chesterfield. He was a distinguished and innovative electrical engineer who had impressed us all with his visionary ideas on how Britain could do far better in translating our ground-breaking ideas in pure and academic science into commercially profitable industrial development. It was a matter of dismay that so many scientific avenues, pioneered in the United Kingdom, had been exploited abroad.

Bowden was frustrated from the week he entered the government. He had reached a modus operandi with Crossman and Stewart he knew not – they simply did not mesh. If I recount a sad little tale, all the more so for being comic, it is to illustrate that those unelected persons, spatchcocked into government without experience of politics, often come to grief. To start with, professional politicians resent ministerial office being snatched away from their number and handed on a plate to persons who have not canvassed one let alone thousands of doorsteps. Secondly, they have little idea of the notion of governmental or, indeed, Cabinet responsibility and the workings of Whitehall. In March 1965, after he had been in office for four months, I ran into Vivian Bowden in a corridor in Westminster. 'How's it going, Vivian?' I asked.

'I've just sacked my secretary.'

'What was wrong with her? Was she slow at typing or not good at filing?'

'You don't understand, I've sacked my permanent secretary!'

'What!' I gasped. 'You, Vivian, have sacked Sir Bruce Fraser?'

'Yes, I've sacked Fraser!'

Now, in 1965, Sir Bruce Fraser KCB was one of the grandest mandarins in Whitehall and in an age when mandarins were virtually untouchable.

'But what did Michael Stewart [his immediate Cabinet boss] say?'

'Stewart?' said Bowden, somewhat contemptuously. 'Haven't consulted him!'

'And Harold? What did the Prime Minister say?'

'Harold? Haven't consulted him.'

A lowly minister of state was naive in the extreme to suppose he could dismiss a permanent secretary. Within a fortnight Bowden had left the government, returning to UMIST to resume his well-received vice-chancellorship. And, as a lowly PPS, I continued my education in the ways of the Civil Service at the hands of that remarkable 'Beatrice Webb-type' lady, Dame Evelyn Sharp – the Dame of the later *Crossman Diaries* – and her senior colleagues, (Sir) James Jones and (Sir) James Waddell.

Mutual respect between politicians and civil servants was more evident in those days than in the twenty-first century. In my opinion, the rot set in during the mid 1980s when a triumphant Margaret Thatcher began to ask whether a civil servant, due to be appointed to a sensitive senior position, was 'one of us'.

The reason I was chosen as his aide is that Crossman, author of *Plato Today* and other books, had little contact with the scientific community and heard that I had organised for some of my parliamentary colleagues to visit the Laboratory of Molecular Biology at the Medical Research Council's Cambridge Unit. This came in the wake of the glamour of the Nobel Prizes awarded to Max Perutz and Sir John Cowdery Kendrew (for their work on proteins and nucleic acids) and to Francis Crick and James D. Watson (for their work on the double helix). The Nobel laureates, joined by future prizewinners Sydney Brenner and Aaron Klug, explained their work and took us on a tour of the laboratory. After a congenial lunch, I asked Perutz if he and his colleagues would care to come to a meal in the House of Commons. 'No,' he said, 'it is kind of you but we are very committed to our schedules.' He paused. 'But we have three German researchers who are going back to Frankfurt next week. Before they go to Heathrow, they would, I think, love to come to Westminster. Would you give them lunch?'

It was arranged. Saying goodbye to the researchers in the Central Lobby, I felt a firm hand on my shoulder. It was James Hoy, Labour MP for Leith and later a fisheries minister in the first Wilson Government. 'I want you to meet my guests, Kathleen Wheatley and her friend, Eileen Murdoch. Kathleen was canvassing for you during your West Lothian by-election.' I thought, 'That's funny. Had I not written a personal thank you to all the helpers who had signed the books in the various committee rooms?' Kathleen was the daughter of John Wheatley QC, law officer and Lord Advocate in Attlee's Labour government and, subsequently, a Judge of the Court of Appeal, Lord Justice Clerk and chairman of the Royal Commission on Local Government in Scotland (some 40 years later, Kathleen herself was to be a Royal Commission chairman). Surely I would have remembered if I had written to the daughter of a well-known judge of the High Court! Never mind the great-niece of John Wheatley, Red Clydesider and Minister of Health in the first Labour government of 1924.

It was love at first sight – on my part but not on hers. It transpired that she had not signed any helpers' book in her dash to get back to Edinburgh rather than travel back with the others to Glasgow. Moreover, it further transpired that most definitely I had not been her preferred candidate. Kathleen was teaching at St Augustine's Secondary School in Glasgow, alongside Arthur Houston who had been on the shortlist at the Labour Party selection conference. Having been unsuccessful, he most generously said to his Labour Party colleagues, 'We must go across to West Lothian and make sure that the Labour candidate is elected.' (That attitude epitomised the spirit of the Labour Party in Scotland in those days.)

It was, by some standards these days, a whirlwind romance. In April 1963, Kathleen and I did not know each other. On 26 December 1963, we were married. To think that, if I had seen off Perutz's researchers on their way to Germany five minutes earlier or one minute later, the next five decades would have been very different. Kathleen and I might never have met.

With Perutz, Kendrew and Brenner, I was to have a lifelong telephone relationship. Both for my work in the Commons and for the purposes of accuracy in my *New Scientist* column, I would seek the views of Perutz on science policy matters, Kendrew on defence (he later became scientific adviser to the Ministry of Defence) and Brenner on medical research matters.

My engagement to Kathleen was not without incident. Sam Campbell, stalwart of the Orange Order and then secretary of Midlothian Labour Party, publicly complained that the Church of Scotland MP for West Lothian was marrying a Roman Catholic. This caused much consternation in the world of Labour politics in Scotland! Kathleen's mother, Nancy Nichol, was the forthright and down-to-earth lady whose portrait (by authoress Dorothy Dunnett) hangs in The Binns dining room and who was not Catholic. I was deeply fond of her – no man's children having a better grandmother. After a convent education in Aberdeen, at the Convent of the Sacred Heart, which did not suit Kathleen's rebellious character, and an honours degree in history at the University of Edinburgh, she took her first teaching job at the 1,700-pupil St Augustine's in the Springburn district of Glasgow. Having cut her teeth there, she was appointed by Miss Steel, headmistress of James Gillespie's in Edinburgh, who presided over a school where an amalgam of teachers provided the model for Muriel Spark's Miss Jean Brodie.

It was a testimony to the affection in which she was held that, when we emerged from our wedding at St Peter's, Morningside, which was conducted by Father Walter Glancy, a prominent member of the City of Edinburgh Education Committee, Gillespie's girls were there in force to wish her well and throw confetti (I reckon Miss Brodie would have been pleased). After a small teetotal wedding – my father-in-law abhorred drink, the cause of so many of the problems which came before him on the Bench – we left for the airport to fly on honeymoon to Egypt.

There was dual thinking behind the choice of 26 December for the wedding. First, the inevitable General Election of 1964 was unlikely to be called in January but could start in late February, if Sir Alec Douglas-Home were so minded. Secondly, when I went to Luxor alone as a young teacher taking the chance of a visit to Egypt, I was befriended by fellow guests at the hotel, Tor Gjesdal, a Norwegian engineer working as a very senior executive official for UNESCO, and his wife. Gjesdal was in Upper Egypt to finalise the plans whereby the Great Temple of Ramses II at Abu Simbel was to be raised so that it would not be submerged in the rising waters caused by the dams on the Nile which were then being constructed. Gjesdal said, 'Get to Abu Simbel before the construction. For all the good that UNESCO hopes to do to save this wonderful monument, magical in the setting sun, it will not be quite the same.'

Besides, it would not have been sensible for Kathleen and me to go to Upper Egypt between March and October, when the heat at Karnak and the Valley of the Kings can reach 135 degrees Fahrenheit. So, with a kindly parting shot from John Wheatley, my father-in-law of four hours, 'She's yours now – look after her!' and jocular ribald comments from Kathleen's younger brothers – John, Patrick, Tony and Michael – we set off for Edinburgh Airport and got on to the plane for London. Suddenly, the fog came down, as it so often does in the Forth Valley. For the only time in my life, once seated and ready to take off, we had to leave the plane – the Viscount turboprop of those days did not have the equipment to negotiate even limited visibility. The only thing for it was to go to Waverley Station, get bacon and eggs in the café and, since the Night Scotsman was fully booked, get a couple of spare second-class sleeping berths on the 'Milk Train' calling at Galashiels, Melrose, St Boswell's, Hawick, Newcastleton, Carlisle, Oxenholme and all stations to Preston before continuing to London. It was a pretty unsettled night.

Somehow, by the skin of our teeth, we caught our booked flight to Cairo. There we were met by a smiling Dr Mustapha Hafez, a senior official of the Egyptian science ministry.

Let me digress for a moment. I have always found it difficult to switch off. I suppose MPs can travel incognito and without fuss but certainly not in countries where a visa is required, or was

required in 1962, such as Egypt, Indonesia or Iran. The authorities wanted know all about me – understandable as only seven
years had elapsed since Eden attacked Nasser over Suez. Often
they want to show an MP and his wife their country. In those
days, a British MP in Egypt was a rare species. Naturally, we had
paid for our flight and our accommodation but Dr Hafez had a
programme for us in his pocket:

Day 1: You will see agricultural developments in Liberation
       Province and means of finding water other than by the
       shaduf.
Day 2: You will visit the eye clinic in Alexandria and meet
       businessmen concerned with the export of cotton.
Day 3: You will go to the steel works in Helwan.
Day 4: You can go to Sakkara and the Pyramids.

My bride was magnificent and rose to the occasion but, on
Day 5, even her jaw dropped a little. As a courtesy, we went to
call on the British Ambassador, the tall, erect, distinguished figure
of Sir Harold Beeley, a leading Arabist of the Foreign Office, who
welcomed us.

After a minimum of small talk, Sir Harold turned to Kathleen
and said, 'Mrs Dalyell, which hotel are you staying at?'

'A new one – the El Borg.'

'Mrs Dalyell, what room number are you?'

'402.'

'Well, Mrs Dalyell, I think I ought to tell you that we know that
all the 01 and 02 rooms in the El Borg are bugged.'

Given the nature of our disturbed first night as a married
couple, it dawned on us that our first-night intimacies were duly
recorded in the archives of the United Arab Republic as Egypt
and Syria then were. Alas, this conclusion was far from fanciful.
Dr Hafez proposed to accompany us to Upper Egypt where he
had arranged for us to be taken round the Aswan Dam by an
engineer, which did indeed prove extremely interesting, However
Kathleen, who had enjoyed the interest of the visits we had made,
pointed out, 'This is our honeymoon – not an official visit!'

I recollected that Harold Wilson had told me of the time when, as President of the Board of Trade in Attlee's government, he was negotiating the wheat agreements with Anastas Mikoyan, Stalin's clever and able trade minister. Wilson arranged a conversation with his private secretary in the bedroom of the Intourist Hotel in Moscow, which they guessed was wired, along the lines of: 'Mikoyan is a nice man, a good man, but I have laid the final offer on the table and, if they do not accept it, we will just simply have to go back to London without an agreement.' Twenty-four hours later, when they had got round to decoding the intercept, the Russians accepted Wilson's offer.

So Kathleen and I had a stilted conversation in our bedroom about how much we liked Dr Hafez, how much we admired the achievement of modern Egypt, how the pharaohs would have been proud of Colonel Nasser and Dr Hafez but this was our honeymoon and we longed for a bit of time on our own to wander around the sites. Two days later, as we were due to depart for Luxor by train, a breathless Dr Hafez appeared. He was very sorry. He could not come with us. There was no hotel accommodation available for him in Upper Egypt. He hoped we would forgive him. We did and thought all the more highly of him and of Egyptians for their consideration for a honeymooning couple. When we arrived in upper Egypt, the hotels, surpisingly, were virtually empty. The Great Hypostyle Hall at Karnak, Medinet Habu, the mortuary temple of Ramses III, and the rock temples of Abu Simbel itself exceeded even our highest expectations.

On our last night in Egypt, back in Cairo, there was a knock on our door after we had gone to sleep. 'Mr Dalyell, will you get dressed?' said an agitated hotel under-manager. 'A very important man wants to see you.'

I was whisked out to Heliopolis, to the private residence of Gamal Abdel Nasser. He entered his drawing room from a side-door and opened by saying, 'We know that your mother and father spoke Arabic. Why don't you?' I promised to try. I failed. I found Nasser deeply impressive and curiously willing to forgive Britain for the Suez debacle but not Anthony Eden and Selwyn Lloyd personally. He was well informed about the Labour Party and anxious to know how Harold Wilson, if he became Prime Minister, would get on with the Americans. He regretted the death of Hugh Gaitskell, whose stance on Suez he admired.

As soon as Wilson was settled in Downing Street, I wrote to him suggesting that Colonel Nasser should be invited to visit Britain. Crossman thought this was sensible. However, the Prime Minister replied, formally, that it was too early and, informally, tugged my shoulder in the lobby and told me that he was not unsympathetic but that he did not fancy the hornets' nest that such an invitation was simply bound to stir up.

Shortly after Harold Wilson had made his seminal speech on 'the white heat of the technological revolution', the Russian Deputy Premier Konstantin Rudnev, who was the Politburo member responsible for science, invited him to send a delegation of six scientists and politicians to the Soviet Union. Only five got on the plane with me – the only politician. It was led by Vivian Bowden, the others being Dr David Schoenberg, director of the Mond Low Temperature Laboratory in Cambridge; Professor Colin Adamson, Professor of Electrical Engineering at UMIST; and Professor Anthony Bradshaw, a metallurgist at Imperial College, London.

Since Crossman himself was unable to go at the last moment, I asked the powerful Culture Minister, Madame Furtseva, who was on a visit from the Kremlin, if my bride of 10 weeks could fill the sixth place on the schedule (paying her own way). This Communist battleaxe, veteran in the hardest school of politics, had a kindly, knowing streak and assented.

So it was that Kathleen arrived two days later. Having got her visa in record time in London, she got on the Moscow plane and had the good fortune to sit next to Henry Brandon, the distinguished commentator on Soviet affairs. From the icy Sheremetyevo Airport, she was whisked off to the hotel where she and Brandon had dinner. Not being too surprised when she did not see me at the airport, she did begin to wonder what was afoot when I had not turned up as expected that evening. The next day I was able to explain that, having been down a mine somewhere in the Dombas we were entertained – Russian fashion – with a score of toasts. When I hesitated about gulping down the fifteenth toast – it was to our wives and loved ones – the mine manager roared with laughter and asked if I did not love my wife. I was to see her two days later in Tbilisi, the capital of Georgia. It was a different world from Moscow. The climate and atmosphere seemed almost Mediterranean and everyone was more relaxed and charming, particularly to the ladies. Kathleen's hand was repeatedly kissed.

The wine was excellent, the champagne even better and the Georgians were jovial good company. We were taken on a tour of the city and told in detail about the exploits of a fourteenth-century hero, Prince Georgivili, whose statue dominated the main square. Not a word about the Georgian who had ruled Russia for a quarter of a century, Josef Stalin – we did not hear his name mentioned throughout our visit. I asked to go to a football match as I had heard that Dynamo Moscow were playing Tbilisi. We were transfixed by the 'Black Octopus', the great Lev Yashin in action. He deserved his worldwide reputation.

We were accompanied by Sergei Gvishiani. A Georgian himself, he was chief executive of the Soviet Council for Research and the son-in-law of the Russian technocrat prime minister, Alexei Kosygin. He was cultivated, intelligent and charming and a hugely knowledgeable football fan. While the delegation went to meetings with representatives of the Georgian Soviet, Kathleen was whisked off to the Pedagogical Institute because they were anxious to record her Scots voice.

Taken into the Caucasus Mountains, amid the good cheer we gained an inkling of the anti-Moscow feeling that was to erupt 40 years later in the aftermath of the break-up of the Soviet Union. On our return to Moscow, we had the most important and memorable of our engagements – a visit to the Soviet Academy of Sciences. There sat the formidable physicist and president of the Academy, Academician Keldysh. He was flanked by Academician Kirillin and the biologist, Academician Millionshikov, both senior officers of the Academy. There was one other Russian in the room. He was Pyotr Kapitsa, who greeted David Schoenberg with a great hug. Kapitsa had been working in Cambridge in the 1930s and, by order of Stalin, was forbidden to return to England.

They were very candid, these scientists. They wanted co-operation with Britain. They hoped that a Labour government would not impede such co-operation on account of the actions of Klaus Fuchs, Alan Nunn May and others who had transferred to them vital nuclear information. Kirillin made the point that he and his colleagues would have solved these problems without knowledge of what the West was doing but it might have taken them three or four years longer. Here was real friendship towards Schoenberg and the other scientists. As a politician, I was conscious that I was not considered one of them. Clearly, our Russian hosts were of the belief that Fuchs and Nunn May had acted selflessly in the interests of humanity, by deterring any temptation on the part of Washington to deliver a pre-emptive nuclear strike against the Soviet Union. In 2011, this thesis was fleshed out in a remarkable book – to which I wrote the foreword – by Alan Nunn May's admiring stepson, the physicist Paul Broda.*

*

I do not share the conventional wisdom that Labour had a great win in 1964. It was a cliffhanger. In truth, the much-mocked 14th Earl of Home did astonishingly well, in at least restoring the Conservative position after a series of scandals that had come to a head with the Profumo Affair.

Had Hugh Gaitskell lived, my judgement at the time was that Labour would have had a comfortable working majority in the Commons. But premature death can determine political events. Wilson, unlike Gaitskell, was widely perceived to be untrustworthy. A sizeable section of the Parliamentary Labour Party had not forgiven him for resigning over 'teeth and spectacles' with Aneurin Bevan in 1951 (when Bevin, Harold Wilson and John Freeman resigned from Attlee's government because the incoming chancellor, Hugh Gaitskell, had insisted on 'injuring the health service' by levying charges on false teeth and glasses) – to position himself in the affections of the Labour Party in the country better. On the other hand, his speechifying on 'the white

---

* *Scientist Spies: A Memoir of My Three Parents and the Atom Bomb* (Matador 2011).

heat of the technological revolution' chimed with the mood of Britain at the time. Personally, I liked him and had voted for him in the leadership election of February 1963.

Having become a really useful, if awkward, member of the PAC (being ever careful in my early 30s to display exemplary good manners towards the permanent secretaries and accounting officers who came before us), I made the most ill-judged decision of my public life – I volunteered to leave the PAC and become an inaugural member of the Select Committee on Science and Technology in 1966. The PAC was supported by a staff of 500, under the Comptroller and Auditor General in the National Audit Office. Other Select Committees had a clerk and a part-time special adviser if they were lucky. Stupidly, I yielded to Dick Crossman's advice that, as one interested in science and technology, I had a duty to join what was then a 'talking shop'.

We chose as our first task an investigation into nuclear power. This was partly because our chairman, Arthur Palmer, an electrical engineer who had represented Wimbledon in 1945, then Cleveland and finally the safe seat of Bristol Central, was disappointed in not being chosen for a government post and wanted to make various points to the Cabinet.

To digress, I can still pinpoint the precise moment at which I became a lifelong enthusiast for nuclear power. It was a morning in September 1947, after I had just turned 15, that my father arranged that I and a lad called Gordon Lorimer, who was staying with us while his father completed his time in the Sudan Civil Service during his holidays from Marlborough Public School, should go down the Kinneil Coal Mine in Bo'ness on the banks of the Forth estuary. The mine manager took us on one of his routine visits. The miners, some of whom had been members of the Home Guard commanded by my father, made us welcome but one – a cheerful 'toughie' who made it plain that he regarded us as softies (despite the fact that Gordon boxed in the Marlborough team) – asked us, 'How would you fellows like to work here all your lives?' To put it bluntly, I would have been horrified at the prospect and, at that time, Kinneil was among the most modern and well-equipped pits in the Scottish coalfields.

During the course of the investigation into nuclear power, I managed to blot my proverbial copybook. It suddenly occurred to me that, following a stream of witnesses from the Atomic Energy Commission and the Central Electricity Generating Board (CEGB), we ought to call on Harold Wilson, now Prime Minister following the 1964 General Election, to explain his thinking. It did not seem unreasonable. After all, as Leader of the Opposition, Wilson had had a great deal to say about 'the white heat of the technological revolution' in general and about the role of nuclear energy in particular.

I made the suggestion that Wilson be asked to pay attention to Arthur Palmer, who hummed and hawed but did not dismiss the motion. I then told the technically well-informed journalist David Fishlock, then at the *Financial Times*, that I had approached the committee chairman. This was picked up by the tabloids and presented as yet more trouble in the Labour Party. I was summoned to the Chief Whip, Ted Short (now Lord Glenamara) who sharply asked me, 'Tam, what on earth do you think you are doing?' while waving the *Daily Mirror* at me. My own boss, Dick Crossman, whose PPS I was, put it more earthily. 'You are behaving above your station in life. Why should the Prime Minister waste his time by coming to your bloody committees?'

On this occasion I had not, as I thought, been awkward, but was merely seeking after the truth of what was possible. I did not mean to be awkward. Journalists revelled in the minor discomfiture that I had caused in Downing Street. Some, who remembered how Wilson had once dwelled on the exciting world of nuclear power, thought my request far from unreasonable. But my next suggestion to Palmer, which he accepted with alacrity, was to have far greater consequences and was to establish my credentials as a fully paid-up member of the 'Awkward Squad'.

The early background was as follows. Some two years previously, Dr Leonard Rotherham of the CEGB had revealed to the PAC the huge and costly operation of the Radar Research Establishment (RRE) at Malvern. My antennae were alerted, as were those of Brian Parkyn, MP for Bedford, who had built up his own chemical engineering company, that Malvern would be an ideal venue for a technology-orientated university. This was thought to be a 'runner'. The Select Committee went to RRE and I went with one or two Committee colleagues to the Service Electronics Research Laboratory at Baldock.

The Select Committee's work went smoothly until I suggested to Palmer and colleagues that we would be failing in our duty if we were not to visit the substantial Chemical and Biological Warfare Defence Establishment at Porton Down. At first, resistance was total. Defence Secretary Denis Healey and his deputy, Fred Mulley, certainly did not want MPs prying into Porton Down. It would be giving hostages to fortune and particularly awkward in that the Labour Party did not like to think its government was sanctioning the use of 'nasties'.

My weakness was that I had been part of a high-profile campaign against the use, in any circumstances, of chemical and biological weapons (CBW). And, I was to learn that an MP cannot combine membership of a Select Committee with public campaigning on an issue connected with the work of that Committee. I stirred Palmer, however, into making a song and dance about the dignity of Select Committees of the House of Commons. Ministers thought a row was not worth the proverbial candle and capitulated.

Off we went to Porton Down. As usual, we took formal evidence, after being taken round those parts of the establishment that seemed pretty innocuous. Some weeks later, members of the Select Committee received printed records of the proceedings, as faithfully recorded by the Hansard reporter who had accompanied us. Carelessly, I thought this was a public document, as were all proceedings in Parliament. It wasn't. It had not gone through the 'side-lining' procedure that allows any witness or questioner to correct and alter, subject to the judgement of the editor of Hansard, any error in transcription. So, for a couple of weeks or so, the hearings were not in the public domain.

A heavyweight and serious journalist, the late Laurence Marks of the *Observer*, asked if he could come to see me about CBW. I gave him a drink on the Terrace of the House of Commons,

where we talked for about an hour and then the Division Bell
went. 'Look,' I said, 'for the purpose of greater accuracy, you'd
better keep these minutes.' Off I went to the Lobby to vote and off
Marks went home. The following Sunday, Marks' story, together
with reference to the Select Committee minutes, filled the front
page of the *Observer*. On Monday, all hell was let loose. Without
warning to me, Arthur Palmer portentously rose in the House of
Commons and demanded a 'leak enquiry'.

In 1967, 'leaks' were an infinitely graver matter than nowadays,
when they are greeted with a shrug of the shoulders as an
everyday occurrence. Up got Boy Scout me and said, 'There
was no need for a leak enquiry, it was I who had talked to
Laurence Marks.' Perhaps I should have kept my mouth shut.
Marks, a deeply honourable man, would not have revealed his
source. A heap of coals descended on my head. A week later, I
was hauled before a specially convened meeting of the Committee on Privileges, then a really august body. It was chaired by that
charming, witty Welshman, Sir Elwyn Jones QC, who had been a
razor-sharp prosecutor at Nuremburg after the war. The first
question came egregiously from Churchill's son-in-law, Duncan
Sandys, who had been Harold Macmillan's Secretary of State for
Defence. 'Mr Dalyell, how much were you paid for leaking the
Select Committee document?'

'Paid!' I said. 'It never occurred to me.'

Then I got a question which was intended to be friendly from
Arthur Woodburn, who had been Secretary of State for Scotland
and was a great friend of my father-in-law, Lord John Wheatley.
Alas, for an 80-year-old, it was long and convoluted and I did not
really understand what Woodburn was asking, so I simply said,
'Yes.'

Ted Heath, the Leader of the Opposition, pounced, 'Mr
Dalyell, do you really mean that?'

Of course, I didn't. I was confused and created a bad impression in the Committee. A person in my position should have
been allowed a lawyer to accompany him.

On reflection that evening, I knew that I had created a
disastrous impression and was not surprised that the Privileges

Committee recommended that I should be brought to the Bar of the House. I was summoned after a special three-hour debate, from which I was excluded and had to sit, biting my nails, in the Commons Library, in which Michael Foot, trying to be helpful, was in fact unhelpful and Willie Hamilton, ostensibly trying to be helpful, was malign. The Speaker put his black cap on and formally reprimanded me. It was the last time the black cap was used, as this ancient procedure was held up to ridicule in the press as 'mumbo-jumbo'. That dreadful Speaker, alas, the first Labour occupant of the chair, Dr Horace King, hugely enjoyed the drama. I was only too relieved not to be expelled from the House.

A number of colleagues were very nice to me in the ensuing weeks. Some Tories, who knew, as I did, that there were no secrets in the document and that we had not been asked to sign the Official Secrets Act, commiserated. Many Labour MPs, either sympathetic to my campaign on CBW or uneasy about what their own constituency Labour parties might say, declined to vote. Tony Benn hid himself in the toilet rather than have his vote recorded. Home Secretary Jim Callaghan, in the most imperious way, told Cabinet colleagues that he did not take part in blood rituals. In fact, of the Cabinet, only Harold Wilson and Peter Shore voted for the Privilege Committee verdict. The upshot for me personally was that Wilson, who was generally well disposed towards me, could not do as he had planned and make me a junior minister at the next reshuffle.

In 1976, just before Alzheimer's had set in and just after he retired as Prime Minister, Wilson told me, 'I owe you, Tam, an apology and one day I will tell you why.' He never did but I do know why. The first apology, however, which I received, came from Sir Harry Legge-Bourke, the senior Tory on the Committee. Sheepishly, he told me that he had been put up by officials in Ministry of Defence, personal friends of his, to complain to Arthur Palmer and goad him into raising the issue on the floor of the House, which had caused all my troubles. I assumed for some years that this was simply vengeance against me for having been so awkward on the Borneo War, Anglo-French Variable Geometry

Aircraft, Aldabra and a host of other issues (of which more later). I was wrong. Their vengeance was altogether more sinister.

By mucking around and having raised the profile of Porton Down, I was in danger of stumbling across a truly terrible Ministry of Defence secret. Years later, it emerged that a young RAF aircraftsman, by the name of Ronald Maddison, had died of poisoning and was the subject of a murder investigation by the Wiltshire Police. The whole dreadful story emerged into the daylight. In the 1950s, the Services had posted notices on regimental and squadron notice boards to the effect that any National Servicemen who volunteered to spend time at Porton Down's 'Research into the Common Cold' Laboratory would be given 15 days' pay with extra leave. Little did they know that the 'research' included the injection of sarin (subsequently classified in UN Resolution 687 as a weapon of mass destruction) into men wearing tank suits and heavy flying kit. For what purpose? For the purpose of conducting tests of the effect of CBW on service combatants. To try to snuff out the possibility of their really scandalous action filtering into a shocked public domain, the Ministry of Defence thought that, to use a colourful Scots expression, they would 'put my gas on a peep' (defuse me) by getting me on the technicality of the leak of printed minutes.

There was a silver lining. Donald Gould, a medical journalist then editing the *New Scientist*, and his deputy, the talented biologist Dr Bernard Dixon, asked me to write a full-page article giving my side of the story. 'Our readers,' said Gould, 'are more interested in the issues raised by chemical and biological weapons than in Parliamentary "mumbo-jumbo".' His readers *were* interested. Gould asked me to do another article of my choosing. I obliged with a full-page on pneumoconiosis, the miners' lung disease, which caused so much distress in West Lothian. Thereafter, he asked me to submit a weekly column. There was no contract – I could have been sacked without compensation at seven days' notice but I was paid, albeit modestly. The column was to last for 37 years.

CHAPTER SIX

Lessons

IN MY FIRST TEN YEARS in the House of Commons, from 1962 to 1972, I cannot pretend it was politically difficult to be pro-civil nuclear power. One of the firmest parliamentary advocates was the MP for Chester-Le-Street, Norman Pentland. A check weighman before he was elected, he was an office bearer of the 45-strong Miners' Group in the PLP. As the guests of Sir Christopher Hinton, chairman of the Central Electricity Board, Pentland, Eddie Wainwright (Dearne Valley), Harold Neal (Dennis Skinner's predecessor in Bolsover) and I went to conventional and Magnox nuclear power stations. Sir William Penney of the Atomic Energy Authority (AEA), meanwhile, took us personally to nuclear facilities, from the high-temperature reactor at Winfrith in Dorset to Capenhurst in Cheshire and from Sellafield in Cumbria to Dounreay on the northern coast of Scotland.

My relationship with Penney could not have begun more inauspiciously. Shortly after I was elected to the Commons, I had visited Chapelcross Power Station in Dumfriesshire with Scottish colleagues Neil Carmichael, Judith Hart and George Lawson, and had been greatly impressed, over lunch, by the deputy director of Chapelcross, a young nuclear physicist called Dr Robert Drew. He expanded on a dream he had that heat generated by Chapelcross created a huge surplus of hot water which went unused into the Solway Firth. 'Now,' said Drew, 'if only it could be used to create heat for greenhouses, think of the benefit it would bring – not least to the coffers of the AEA.'

I suggested he put his imaginative proposal in writing to me. This he did. I remember scribbling off a note to him on the morning of my wedding, rashly promising to raise his ideas 'at the highest level'. On return from honeymoon, I wrote to Sir William Penney, by then chairman-elect of the AEA, asking to see him and enclosing a copy of Drew's ideas. He agreed to see me at his offices in King Charles Street. I phoned his private secretary to ascertain whether my interview would be 30 minutes, 45 minutes or perhaps an hour. The response came back – three minutes, five at the most. I managed to suppress my self-importance as a duly elected Member of Parliament and went. Well, the interview lasted nearer two minutes than three. 'Mr Dalyell,' Penney drawled, 'it is not the business of the Atomic Energy Authority to grow tomatoes.'

I stuttered, 'But . . .'

'Mr Dalyell, there are no "buts". It is not the business of the Atomic Energy Authority to grow tomatoes.'

With that, I was escorted out of the room.

Some months later, when I had got to know Penney, over a convivial dinner in a Thurso hotel, on a parliamentary visit to Dounreay, I asked him, 'Bill, why did you treat me so abruptly and cursorily when I came to see you about Chapelcross?'

He chuckled. 'It was not about tomatoes. It was not a silly idea at all to link greenhouses with Chapelcross. But when I got your letter and Drew's submission, I consulted Roger [Sir Roger Makins, the outgoing Chairman, former Ambassador to Washington and much else], who was well disposed towards you. We decided that, for your own good, we should teach you a lesson. It was not the tomatoes which annoyed us – it was the fact that you were using your position as an MP to catapult the views of a junior member of the AEA into the chairman's office.'

I learned the lesson and, thereafter, made sure that the normal channels of communication within an organisation should be afforded their proper place. Quite simply, MPs should be extremely careful before leapfrogging their cause to the top of the tree for action.

My visit, along with five parliamentary colleagues, was the first

of half a dozen to the Dounreay Fast Breeder Reactor site before
the decision for closure was taken. It was a truly dreadful decision.
It was governmental vandalism. It was British short-termism at
its worst. Britain led the world in fast-breeder technology but
Whitehall and Westminster succumbed to the financial exigen-
cies of the moment. There was no regard for the long-term
benefit likely to accrue to Britain (and humankind) in the future.
There was little regard for the dismay of those who worked at
Dounreay, many of whom had moved house and family to the
northernmost coast of Scotland.

I met sad scientists, engineers and support staff who just felt
that their life's work had been for nothing. I do have views about
several individuals – parliamentary colleagues, and friends
among Whitehall mandarins – who should shoulder the responsibility for the destruction of the British fast-breeder reactor but,
as I do not know the full story of what happened in Cabinet
committees and in the Department of Energy, it would be wrong
to identify named persons as culprits. Besides, I find the blame
culture distasteful. So many hopes had been dashed, prematurely
and needlessly.

*

On the day I became an MP, I was told that I should fire off a
letter on any Social Security problem which was raised with me to
either of the Parliamentary Secretaries at the Ministry of Pensions
and National Insurance, one of whom, Lieutenant Commander
Lynch Maydon, MP for Wells and a distinguished submarine
commander, was less obscure than his colleague, the MP for
Finchley, then Joint Parliamentary Secretary – a youngish
woman by the name of Margaret Thatcher.

I was given the impression that a letter signed by a minister
would inflate my 'street cred' with my constituents (I admit that,
in 2009, a letter which had obviously become a family heirloom
was produced in Whitburn by the granddaughter of a lady, on
whose behalf I had written to ministers in June 1962, bearing the
signature 'Margaret Thatcher'.) In July 1962, however, I was
taken quietly aside by that wise old owl James Bennie, who was in

charge of what was known as the National Assistance Office (or, more colloquially, 'the Broo') in Bathgate. 'Look,' he said, 'you are entitled, as an MP, to write to the minister but you must understand that every letter you write comes back to us for advice as to how they should frame their reply. In the circumstances, I have to justify every action of my staff in the office. This means that I cannot be flexible. Who loses out? If you write to me direct, I will be able to give you an answer much more quickly and more than likely more favourable to your constituent.' This was true. After six weeks I ceased to add to the in-tray of Commander Maydon and Mrs Thatcher. Bennie had indeed taught me a lesson, applicable to my broader work as an MP.

Of course, an MP has a duty of care for the community that sends him or her to Westminster. The issue is how that duty of care is to be interpreted. One of the heavyweight Cabinet ministers of the 1950s and early 1960s, Duncan Sandys, Churchill's son-in-law and successively Housing Minister, Defence Secretary and Commonwealth Secretary, famously retorted to a constituent, who opined that Sandys was not doing enough to resolve her street cleaning problem, 'It is my job to represent Streatham in Westminster; it is not my job to represent Westminster in Streatham.' In other words MPs should not meddle in matters that properly pertain to local government. In this matter Sandys, whom I found as a young MP curmudgeonly, ponderous (just as I am now, according to my wife) and extremely able was right. MPs should confine themselves to their responsibilities in relation to constituents dealing with government departments and not stray into the world of local government. One of the causes, about which I feel most vehemently, is that the dignity and responsibilities of local councils ought to be restored.

In the first few days that I was an MP, I was handed a lesson that I have never forgotten in 43 years. I was elected on a Thursday in May 1962 but the announcement of the result was made only on the Friday. On a glorious Saturday evening, 30 hours after the result of the polls being announced, I took a walk round the village of Linlithgow Bridge, to thank electors for their support. At every house where I knocked on a door, they were very nice to me. On the Monday morning, I had a phone call from the editor of the local paper, the *Linlithgow Gazette*, Arthur Brown, who in his younger days had been brought up on the *Manchester Guardian*, under C. P. Scott and A. P. Wadsworth, great editors both. The conversation went like this:

'I hear you were in Linlithgow Bridge on Saturday evening. What did they say to you?'

'They were lovely to me.'

'What complaints did they have?'

'They didn't have any complaints.'

'I don't believe you. I know those people in Linlithgow Bridge and have lived among them. It is impossible that they do not have complaints.'

'Well, one or two of the ladies told me that they did not like dogs doing their regular business on Justinhaugh Green, in front of their houses.'

The following Friday, the weekly *Gazette* was published. There was an item, in tiny print on page 11, saying that I had had complaints about dogs' mess. On Saturday, at 8 a.m., my telephone rang. It was the unmistakable gravelly voice of Councillor James Boyle, my agent at the by-election and soon to become county convener, an individual who, had he so wanted, could have got me deselected at the General Election due in 1964. 'Tam,' he said, 'Westminster, your business. Dog shit, mine.' Whereupon the telephone was slammed down. That was the first and only occasion I had a brush with West Lothian Council.

In relation to local government queries, MPs do have the role of advocacy but I don't think it should go further than making sure that officers of the council actually reflect on the case to which the MP brings their attention. That was why, on almost every one of the thousands of letters that Kathleen and I wrote to officials of the council, we ended up with the same words: 'Could you do what you deem right?'

But emphatically it *is* the duty of an MP to deal conscientiously with constituents who have problems with government departments and, indeed, it was harrowing constituency cases which ignited some of my most significant parliamentary campaigns. Our modus operandi was that Kathleen and I would deal with 99 per cent of generally routine cases competently and expeditiously. But there were some individual matters which we thought should be taken much further through the parliamentary process not only for the good of individuals who came to us but for the general good of people in Britain. My first such campaign concerned usury, the illegal practice of lending money at unreasonably high rates of interest.

At my regular Saturday surgeries, I became increasingly uncomfortable about the actions of a particular firm of moneylenders, operating out of Glasgow, who would lend small sums at times of family crisis and bereavement and then send in thugs, calling themselves bailiffs, if the extortionate interest could not be met. This, to me, was blatant usury. There was no other word for it. I made a speech in the Commons, bringing examples of the exploitation of vulnerable constituents to the attention of the House under the protection of Privilege, a system under which a Member of Parliament could not be sued in the courts for something that he had said in the House of Commons. Outside the House of Commons, of course, an MP was subject to libel laws. I threw in a line to the effect that, for all their cruel reputations, the caliphs of ancient Baghdad would not have tolerated what was going on in parts of West Lothian as the result of the greed of moneylenders.

This phraseology tickled the fancy of the Parliamentary Gallery correspondent of the Press Association, the duty sentinel reporter in the Commons doing his late-night stint. The 'caliphs of ancient Baghdad' went out on the wires. Cartoons followed – imaginary caliphs were such fun to draw as one national newspaper cartoonist put it to me – but my point was made and it contributed to the consumer protection legislation introduced during the course of the 1964–1970 Labour governments. As the Sheffield Hillsborough MP, George Darling, himself an industrial journalist and a minister at the Board of Trade, put it to me, 'All I remember about your campaign were the cartoons.' But the cartoons proved sufficient.

Another campaign – not wholly resolved after 40 years – was also sparked by a constituency experience. When we were engaged, Kathleen and I would, from time to time, take a quick bite to eat at the Victoria Café on the High Street of Linlithgow. We became friends with the owners who served us, Mr and Mrs Allen. One day, sobbing, Mrs Allen came and sat down beside us. She had a tale of woe to tell and invited us into her back kitchen to meet her 23-year-old son Grant, a teacher at Bo'ness Academy, where I had been a member of staff just three years earlier. He had been on kidney dialysis and had been told that, if he were not given a transplant soon, he would die. Could I, as an MP, do anything to facilitate the provision of matching tissue? Of course I took the case up with the medical authorities and made a personal approach to Michael Noble, the then Conservative Secretary of State for Scotland. Alas, as the weeks passed, no matching tissue was forthcoming and Grant Allen died. I promised his parents that I would do everything possible to help others in a similar position to their son.

Along with some parliamentary colleagues I was instrumental in persuading the government to set up a committee to examine the entire issue of organ donation. This was chaired by the distinguished president of the Royal College of Physicians, Sir Hector MacLennan, whose son Robert would later become a Scottish Labour MP and leader of the SDP in Scotland. He reported in 1969. The snag was that, although he was himself persuaded that more organs would be forthcoming under an opting-out system, he thought that public opinion required that a voluntary system of opting-in – that is, making a positive choice that one's organs should be donated – should be tried first. Opting-out meant that the organs of anyone who had not taken the trouble to say to the transplant centre in Bristol 'no, not mine' could be taken and used for transplants.

What struck me was that so much matching tissue, which would have saved Grant Allen, went to dust in the incinerators of crematoria. Also, personal contact and anecdotal evidence suggested that many relatives would willingly have given permission for organs of loved ones to be used if they could have thought about it in the cold light of day. The basic trouble was that decisions had to be taken at the moment of maximum grief. I spoke to a number of constituents who regretted, in retrospect, that the organs of their loved ones had not been used so at least part of their body would have been kept alive to give life to someone else.

During the summer recess of 1969, I determined to find out for myself whether it really was the case that public opinion demanded a voluntary system. So, over a marathon 42 days, I visited 1,000 homes in West Lothian, asking questions on a delicate, personal subject. I reckoned that people would talk more thoughtfully to their MP, whether they had previously met him or not, than to a pollster.

The results, which were taken seriously by the Secretary of State for Health, Dick Crossman, and by the powerful Chief Medical Officer Sir George Godber, were encouraging for those in favour of legislation: 364 out of 1,000 had no qualms about their organs being used, if useful in the event of their decease; 312 out of the 1,000 would prefer the voluntary system to be tried first. There were 216 'don't knows' and 108 were against transplantation, including three separate state-registered nurses, who said, 'Mr Dalyell, before you talk about transplanting kidneys, just make sure that you are providing us with the facilities to get the hernias sorted!' In the course of going round, I encountered many moving attitudes. A lady from Stoneyburn said to me, 'You can have any of my body parts you want, except my heart. My heart belongs to my husband.' Time and again I came across the juxtaposing of heart and soul.

So in 1971 I introduced a Ten Minute Rule Bill (under which an MP can speak for 10 minutes to introduce a bill which hardly ever gets as far as committee, let alone making it on to the statue book) which proposed that a hospital could take the organs of anyone who had not specifically 'opted-out', once clinical death had been established by two doctors, neither of whom was a renal surgeon and likely to benefit. I had the enthusiastic encouragement and expert help of Professor Sir Roy Calne, FRS, a pioneer of liver transplants and much else at Addenbrooke's Hospital in Cambridge.

As usual on such occasions, the Chamber virtually emptied after questions. On this occasion, one particular colleague did stay to listen. It was the Prime Minister, Ted Heath. Two days later I passed him in the corridor. 'I reflected on what you said about the need for legislation on transplants,' he told me. 'Personally, I'm sympathetic but you'll never get it past Keith Joseph [the Health and Social Security Secretary].' I did not and subsequently found out that what really scuppered the 'opting-out' system was the opposition of two eminent transplant surgeons, Michael Woodruff from Edinburgh and Robert Sells from Liverpool. They took the view that, if the voluntary element was downplayed, then fewer rather than more organs would become available.

*

Having first visited Canada as an undergraduate in 1953, I returned 14 years later when Kathleen and I went to Expo '67 in Montreal. The British pavilion director was General Sir William Oliver, who gave us lunch, his wife saying to Kathleen, 'If we had realised how nice you and Tam were, we would have invited you to stay with us!' The Montreal Expo, with the outstandingly inventive Czechoslovak pavilion, showing what Communist countries could do, proved a huge success, except for the city fathers of Montreal, who were saddled with crippling debt for years to come.

From Ottawa, we went to Chalk River, a research centre for civil and military nuclear power, taken by Renee Whitehead, science adviser to the Canadian prime minister, whom I had met at a Ditchley Conference and who, with typical Canadian generosity, invited us to stay in his home. Attendance at a session of the Canadian Parliament convinced me that a chamber where every MP had his or her allocated desk led to stilted exchanges. For, despite that bull of a man John Diefenbaker's passion, it seemed no atmosphere could be generated. In comparison, in those days, the House of Commons atmosphere could yield concrete results such as stiffening Harold Wilson's resolve not to accede to Lyndon Johnson's pressing request to send a

'battalion of bag-pipers' as a token of the British government's
support for the American cause in Vietnam.

In 1967, at the invitation of Ontario Hydro and Quebec
Hydro, I went with Jack Cunningham, the MP for Whitehaven
(with a PhD in chemistry), and Jim Callaghan's PPS, to the
CANDU nuclear power stations at Pickering and Bruce on Lake
Michigan and to the huge installations at Trois-Rivières and
Gentilly. When we returned, Jack and I urged ministers to think
in terms of co-operation with Canadian systems but, at that time,
they were wedded to the British advanced gas-cooled reactor (the
AGR) and American Westinghouse reactors. I shall always think
an opportunity was missed – not least because the Canadian
system minimised the problem of nuclear waste.

It was also Ditchley Park that gave me the entrée to federal
Washington. One of the participants was Bill Carey, who had
responsibility for the science and space programmes in the
Bureau of the Budget. He said, 'Come and stay with me and
I will get you interviews with anyone in Washington, other than
Lyndon Johnston [the then president].' Carey was as good as his
word. Meetings were fixed with Hubert Humphrey (whom his
president called the 'greatest co-ordinator of tongue and brain in
all America'), Glenn Seaborg, chairman of the Atomic Energy
Authority, Ed Wenk, Jr, secretary of the Marine Science Council,
Don Hornig, the president's science adviser, crusty old Senator
John L. McClellan of Arkansas, who held the key position of
chairman of the Senate Appropriations Committee, and Budget
Congressman Henry Reuss. The truth became apparent to me
that a young MP such as I, had he been guest of the State
Department, would not have been given the time of day, but
everyone in Washington was anxious to please the Bureau of the
Budget. It wasn't for my status or brown eyes that I was accorded
such treatment.

One man I did not ask to see was the economist Walter
Rostow, who had become Lyndon Johnson's key policy adviser
on Vietnam. But, on hearing that a young British MP was
peregrinating round governmental Washington, Rostow phoned
Carey to summon me. 'You'll have a rough ride, warned Mary

Carey, my host's wife. 'Walt takes no prisoners.' She was right. I went to Rostow's suite of offices in the basement of the White House itself. Without even one polite nicety, Rostow told me to sit down and barked, 'I am told that you are in favour of the British withdrawing from Singapore and related bases.' I said I was. Then he spluttered into a tirade, only one word of which I clearly recollect, which was that I and any who thought like me were 'lily-livered'. In vain, I tried calmly to argue the case for withdrawal from East of Suez. After about 10 minutes, the telephone on Rostow's desk rang. He lifted it up and let forth an impatient 'Yeah'. Seconds later, I never heard anyone change their tune so quickly as the impatient 'Yeah' was followed by an obsequious 'Sir'. Two burly marines bundled me out of the office in a flash. It was obvious to me that the only man in the world Walt Rostow would address with an obsequious 'Sir' was Lyndon Johnson. I never met Rostow again.

Shortly afterwards in the Commons Lobby, Harold Wilson, who liked to show off to his parliamentary colleagues that he knew everything they had been up to, whispered to me, 'I hear you saw Walt Rostow. His brother, Eugene, is a friend of mine. Says power has gone to Walt's head. I never did care for him.' Ensconced in the White House itself, Rostow was more influential and more of a blind hawk than Defense Secretary Robert McNamara and Secretary of State Dean Rusk, let alone any of the generals who had to command the actual fighting in Vietnam.

Had I simply met these powerful Americans, I would not record it here as it would have seemed to be name-dropping without purpose. However, to have established contact with them was a pre-requisite for the success of the campaign of which I am proudest in my life, Aldabra. The circumstances were that I got a letter out of the proverbial blue from Professor Sir Ashley Miles, then Professor of Experimental Pathology at the University of London, and Biological Secretary of the Royal Society. Miles said he was approaching me as a fellow graduate of King's College, Cambridge (although there were 30 years between us) and as a result of articles that I had written for the *New Scientist*. Could I do anything in parliament to protect the remote Indian Ocean atoll of Aldabra from the ravages that would inevitably follow from the construction of a proposed RAF staging post, destroying a unique pristine ecosystem?

Sir Ashley Miles told me that some of his Royal Society colleagues and young marine scientists were dismayed. Aldabra's beaches were where the giant tortoises of the Indian Ocean buried their eggs in the sand; Aldabra was also almost the only undisturbed habitat of the pink-footed booby and the flightless rail, a vulnerable dodo-like creature. I asked Sir Ashley to lunch in the Strangers' Dining Room. He brought with him a then young zoology lecturer at Cambridge (later distinguished professor at the University of Berkeley in California), David Stoddart, who had actually been on one of the few expeditions to land in Aldabra. With Stoddart, it was the beginning of a lifelong personal friendship.

I decided there and then to go much further than putting down one or two desultory Parliamentary Questions, which could be easily fobbed off. After Sir Ashley had had to go back to Carlton Gardens (the headquarters of the Royal Society) for a meeting of its council, to which he had promised to report my sustained interest, I sat down with Stoddart and devised 70 PQs to different ministries on Aldabra. Any MP who seeks to conduct a seriously effective and awkward campaign must have an enthusiastic expert, committed to the cause, to whom he can turn at any moment. On this occasion, Stoddart was mine. I spattered the parliamentary order paper with questions about Aldabra, helped in one way by a name which lent itself to ribaldry. For example, on 21 November 1967, I had given a fortnight's notice that I would ask the Foreign and Commonwealth Secretary:

1) What discussions he had had with the Government of Tanzania?
2) What discussion he had had with the Government of India on the proposal to establish a staging post base in the Indian Ocean at Aldabra?

It earned me the nickname for some months, among my Scottish colleagues, of 'Aldabra dafty Tam'. And I recognise that had I been campaigning for Henderson Island, for example, a jewel beyond Pitcairn Island off the coast of Chile, I would have been more easily ignored.

Forty years later, it is fascinating to read the Foreign and Commonwealth Office memorandum, authored in November 1967 by Alan Campbell (later UK Ambassador in Rome):

> The Tanzanian Government has said nothing to us about their reasons for supporting the resolution. We have however been approached by the Indian Government in both New Delhi and London. We have explained to them that neither the Seychelles nor Mauritius considered themselves 'dismembered' by the creation of the British Indian Ocean Territory and we have repudiated the view that the establishment of military installations in the area of the kind we have in mind would be contrary to General Assembly Resolutions . . . No decision about Aldabra has yet been taken but we remain ready to continue explaining our general policy towards it and our other islands not only to the Indian and Tanzanian Governments but to any Commonwealth Government which may enquire.

I asked to see the Prime Minister. His private secretary replied saying that the Prime Minister had said that I must go to see George Brown at the Foreign Office. I went. Going through the door into his room – it was late afternoon or early evening – he greeted me with a booming but not unfriendly, 'How's my favourite pink-footed booby?' He would not take it seriously. I did not realise then, as I was to discover later, that relations with Denis Healey as Defence Secretary were far more important than the health of ecosystems in the Indian Ocean. Healey would not see me but palmed me off with his Minister of State, Fred Mulley, a decent and able man but he was not prepared to contemplate scuppering the plan for a quicker way for troops going to Singapore by air than by sea.

I also went to see James Callaghan, by that time Home Secretary, who told me 'not to be a chump', by which he meant (as kindly fatherly advice) that, if I wanted to be a junior minister – which I did – I should not be awkward. Roy Jenkins, as Chancellor, gave me short shrift taking one and a half minutes to tell me, standing in the doorway of his Commons office, that the Treasury could not get involved in deciding the spending priorities of a department's overall budget. Barbara Castle, meanwhile, said she had enough problems with railways, motorways and breath tests to take up the cudgels in Cabinet on behalf of Aldabra. Dick Crossman was also no good. Although he sympathised with doing anything that would help unhinge the government's East of Suez strategy, he had zero interest in wildlife considerations. He told me, 'I can't be seen by my Cabinet colleagues as a pawn in the hands of my PPS and his nostrums.'

The charming Sir Elwyn Jones, the Attorney General, said that he had discussed my letter asking to see him on the subject with Gerald Gardiner, the Lord Chancellor, and they had concluded that the decision for a staging post in the Indian Ocean in no way contravened the nebulous Law of the Sea as they understood it. One minister and his officials did listen properly. This was Bob Mellish, later Labour Chief Whip but then Minister of State for Public Buildings and Works. He knew me well, as I had been the PPS in the Housing Department when he was Parliamentary Under-Secretary for Housing, working under Crossman. The conversation in his office went like this:

'What's bleeding Aldabra got to do with me?'

'Bob, you are going to have to build the bleeding runway. That's what it's got to do with you.'

'You don't say.'

'I do say. Look, do you know about the nature of coral limestone?'

'Haven't a bloody clue.' One of his officials wriggled uneasily.

'Well, I'll tell you. It is brittle hard on top. Underneath, after a few inches it is soft. It is quite unsuitable for runway construction.' I had been well briefed by David Stoddart.

'Is Mr Dalyell right?' Mellish barked at his officials.

'Well, um, yes, minister, in the circumstances.'

'How do we build a runway without in-fill?'

'Well I suppose,' I mused, 'you could pay for ships to bring 160,000 tonnes of rock from Mombasa or Lourenço Marques on the African Coast.'

'Who would pay?'

'Your department, Bob.'

'Crikey! I'd better look into this.'

The following week, I encountered Bob Mellish in his normal place, sitting alone at the table for six in the Members' Dining Room, before other regulars at the table, such as George Strauss, Charlie Pannell and Douglas Houghton, arrived.

'Have you looked into Aldabra?' I asked him.

'Yes, darling,' was his reply, an East-End Cockney form of address he used for junior male and female colleagues alike. 'You're probably bleeding right,' he told me, 'it's a madcap scheme. But the Ministry for Public Buildings and Works is not going to win against all those departmental chieftains, whom you have already got across by trekking round the Cabinet. You and your dodos!'

Quite clearly my campaign was hitting the buffers – it was going nowhere. The merits of the case were secondary in the eyes of otherwise good colleagues, who thought that I was 'acting above my station in life'. The PLP was far more hierarchical in the early 1960s than nowadays.

At this point, I decided to be really awkward. I knew what I was doing and I knew that it might infuriate senior members of the government. Along with a short covering letter, I sent photostats of my 70 PQs on Aldabra to Senator Hubert Humphrey, Vice-President of the United States, Glen Seaborg, Ed Wenk, Don Hornig, Senator John L. McClellan, Congressman Reuss, Congressman John Blatnik of Minnesota and Bill Carey – all my Washington contacts – pointing out not only that the ministerial answers were unsatisfactory but also often plain ignorant.

They reacted, as I had anticipated, and passed the documentation to the Defense Secretary, Robert McNamara, and to the Secretary of State, Dean Rusk, saying they had met with this young British MP – he seemed a serious man – and what was all this about the threat to the tortoises, etc. Healey confessed to me years later that McNamara had contacted him. However, before Healey could reply, I had a stroke of luck. I happened to hear from a friend on the staff of the *New Scientist* that Dillon Ripley was passing through London. He was Secretary of the Smithsonian Institute, one of the pivotal positions at the epicentre of the American scientific establishment. Through Sir Ashley Miles and the Royal Society, I fixed up to go to see him at midnight in his room at the Cavendish Hotel before he was due to fly on to Tunis the following morning. Unlike British ministers, Ripley was interested in the merits of a staging post on Aldabra. Having listened carefully, he said quietly, 'Leave me your PQs and I will undertake to raise them with President Johnson next week.' I did not realise that, under the American Constitution, the holder of the office of Secretary of the Smithsonian has a direct right of access to the President of the United States on any scientific matter.

Ripley was as good as his word and sent me a copy of a handwritten letter which he had addressed to the Prime Minister:

My dear Mr Wilson

As head of the Smithsonian Institution in Washington, I happen to be in London and have asked to see Tam Dalyell as I had come to know from U.S. colleagues that he was interested in the question of the future of Aldabra Island. He tells me that it may well be that H.M. Government will make public their decision on the future of this island very soon.

It, of course, does not behove me to present any arguments pro or con to yourself but, in the process of discussions in this matter in Washington, it does appear to me that no lasting decision should be made pending further evidence and further study. I have every intention in my capacity as Secretary, to bring this matter to the personal attention of Mr Johnson on my return from an official mission to Tunisia in a week's time.

Yours truly again
S. Dillon Ripley

P.S. I have of course discussed this matter with Mr McNamara and Mr Rusk.

S.D.R.

On 8 December 1967 I wrote:

Dear Prime Minister

You may want to know that apart from an undertaking to send a copy of Dillon Ripley's letter to the American Ambassador, only Dick Crossman is aware of this letter. I do not intend to show it to anyone else in the Government, let alone the Press.

Yours sincerely,
Tam Dalyell

Forty years later, the National Archives in Kew has shown me the letter. In green ink, at the top of my letter, Wilson has ticked and written, 'Should it not be seen by the S/S [Secretary of State for] Defence? Ask Tam if he has any objections?' There followed a letter from Michael Palliser, then private secretary to the Prime Minister, to Ewan Broadbent at the Ministry of Defence, saying, 'Dalyell told me that he would not wish to embarrass Mr Ripley by the news getting back to Washington that he had written to the Prime Minister about this but, subject to that, he has no objection to Mr Healey being aware of Mr Ripley's letter, more particularly since Mr Ripley claimed to have discussed the matter with Messrs Rusk and McNamara and to be bringing it to the attention of the President.'

The Commons gave me a good-natured, if slightly jocular, cheer when Harold Wilson announced that the Aldabra proposal had been cancelled. Weeks later, Crossman told me exactly what had happened. Harold Wilson had had a phone call from Lyndon Johnson: 'Hey, Harold, what's all this about tortoises and boobies that Ripley, McNamara and Rusk are pestering me with? Can't you drop it? I've got enough problems.' Umpteen well-directed PQs simply did not make the impact on government policy that was immediate in a way that an irritated phone call from the President of the United States had done. I continue to keep in touch with the development of Aldabra as a protected scientific gem through Professor Stephen

Blackmore, Regius Keeper of the Royal Botanic Garden in Edinburgh.

Years later, when he had just ceased to be ambassador to Japan, I met Sir Michael Wilford at the house of Sir Julian Ridsdale MP, Stanley Baldwin's nephew, who for 30 years was the active secretary of the Britain–Japan Group. Wilford recalled that, in October 1967, he had put the government's case for the Aldabra staging post. Wilford said with a smile, 'Thank heaven for awkward MPs like you. They can be a bloody time-consuming nuisance but they have great uses in the ecology of politics. Aldabra would have been an expensive white elephant and put us on the wrong side of every conservation body.' Likewise, Michael Palliser later told me, at a Foreign Office reception, that he and his colleagues were grateful Aldabra had been propelled into their consciousness by a determined MP.

*

Ireland was another pressing issue at this time. En famille, with Kathleen's parents (Lord) John and Nancy Wheatley, and our infant son Gordon, we went on holiday in August 1966 to Ireland. The bush telegraph had told a prominent politician that a Westminster MP was staying at the local hotel in Fahan, and I had an urgent request from the hotel owner asking if I could see her friend alone.

A private room was provided and in came Eddie McAteer, a prominent Northern Irish politician at the time. What did he do? Pulled down his trousers and his underpants and displayed his testicles. Non-medic that I am, I was horrified by their bruising. 'This is what they do to you in this country,' he said, his voice bursting with anger. 'What are you Westminster people going to do about it?' When I recounted to my father-in-law (whose father had been born in Ireland) why Eddie McAteer had wanted to see me alone, he said gently that I should not be too surprised.

Three years later, in 1969, I was surprised again. With the outbreak of 'The Troubles', I thought it was the duty of Scots MPs in general and me in particular – as MP for West Lothian, I represented, with the exception of Harold Wilson in Huyton, more second-generation Irish than any other constituency in Britain – to visit Northern Ireland and see for ourselves. I soon discovered my Scots parliamentary colleagues would not touch Northern Ireland with the proverbial barge pole.

Vividly I remember the embarrassed fury of my parliamentary neighbour and a leading lady of the Labour Party, Judith Hart, when I told her that she ought to be as interested in Ulster, which was 90 miles from our constituencies, as she was in Chile, which was 12,000 miles away. 'Judith,' I told her, 'if you've got time to share platforms up and down the country with Madame Allende and the Chilean Ambassador, surely you've got time for Northern Ireland?' I was met with a cryogenic, 'Tam, grow up.' At the time, I brimmed with righteous indignation at Labour MPs who would campaign against apartheid in South Africa, American policy in Vietnam and human rights in a dozen countries but declined to get involved in delicate issues on their own doorstep.

In these circumstances, I determined to visit Northern Ireland. Believing in good manners towards ministers, I dropped a note to the Minister of State responsible for Northern Ireland, my friend and contemporary Elystan Morgan, telling him of my ancestor's experience at Carrickfergus (General Tam), my holiday experience with the bruised testicles and constituency interest and informing him of my intention to visit the Province.

That same day, I picked up a phone message in the Members' Lobby of the House of Commons. It came not from Elystan Morgan but from the Home Secretary James Callaghan – a laconic 'Come and see me at once'. So I rang his private secretary Brian Cubbon (later Permanent Undersecretary of State at the Northern Ireland Office, 1976–79), who was always well disposed towards me. 'I think, if I may say so, Mr Dalyell,' he said, 'that you will be well advised to drop anything you are doing and come across and see the Home Secretary. He is not pleased with you.'

Thus, I was ushered in to the long, sepulchral room that Home Secretaries then occupied. Seated at the far end at his desk was James Callaghan. He took a little time to finish what he was doing and, after a couple of minutes, looked up and said, 'Elystan tells me that you want to go to Northern Ireland. Tam, what good do you think you can do for the people of Northern Ireland that I cannot do as Home Secretary?' No one could use silences more effectively than Callaghan – he was a master of the deadly, but sometimes slightly unfair, question. I was reduced to a watery smile – my off stump had been bowled over. Twenty years later, I might have retorted, 'Well, Jim, quite a lot.' But, in 1969, I was young and, I confess, in some awe of the holders of great offices of state on their home turf.

Callaghan then switched from bully to charmer. 'Look,' he said, 'I just don't want any Scottish MP to become involved in the explosive affairs of Northern Ireland. I don't take Gregor [Gregor Mackenzie, MP for Rutherglen and Callaghan's faithful PPS] when I go, I take Roland [Roland Moyle, MP for Lewisham].'

At that point in time, Callaghan was right and I was wrong. I did not go. Scotland was tinder dry and The Troubles could easily have spread to the land of Glasgow Rangers and Celtic. Indeed, I made up my mind to oppose devolution for Scotland, tooth and nail, on the sweaty summer evening when I watched Glenn Barr, the Ulster Protestant leader, and his Ulstermen's reed pipe band, making its way along Linlithgow High Street and past the very church of St Michael's where General Tam and his father worshipped and where their signatures are on the National Covenant. I believed – and still believe – that it is much better for Scotland to be fully part of Britain and not to be hived off as an inward-looking community, as in Northern Ireland at that time.

Two years later in 1971, with hesitation yet becoming ever more intransigent, I was determined to go to Northern Ireland. By that time, it had become mercifully apparent that any religious or tribal divide between Catholics and non-Catholics was unlikely to erupt in Scotland. Furthermore, when I went to see the incoming Conservative Home Secretary, Willie Whitelaw, he was all for MPs acquainting themselves with the facts on the ground. One of Whitelaw's favourite words was 'splendid'. He must have used it a dozen times over my proposal to go. So, off I went with James Lamond, MP for Oldham and erstwhile Lord Provost of Aberdeen who was an extreme left-winger suspected of being a 'fellow traveller' (i.e. sympathetic to communism). (My friend, Dick Mabon, who at that time had recently been Minister of State at the Scottish Office, bestowed what was meant to be friendly advice: 'Tam, if you fly with the crows, expect to be shot with the crows.')

Lamond and I met up with our friend Harold McCusker, the Ulster Unionist MP for Armagh; we were among comparatively few Labour MPs who deemed it important to have good human relations with representatives of the Protestant *and* Catholic communities. With Whitelaw's blessing, we went with McCusker to the Maze Prison. Here I was brought face to face with the feuding aggressiveness of Irishmen that had nonplussed Ensign Dalyell and the Earl of Stafford 330 years earlier. The nervous prison officers conducted us straight to the totally un-nervous boss man, 'Gusty' Spence, a leader of wit and charm, who had been convicted of several murders and suspected of many more. 'Would you, Mr Lamond and Harold care for a cup of coffee?' he inquired. We thought it polite to accept, whereupon Spence barked over his shoulder.

A fellow prisoner came at the double: 'Corporal Spence, sir, your wishes?'

'Coffee all round,' commanded Spence.

Five minutes later, two fellow prisoners, immaculate starched napkins over one arm, served us coffee. This convivial meeting encapsulated the whole hierarchical guerrilla structure of one of the Northern Ireland factions. Apart from the substance of the hour-long discussion, an uncomfortable impression was forming in my mind of how much those in the position of Spence positively enjoyed the conflicts and being in the centre of world-wide attention. His parting words to us were, 'And now, you will be going to see the others.' We were. The 'others' were the hard men on the other side, the IRA and Provisional IRA. They were no less hospitable, witty and charming to Lamond and me. McCusker thought it advisable not to accompany us to this meeting. Self-evidently, the detainees from the IRA and the Provisional IRA revelled in the 'struggle', which they believed to be a justifiable political cause and not a criminal activity. To all intents this was civil war.

Less agreeable was the visit, the following day, to the women's prison in Armagh. Indelibly etched on my memory was the encounter with 19-year-old Elizabeth McKie, a gunrunner. She hissed at us, 'I don't mind if Dr Paisley is the Prime Minister of Northern Ireland – as long as you Brits get out.' Miss McKie was from the Provisional IRA. I shook my head in despair and disbelief as my forbear Ensign Dalyell must have done centuries before. Did I continue to pursue my public and active concerns about Northern Ireland affairs? I did not. Why?

A major consideration was due to a threatening letter I had received shortly after my visit with Lamond. Like most MPs, I received threatening letters from time to time, and discarded them light-heartedly. However, this particular letter was ominously different. It was postmarked 'Coleraine' and stated all too plainly that, if I continued to meddle in Ulster's affairs (the use of the word Ulster in this particular context would be an indication that it came from a UDF-related source), there were means of destroying our home. Details not just of the location but also of the layout of the House of The Binns could easily have been noted by a legitimate visitor to the house.

Our home in Scotland was open to visitors and I had no right to put them or the National Trust for Scotland at risk, still less Kathleen and our young children, Gordon and Moira. I smelt that the writer meant what he said. I immediately drew the attention of Lothian and Borders Police to the letter. They offered protection. But could an MP accept round-the-clock protection from a hard-pressed police force for five days a week, while parliament was sitting and I was in London? And, truth to tell, I did not see myself as effectively resisting terrorist action. I, thereafter, left the problems of Northern Ireland to dedicated colleagues such as Kevin McNamara, Stan Orme and Paul Rose. Publicly, I sympathised with the Troops Out Movement, believing, as General Tam did, that there was little we could do from this side of the water to resolve the historic problems of Ireland.

*

It was the pathetically sad case of a Mrs Lynch of Blackridge, whose husband had run off leaving her almost destitute, which led to the Mechanics of Payment of Aliment Bill, presented to the Commons on 24 February 1971, which contributed to Social Security measures, providing an improved, if not perfect, settlement for women whose husbands had left them. Blackridge, a small mining village in the western part of West Lothian, was a community where everybody knew everybody else's business. It was also a community at that time with sharply divided religious adherence. The fact that the Roman Catholic Society of St Vincent de Paul and the Order of the Eastern Star, the female wing of the Masonic Lodge, both told me of their sympathy for Mrs Lynch reinforced my determination to explore what could be done.

My first port of call was the chairman of the Board of Inland Revenue. Normally, in those days, such an august personage would not have given time to a 'rookie' MP but he had come before the Public Accounts Committee, of which I was a member, very much the dour Scot, the lad o' pairts, who had scaled the heights of the United Kingdom power structure, and, one afternoon, as the Committee ended, Sir Alexander Johnston came up to me and said cheerfully, 'I have heard of your teaching practice time at Heriot's.' I expressed surprise. 'You see,' he explained, 'I'm a friend of the headmaster, William McLachlan Dewar, and I have kept close connections with my old school over the years.' I replied that Dewar was a remarkable headmaster, which clearly pleased Sir Alexander.

Thus it came about that, three years later, he agreed to see me personally in his office in Somerset House, surely the grandest and most elegant office surveying the Thames in all London. This outwardly dour Scot turned into a warm human being, who cared about the circumstances of divorced and separated women. He was blunt about my likelihood of success but encouraged me to campaign. The central issue was how to cope with a situation where money was awarded but not paid. It was one of the saddest scenarios in the Britain of 1971.

The plight of divorced and separated women was harrowing

enough, and their financial situation would in most cases be
serious even if maintenance awards made in court were, in fact,
actually paid. But I found – and, talking to parliamentary
colleagues, it was the same for them – that, in many cases the
award of alimony was little better than a legal fiction. I came to
think that the sum decreed by the court was more likely to
determine not what the wife received over any period of time but
the extent of her husband's arrears. Other cases from my weekly
surgeries showed that, even where the husband began the payments with every intention of continuing them indefinitely, he
was all too likely to lapse, particularly if he started a second
family. Most of my constituents' income did not easily run to the
support of two families; it was natural though reprehensible that,
as the pressure became more acute, the husband often began to
ignore his financial obligations to the wife and family he had left.
When this happened, it seemed to me that, in a range of
constituency cases, apart from Mrs Lynch, it was far too easy
for him to get away with it. Tracing was a nightmare. As an MP, I
also had the dilemma that, through my work, I just happened
sometimes to know where the absconding husband was hanging
out or working. Was it my business to disclose this information to
the wife? I fear that often my way out of the dilemma was to have
a quiet word with a police superintendent friend, who would use
his discretion and sometimes shame defaulting husbands into
coughing up. Of course, the woman awarded the alimony could
go back to court, if the alimony was not paid over a period of
time. My experience was that courts, in practice, often decided to
wipe out some of the arrears as a bad debt. Actually, it was no
easier to force the husband to comply with the second order than
with the first. The court could make an Attachment of Earnings
Order. But, lo and behold, in such circumstance I found that the
husband just moved from one job to another. A wife who was in
receipt of Supplementary Benefit could agree to transfer her
alimony payments to the Supplementary Benefit Commission. By
doing so, she could receive a full entitlement from them and it
would be up to the Commission to obtain the payments from the
husband – if they could. On one of my regular visits to 'the Broo',

the local name for the benefits office, in Bathgate, the manager said wryly, 'I am not Scotland Yard. How on earth are my staff expected to find absconding husbands and then extract money from them?'

Besides, the Supplementary Benefits Commission route was of no use whatsoever to working wives or those who were ineligible for benefits for other reasons. It also came home to me that there were many wives, whatever their plight, who wanted to maintain their pride, which required that they go nowhere near the Commission. 'I would rather be dead, Mr Dalyell, than be spied by my neighbours going to the Broo' was the sentiment conveyed to me in various forms, dozens of times. The issue was what could be done to obtain what was no more than their legal due for these women. In the bill I put before the House, I proposed that the responsibility for collecting the payments should be transferred to the Inland Revenue.

I anticipated that they would resist on grounds both of principle and of practice. Forty years later, I have seen their internal memorandum, thanks to the National Archives at Kew. In a sentence, a turgid memorandum comes to the conclusion that the Inland Revenue would not touch my bill with the proverbial barge poll. And, of course, they had the support of the Treasury. However, I do not know whether after four decades to be mildly amused or angry at the way in which the Treasury and the Home Office officials squabbled over which department should have the responsibility of subjecting the bill to the scaffold. Neither fancied the opprobrium they would incur in certain quarters.

My view was that it was altogether too easy to accept objections from the administrative machine as the ultimate veto. There is strong resistance – I understand it – to using the machinery of the Inland Revenue for any purpose other than the collection of taxes – 'this is the thin end of the wedge' line of argument. Once you start using the Revenue for anything else – the collection of fines or civil debts, for example – so it is contended, it will become impossible to stop until the system has become quite overburdened. The tax collector should stick to his tax-raising forms. But, in letters to Keith Joseph, the Secretary of State, and Mark Carlisle, Minister of State at the Home Office, and personally read by them, as I now know from the annotations preserved at Kew, I asked why this canon of administrative practice was not to be measured against the manifest injuries suffered by women in the position of Mrs Lynch and by the grave situation created by the rapidly increasing number of divorces.

I conceded that, in certain respects, the Inland Revenue was overstretched but asserted that, once the initial arrangements had been made for collecting alimony through the tax system, there would be no extra call upon the more specialised services of the Inland Revenue. I thought, and still think, it would have been quite a simple business to make the necessary adjustments to the tax coding. I was told by a sympathiser in the middle echelons of the Revenue, whom I promised never to name, that the objections of Somerset House (headquarters of the Inland Revenue) were lazy hogwash and, in particular, since there would be no frequent changes in liability to payment, there was no need for the nightmare of complex assessment. Any changes to payment would be assessed, not by the Inland Revenue, but by the courts.

A Ten Minute Rule Bill can have up to a dozen supporters; mine were all serious MPs who did not give their signatures lightly. A note which I have seen at Kew 40 years later, by Mr R. L. Jones of the Home Office, reveals the Legislation Committee of the Cabinet decided there was 'no reason to oppose Mr Dalyell's Bill' but that Whips should ensure it received an opposed Second Reading. In other words, the bill should be buried as quietly as possible by the practice, which brings parliament into disrepute, of the Whips shouting, 'Object!' – or, more likely, muttering, 'Object' – at the fag-end of business on a Friday afternoon. Many sensible proposals have been snuffed out by this nefarious practice.

However, I would be doing an injustice to Tory ministers to suggest that they were unsympathetic. Mark Carlisle, then at the Home Office, saw me. We had been friends since I was chairman of the Cambridge University Conservative Association, and he bore me no ill will for turning up as a Labour MP. He said he was a friend and a political opponent in that order. I also saw John Nott, Minister of State at the Treasury. The beaver-like journalist David McKie wrote in the *Guardian* that, having talked to Nott, he found him 'sympathetic to Tam Dalyell's cause'. I approached Keith Joseph (a fellow of All Souls), asking for a meeting. He sought me out after a Commons division and said, 'You need to be educated in the issue of alimony. I promise you, we are not being obstructive but I will arrange for you to see the chairman of the Inland Revenue and the best of luck in making an impression on him. We hope that the Finer Committee will provide answers.'

By appointment, I went along to the same gorgeous office in which Sir Alexander Johnston had met me four years earlier. Sitting in his chair was Sir Arnold France, an extremely able, clever and welcoming Treasury mandarin, who greeted me as a fellow protégé of Sir Edmund Compton, the Comptroller and Auditor General, who had mentored me when I first joined the Public Accounts Committee in 1962. I began by suggesting that if the Treasury/Inland Revenue objections were so rigid, there was another possibility. Surely alimony could be paid through the National Insurance system. It would, in effect, be a surcharge on the stamp. I put it to him that such a route might be feasible only for so long as all National Insurance payments were not made earnings related and therefore collected through the Inland Revenue. Sir Arnold countered that this would provide more administrative difficulties than if the National Insurance method were adopted and just the same objections to using that system for a wider purpose. France added that there would be more invasion of personal privacy because a surcharge on the stamp would be more evident to an employer than the adjustment of the tax coding. He then offered me a cup of (delicious China) tea, and revealed that my kite-flying bill and speeches had contributed to the government's decision to set up a commission of enquiry into one-parent families. Chaired by the Vice Chairman of the Board of Governors of the London School of Economics, Morris Finer, this reported in 1974 and paved the way for a better, if a far from

perfect, deal for divorced or separated women. My persistence
had not been in vain.

One thing I have learnt over a long political life is the
importance and value of persistence. Believing deeply in issues
and campaigning hard to achieve a fairer system, it has often
been a great frustration to politicians that they have not succeeded. But often, over time, the arguments have made their
impact and changed the course in the direction I was pursuing.
Time and again, despite public perception, I have been impressed by the calibre and commitment of so many of our public
servants. Wise, thoughtful men and women need to be persuaded
to consider the consequences and risks – they need thinking time.
The documents which, as a result of the Thirty-year Rule, have
become available to me in the National Archives, if lengthy and
written in turgid prose, confirm that the Civil Service did indeed
use their thinking time to good effect. They were always conscious, and rightly so, of the law of unintended consequences.

*

Some controversies arrive out of the blue, unheralded and
unintended and certainly uninvited. A prime example was the
row which ensued after I seemingly had gone out of my way to
criticise the role of the Argyll and Sutherland Highlanders in
Aden. Forty-five years later, I am still subject to the anger of
militarily orientated people and, indeed, others who abhor the
criticism of serving British soldiers. My constituent Ross Stephen-
son, of Mike's Taxis, the local firm that, from time to time, take
me to the excellent St John's Hospital in Livingston, was with the
Royal Engineers in the Crater district of Aden and reasoned with
me, saying, 'What were we to do? If we had not used grenades,
they would have got us. Colonel [Colin] Mitchell was quite
justified in being aggressive. It probably saved my life and the
lives of those around me.' I am sensitive to such a rebuke.

It all began, in my case, with an ill-attended Commons debate
on the future of the Scottish regiments in 1968. George Younger,
a Conservative backbencher at the time, was speaking, trying to
snuff out any proposal to amalgamate the Argylls on account of

what they had recently done in Aden. I intervened to defend the Scots Greys and added, impromptu, that the Argylls should not crow too much about Aden, where they had been undisciplined and acted contrary to orders. I said I knew that the Military Commander, General Philip Tower, and the overall Commander, Admiral Sir Michael Le Fanu, Commander-in-Chief in the Middle East 1965–68, were angry with the Commanding Officer (CO) of the Argylls, Lieutenant Colonel Colin Mitchell, for having flouted their instructions.

All hell was let loose in the Scottish press. I had insulted the CO whom the *Scottish Daily Express* had affectionately dubbed 'Mad Mitch'. 'How dare a National Service, donkey walloper [Cavalry] trooper insult such a courageous hero,' roared the *Scottish Daily Mail*. The Labour-leaning *Daily Record* was equally censorious. On the other side of the coin was the indubitable fact that events at Crater had harmed Britain's reputation throughout the Arab world. Stories of kilted, gung-ho Jocks mowing down innocent Aden civilians were embellished. The fault was not so much that of the troops, as that of the politicians who put them in that position. It was conveyed to Mitchell by top brass in the Ministry of Defence that he had no promotional future in the army.

But I, by my intervention, had created the conditions in which Mitchell became something of a folk hero in Scotland. He was persuaded, he confessed to me later 'against my better judgement', to become a Tory candidate in West Aberdeenshire and Kincardine where, such was his glamour, he ousted a strong Liberal MP, James Davidson, an ex-naval officer and qualified Russian interpreter turned local farmer. The press gave the impression that his first action on coming to Westminster would be to seek me out for a (physical) fight in the corridors of the House of Commons. Not a bit of it. On the contrary, he thanked me for being the unwitting instrument by which he became an MP. Alas, Mitchell soon became 'cheesed off' at being a government backbencher. Some of the Tory grandees with military backgrounds, DSOs and MCs and Bar, did not take to him on account of what their friends among the generals had told them of Mitchell's intolerable insubordination. In February 1974, he did not seek re-election and went off to become director of the Halo Trust, personally disconnecting booby traps and landmines. I admired him for this and wrote an affectionate obituary of him in the *Independent*. In politics, relationships that start aggressively can become healthily good.

CHAPTER SEVEN

The East

ONE OF THE bonuses of having something of a reputation as an MP for probing in controversial areas is that one becomes the recipient of a vast amount of correspondence from people with all kinds of bees in their bonnets and who ask for all sorts of unrealistic – and often absurd – things to be done. One develops a knack for weeding out the dross. So when, in the early autumn of 1970, I began to read the contents of a letter hand-written on airmail paper and postmarked London, I quickly realized I was dealing with a very serious matter indeed.

After referring to my successful and sustained efforts on behalf of Aldabra, the writer asked if I would focus attention on the terrible injustices being perpetrated against the vulnerable islanders of Diego Garcia and the Chagos Archipelago. The writer had huge concerns about an American base in the Indian Ocean but there was no mention of marine or wildlife concerns. I thought, and still think, it could have come from a thoughtful Mauritian student I had known at Moray House Training College in Edinburgh and whom my mother and I had invited for meals at our house. I could quite imagine why he wished to maintain a cloak of anonymity as he had become an upwardly mobile administrator in the government of Mauritius and would not want to antagonise his prime minister, Seewoosagur Ramgoolam, a bosom buddy of Harold Wilson.

My next step was to return to some of those, such as Sir Ashley Miles and Professor David Stoddart, who had been so helpful in the Aldabra campaign. Their attitude was: 'We don't really know. We have to be careful about not seeming to oppose everything the government does as it engenders opposition when it really matters – as over Aldabra. But you had better find out!' My opening question on 12 November 1970 was to ask Reggie Maudling, standing in for Edward Heath at Prime Minister's Questions, about the discussion with President Nixon on a joint UK/US base at Diego Garcia in the Indian Ocean. 'Details of exchanges with President Nixon,' Maudling replied, 'were confidential.'

Passing him in the corridor he said, with the good humour for which he was much liked, 'Tam, I've been learning some new geography from you!' I told him not quite so cheerfully that he had fobbed us off. Even more cheerfully he said, 'What do you expect?' and ambled along on his way.

On 15 December, undeterred, I asked Heath himself about his discussions with Senator Percy of Illinois as personal envoy of President Nixon on the issue of a joint UK/US staging post based in the British Indian Ocean Territory (BIOT). Heath said he had not talked to Senator Percy about BIOT. The fact that he hadn't demonstrated how low down Diego Garcia was in relation to the priorities of the government. But my question elicited, for the first time, the thin edge of the wedge, with his reply: 'But I am now able to state that, in accordance with the terms of the United States/United Kingdom Exchange of Notes of December 1966, published in April 1967, HMG have agreed to the construction by the United States Government of a limited naval communications facility on Diego Garcia Atoll in the Chagos Archipelago. The United Kingdom will assist in its manning. It will provide communications support to US and UK ships.'

There was no indication whatsoever that, soon and for at least the next 40 years, Diego Garcia was to become the largest base for American forces outside the continental United States.

On 4 February 1971 my friend and colleague Lewis Carter-Jones asked the junior minister in the Foreign Office, Anthony Royle, MP for Richmond in Surrey, when the governments of India and Ceylon were formally told about the proposed base at Diego Garcia. Carter-Jones was one of the MPs I most admired and respected. This was on account of his relentless personal research into mechanical and electronic devices which would enhance the quality of life of the elderly and the disabled and his promotion of the use of such devices by NHS trusts and local authorities. But Carter-Jones was also the right man to ask the question since he was an official of the Curry Club. This was an organisation which met every month in the ample rooms of the Indian High Commission. Over a delicious buffet curry lunch, members would hear a short speech by the Indian High Commissioner of the day and then participate in a discussion of outstanding issues between India and Britain. I asked Carter-Jones, one of my squash partners at the time, to put the question for two reasons. As secretary of the Curry Club he had an obvious locus and an obvious locus is a great help to being taken seriously in politics. The second reason was that I was sensitive to the weaknesses of being perceived as a 'one-man band' on Diego Garcia, and the issue would be taken more seriously if well-regarded parliamentary colleagues also put questions. The answer was just as we guessed it would be.

India and Ceylon had not been informed about the proposal to create a base until the very last moment before the public announcement. At best, this was but an example of the gaucheness which pervaded the attitude of the West towards the emerging great states of Asia. We simply should not have been back in the eighteenth century when Captain Thomas Dalyell was sailing these seas. India and Ceylon had a right to know what was happening in their own backyard. It was the long-held belief of the Indian government that the Indian Ocean should be a demilitarised zone. It transpired that the government of Australia had been not only informed but consulted well in advance. Now, in the 1970s, cross-party friendships were both more frequent and more acceptable than today (this may partly have been on account of the fact that, as young men and women, Tory and Labour people had fought alongside one another against Nazi Germany). In any event, Anthony, later Sir Anthony, Royle and Lewis Carter-Jones had both been wounded in the war and were mates in the All-Party Disabilities Group. Royle, a Foreign Office

Thomas Dalyell (1570–1642) of Edinburgh, merchant adventurer trading in butter used as axle and cannon grease, married Janet, daughter of Mr Edward Bruce. Bruce was Scottish Ambassador to the Court of St James and negotiator, with Robert Cecil, on the Scottish King's succession to the English throne in 1603. Living in Fetter Lane from 1603 to 1612, Dalyell made money to return to Scotland and built most of The Binns, basically through 'cash for honours' patronage in his position as Deputy Master of the Rolls.

Tam Dalyell (1615–85), taken prisoner at the Battle of Worcester (1651), escaped from the Tower of London (1652), commanded the armies of Tsar Alexis Mikhailovitch at Smolensk, the gateway to Moscow. He returned as Charles II's Commander-in-Chief, Scotland (1666) and raised the Scots Greys in 1678.

Magdalene Dalyell, 'Lady of Binns' (1672–1732), General Tam's favoured and formidable granddaughter. She settled the estate following the death of her husband, James Menteith of Auldcathie, on her eldest son, and in 1727 sailed across the Atlantic to join her younger son at Rappahannock, Virginia. She was the grandmother, at five removes, of Harry S. Truman. In 2004 Kathleen and I went to Independence, Missouri for the 120th anniversary of Truman's birth, and presented an armorial plate and Dalyell tartan to the Presidential Library.

Sir John Graham Dalyell (1775–1851), prolific author on flora, fauna and musical instruments, teacher of Charles Darwin at Edinburgh University, persona of the Scottish Enlightenment, friend of Sir Walter Scott, whose abiding interest was the reproductive system of the common leech.

Aged two, being inspected by Colonel Piggott-Moody in 1934, when the Royal Scots Greys camped at The Binns during a recruiting drive. In 1984, the Colonel of the regiment, (later Field Marshal) Sir John Stanier, quipped, 'In 1934 all of us could ride; none of us could drive. In 1984, all of us can drive, none of us can ride!' I used to phone Stanier weekly during the Iraq War for military advice.

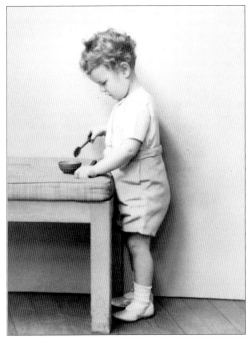

Aged four, pretending to make the porridge. This picture was taken to send to my mother, who had left me aged three weeks to accompany my father to his job as HM Political Agent in Bahrain.

Aged five with the Sheikh, head of the Khalifa family of Bahrain, who had come to Britain on an official visit, and was my parents' guest at The Binns. Both my parents were fluent Arabic speakers.

With my mother and father on 1 September 1939, the day Hitler's armies marched into Poland. Within days, my father volunteered to be liaison officer between the RAF and the Ack-Ack guns at Turnhouse, now Edinburgh International Airport. He was on duty the day Rudolf Hess landed in Scotland, on what is now believed by some serious people to have been a peace mission.

With Willie Martin of West Lothian County Roads department during the tarmaccing of The Binns drive in 1939.

In 1944, the National Trust for Scotland asked my mother, Eleanor Dalyell, whose house it was, for The Binns as their first property under the Country House Scheme initiated in the 1930s by the English National Trust. She gave it with an endowment. In April 1946, the day before the house opened to visitors, she handed over the property, with a token clod of earth, receiving one penny 'Blench Duty' from the 34-year-old Earl of Wemyss (extreme right), the Vice-Chairman of NTS, deputising for the ill Chairman, Sir Iain Colquhoun of Luss. My father and NTS thought that this form of Sasine ceremony was in the Celtic tradition – alas, as we now know, it was Anglo-Saxon.

Lochboisdale, August 1945, fishing for sea-trout on Lower Kildonan Loch. My father adored trying his own flies to tempt the fish, or using flies such as the Peter Ross, which he bought from the South Uist Gaelic-speaking hotel-keeper Finlay Mackenzie, or our friend the ghillie Peter MacLennan.

Friends from Tom Brocklebank's Eton House: Me, Robin Shuldhman, Freddie Nicolle (later a distinguished plastic surgeon), Ian Maclean and Michael Talbot-Ponsonby.

Me as a member of a Centurion tank crew, in B.A.O.R. In the kindly – and accurate – judgement of Willie Whitelaw's brother-in-law, Colonel Aidan Sprot of the Royal Scots Greys, 'Unlike his famous ancestor, General Tam Dalyell, the founder of our regiment, this Tam was not cut out to be a soldier!' He was speaking on the record to my biographer, Russell Galbraith.

Bo'ness Academy Under-15 Squad, winner of the Scottish School Cup 1960. Back row (left to right): Eric Slater (later headmaster of Ellon Academy), Brian Cairns, Tarry McAdam, Drew Duff (goalkeeper), George Fairclough, Sandy Oliver, 'Sinky' Sinclair, John Watson, me. Front row: Frank King, Jimmy Smith, Douglas Raeburn, Dennis Setterington (later friend and team-mate of Sir Alex Fergusson when both were playing for Glasgow Rangers FC), 'Bugle' Sneddon, Richard Snedden, Leslie Grant.

Above. School camp at Aberfoyle, 1957. Me with some of the West Lothian Schools contingent. Acting as a school camp teacher was a confidence-building experience for me.

Right. With pupils on the ship-school *Dunera*, preparing for a shore visit. During my time as Director of Studies, *Dunera* docked at Corunna, Gibraltar and Lisbon on the first voyage and Bergen, Oslo, Copenhagen and Hamburg, and Amsterdam on the second. Subsequently we went to Tenerife, Funchal, Vigo, Malaga, Lorient, Malta, Naples, Palma, Dubrovnik, Iraklion and Piraeus. Between 1962 and 1982 British India Steam Navigation Company's ship-schools, *Dunera, Devonia, Nevasa,* and *Uganda* carried over a million pupils.

The summer school holidays of 1958 and 1959 were devoted to staying five days each week each in Galashiels/Melrose, Hawick, Jedburgh/St Boswell's, Kelso and country area, Morebattle/Newcastleton/Yetholm and Kirk Yetholm, Peebles and Selkirk, and canvassing on my bike. I was the only Labour candidate to have won over 10,000 votes in the Roxburgh, Selkirk and Peebles constituency.

With my fellow 'Black Bitch' (the name given to anyone whose parents or grandparents are Linlithgow-born), Mrs Bessie Braddock, the redoubtable Liverpool MP, at the road sign which marks the entrance to Linlithgow. Her mother and grandmother, of the White family, lived for generations above the Mercat Cross in the town centre.

Above. Jubilant supporters after the declaration of the poll in the West Lothian by-election, May 1962. (Scotsman Publications)

Right. Wedding day, 26 December 1963, with my formidable father-in-law, John Wheatley, High Court judge for a third of a century, whom I liked very much. Kathleen took in her stride much publicised complaints from the leading Edinburgh kilt-shop owner that I was wearing the wrong kind of jacket, and from the Secretary of Midlothian Labour Party that the MP for West Lothian was marrying a Roman Catholic.

Left to right: Eric Lubbock, now Lord Avebury, then MP for Orpington; R.H.S. Crossman, MP; Anthony Buck, MP; me; Dr R.R. Matthews, Director of Dounreay; and Sir William Penney, FRS, Chairman of the Atomic Energy Authority, at the Dounreay fast breeder reactor, 1963.

Kathleen in animated conversation with Vice President Hubert Humphrey in 1966. Humphrey was dubbed 'the greatest co-ordinator of mind and tongue in the United States' by President Lyndon Johnson. Watching somewhat dumbstruck are the influential Congressman John Blatnik of Minnesota and me.

The word 'Binns' comes from the Old Scots word 'bynnis' meaning 'twin hills'. The house is on one of two (extinct!) volcanoes overlooking the Firth of Forth and the naval dockyard at Rosyth.

Photograph for 1970 election address. Kathleen, me, Gordon (aged five), Moira (aged two) at The Binns. Forty and more years ago, West Lothian electors would have thought it odd not to have a family photograph and a message from Kathleen. The County Convener, Peter Walker, vouchsafed that, on due reflection, he reckoned Kathleen's message got more votes for Labour than my policy 'blurb'.

With Willie Hamilton, scourge of the Royals, at the European Parliament in Luxemburg in 1977.

The West Lothian Question – the dreaded WLQ – which still in 2011 has gone unanswered and causes continuing problems.

With Emmanuel Shinwell, my predecessor as MP for West Lothian between 1922 and 1924, and 1928 and 1931, Cabinet Minister for Fuel and Power, later Defence in the Attlee Government and Chairman of the Parliamentary Labour Party 1964–67, nominated by me, as the then youngest MP, at Harold Wilson's request.

Right. A Gala Day in West Lothian at the local summer rituals, which I enjoyed, with TV presenter of BBC Scotland and STV John Toye. This was one way of getting round the constituency.

Bottom. The trial of Clive Ponting, 1985, at the Old Bailey. Left to right: Jonathan Caplan, QC (Ponting's Junior Counsel); me; Clive Ponting; Sally Ponting; Brian Raymond (Ponting's solicitor from Bindmans LLP); Bruce Laughland, QC (Ponting's Senior Counsel); Timothy Langdale (Junior Counsel for the Prosecution); Roy Amlot, QC (Senior Prosecuting Counsel to the Crown at the Central Criminal Court); and the judge, Mr Justice Sir Anthony McCowan (later Lord Justice of Appeal).

Left. With David Bellamy in 1988 during the campaign to save hard-woods in the rain forest.

Below. Interviewed by BBC Radio. Standing, left to right: Brian Smith (Blackburn Labour Party); Brian Fairley (Whitburn), my agent for seven out of twelve General Elections; and Matt Sommerville (Bathgate Labour Party). For a politician who wants to make a political argument rather than simply harvesting votes, 'steam radio' is more important than TV. The programmes which mattered to me were *The World at One*, the *PM* programme, *The World Tonight* and the *Today* programme, described by Brian Redhead as 'slipping a word into the nation's ear'.

Left. This cartoon appeared during the Westland Affair in 1986, prompted by Mrs Thatcher's statement before the crucial Commons debate, 'I might not be Prime Minister at six o'clock tonight'.

Right. At Altamira on the Xingu River in 1987 with the chiefs of the Kayopo tribe, Riuini and Megaron, at the rally of the Amer-Indians. I was invited (at my own expense) by Charles Secrett of Friends of the Earth.

Middle right. With Sir James Black, FRS, at The Binns in 1990. Like tens of thousands of others, I owe my life to his work on beta-blockers, for which he was awarded a Nobel Prize for Medicine.

Bottom. In 1993, with the Governor of Baghdad, and George Galloway, who asked to come with me, and was extremely impressive throughout our stay. At that time George, MP for Glasgow Hillhead, had been more critical of human rights in Iraq than any other MP.

Above. With Riad el-Taher, my Esher friend who facilitated my visit to Iraq in 1993, and Tim Llewellyn, veteran Middle East correspondent of the BBC outside the Great Mosque at Karbala.

Left. Time and again, I challenged Blair, Straw and Hoon as to the provenance of the Iraq Dossier. When General Colin Powell came to a packed Commons meeting, I asked him if he was sure about his Intelligence. His assurance – later to be bitterly regretted – was emphatic. (Peter Brookes/ The Times/NI Syndication)

Bottom. Receiving an honorary Doctor of Science degree at the University of Edinburgh. Left to right: Sir Ronald Oxburgh, FRS, Professor of Mineralogy and Petrology, University of Cambridge 1978–91 and Rector of Imperial College, London 1993–2010; me; Sir Robert May, then Royal Society Professor of Zoology at Oxford and later President of the Royal Society 2000–2005.

Top. With Mrs Alice Mahon, MP, viewing the destruction wrought by NATO bombing in Belgrade. As in Kosovo, we found wanton destruction by British and American air power, ordered by leaders too ready to engage in bombing and who provoked hatred of the West.

Above. I was impervious to being undermined as an MP by those who put it about that I was a bore. One has to learn to be boring. The New Labour front bench did become very, very exasperated and angry with me.

Right. With Max Perutz, OM, Nobel Prize-winner for Chemistry for his work on deoxyribonucleic acid, at The Binns in 1999. Over 35 years I was in regular telephone touch with him, for advice, not only on scientific matters, but on issues such as asylum. It was on the clear understanding that I never would quote him.

junior minister, took Carter-Jones aside and said, 'Lewis, you can ask PQs on any subject you like as far as I'm concerned – except Diego Garcia and these wretched Indian Ocean Territories. And, for pity's sake get your friend Tam Dalyell to sail away elsewhere, out of the Indian Ocean!'

I do not make a party point since I got no encouragement whatsoever from the three ex-Labour Foreign Secretaries whom I approached. Patrick Gordon Walker, Foreign Secretary fleetingly from 1964–65 and Secretary of State for the Colonies in the Attlee Government, replied with avuncular gentleness, 'It is not always wise to be too inquisitive.' George Brown was, as was his wont, far from gentle. 'We don't want people like you buggering up the Americans if they want to build a base in the middle of the Ocean so don't meddle!' This was rich coming from one of the greatest political meddlers of the age, who appropriately gave the title *In My Way* to his autobiography. Michael Stewart, Foreign Secretary, was characteristically circumspect when he said, 'You have to put the American requirements into the global geo-political context!' He at least had some concern for the people of the Chagos Archipelago, subsistence fishermen and coconut growers who were being uprooted. The only real sympathy I received was from Ben Whitaker, a fellow Old Etonian who was created Junior Minister for Overseas Development at the fag-end of the 1964–70 Labour government. Whitaker later became secretary of an organisation which championed indigenous peoples all over the world.

For any serious campaigning MP, it is not sufficient simply to bang down questions on the parliamentary order paper. There is an obligation and, indeed, a courtesy of offering to go and see ministers in their offices about the topic of the campaign. This has the advantage that at least the civil servant directly responsible hears what the MP has to say. Parliamentary Questions properly used can often be a peg on which to hang a ministerial interview. An uncovenanted bonus is that, if the MP has taken the trouble to propel himself along to the department, the officials, usually drafters of the replies, will take more trouble with the replies to future questions.

So it was that I put down a battery of PQs for answer on 17 December to the Ministry of Defence, which were answered by Peter Kirk, army minister under Sir Alec Douglas-Home at the time he was Prime Minister. I went to see him in January. Son of an erstwhile Bishop of Oxford and a former president of the Oxford Union, Kirk was a driven and ambitious politician – the epitome of earnestness, he was without a lazy bone in his body. But his attitude encapsulated a problem of the last third of the twentieth century – colonial issues simply were not centre stage, at precisely the time it mattered most.

Kirk's mind was on Europe. He was a passionate European and soon to be the first leader of the Conservative group in the European Assembly in Strasbourg. Having to see an MP about remote territories in the Indian Ocean was a chore that he could well do without. When I first became an MP, the Secretary of State for the Colonies, whoever they might be, was an important Cabinet minister in a 'hot-potato' seat. As soon as the Colonial Office was subsumed into a sprawling Foreign and Common-wealth Office (FCO), interest waned. Had it not been so, I suspect action would have been taken to pre-empt the circumstances in which the Falklands situation later exploded into armed conflict. For politicians chiefly concerned with ascending the greasy ministerial pole, there was little mileage to be gained from fussing about abstruse colonial affairs.

And like the unfortunate but conscientious junior minister Bill Whitlock when he had to retreat from a riot, one could be held up to ridicule and become expendable over a tinpot situation in the West Indian island of Anguilla. So what was going on behind the scenes in Whitehall? Again, thanks to the 30-year rule, we get an inkling of the deviousness of authority, which would not have been unfamiliar to Captain Thomas Dalyell in his dealings with the eighteenth-century East India Company.

My friend the *Times* columnist Matthew Parris, whom I first knew as a brave Tory MP, and I have browsed through the relevant archives. We stumbled across a letter dated 13 November 1970 from a Foreign Office official to the then governor of the Seychelles, one Sir Bruce Greatbatch. The official in question was a Miss Emery, working in the Pacific and Indian Ocean department at the FCO. She tells Greatbatch that it had been 'decided' (exactly by whom and when is unclear) that all 2,000 inhabitants of the 65 islands of the Chagos Archipelago, a people known generically as the Ilois, would have to be 'removed'. They were to be sent – and later were sent – for settlement in Mauritius, a thousand miles away. There was also specific and – I do not complain unduly – disparaging reference to me.

She penned to Greatbatch, 'As you will have gathered, there has recently been a revival of public interest in the British Indian Ocean Territory.' She went on, 'We shall continue to try to say as little as possible.' This obviously was the tenor of the advice that Reggie Maudling received before he had to answer Prime Minister's Questions. Miss Emery's reason, which I suspected at the time, confirms my instinct. It was, in her words, 'to avoid embarrassing the United States Administration'. Time and again, this was a paramount imperative which determined British actions, often in dubious situations. Emery proceeded with a sentence which she cannot have imagined would ever emerge into the sunlight of public scrutiny: 'We are also concerned, at present, not to have to elaborate on the administrative implications for the present population on Diego Garcia of establishment of any base there.' Administrative implications! This is vintage Sir Humphrey Appleby in the TV series *Yes, Minister*. Translated into plain English, 'administrative implications' is a euphemism for 'being turfed out of one's homeland'.

But it was what came next in Emery's epistle to Greatbatch that had both Parris's and my eyeballs straining to leave their sockets. She had the gall to write, 'We would not wish it to become general knowledge that some of the inhabitants have lived on Diego Garcia for at least two generations and could, therefore, be regarded as "belongers".' At this point, Emery returns to my PQs: 'We should therefore advise Ministers, in handling Supplementary Questions, to say that there is only a small number of contract labourers from the Seychelles and Mauritius engaged to work on the copra plantations on the island.

'Should a Member [Emery doubtless meant 'that bloody pain-in-the-arse Dalyell] ask about what would happen to these contract labourers, in the event of the base being set up on the island, we hope, for the present this can be brushed aside as a hypothetical question – at least until any decision to go ahead with the Diego Garcia facility becomes public.' In the sunset of my life, I cogitate on public attitudes mid-term 40 years ago. All right, Miss Emery thought her letter was confidential. But this intelligent and highly educated high-flying lady seems entirely at ease with the nature of the advice. I do wonder if it struck Miss Emery how cynical and knowingly misleading her advice was. And I wonder how often such cynical advice in different circumstances, such as during the run-up to the Iraq War, has been proffered to politicians. In my experience, most ministers are reluctant to antagonise civil servants in the department for which they have responsibility on the factual basis of advice. Of course, they will interrogate civil servants if the political consequences are deemed unpalatable, seeking for easier alternative strategies, but this is rather different from interrogating them about facts and the basis on which they establish facts.

Moreover, Emery's letter to Greatbatch was no one-off. We discovered from the National Archives that she copied it widely. All were made aware of the line of the British government on these most 'disposable people', the Ilois. Let us be clear about what that line was; let us not mince words. Ministers were being asked to lie to Tam Dalyell, but not only to Tam Dalyell, but to the House of Commons as a whole. The message was brutal. Fob off Dalyell, no matter that the inhabitants of a British territory must be removed from their native islands and with the minimum of public fuss. I was flattered by the later complaining observation in the National Archives: 'Mr Dalyell is not, however, giving up.'

The sentence which sizzles with impropriety in Emery's epistle is: 'We shall therefore advise Ministers . . . to say that there is only a small number of contract labourers from the Seychelles and Mauritius . . . on the island.' This is blatantly not true. It is phrased in such a way as to say that the Ilois were not, to use the crucial word, 'belongers'. I discovered 40 years later that Kirk and, yes, Maudling and Heath were being actively advised to mislead me. Emery was making sure that ministers were singing from the same hymn sheet. I now wonder what ministers knew of the deception. If I had died, as I might well have done, but for cardioversion, warfarin and modern medicine, some time before my late sixties, I doubt if anyone would have been interested enough to excavate the truth.

The personae I was interrogating to their great discomfort were significantly older than I was. By the time the truth emerged, they were either too old to be involved in the controversy of defending themselves – or had passed on. Foreign Secretary Sir Alec Douglas-Home, as he then was, has long since joined his ancestors in a Berwickshire vault. Peter, Lord Carrington, an honourable and frank man, then in his late eighties, shrugged his shoulders and told me, 'I judged truthfully that, as Defence Secretary, as far as I can remember, the issue of Diego Garcia inhabitants never came up on my radar.'

Lord Greenhill of Harrow, then Sir Denis Greenhill, catapulted by George Brown over the heads of some more senior colleagues into becoming Permanent Under-Secretary of State at the Foreign Office in 1969, recognised a soulmate and greeted me, on being first introduced at an FCO reception in 1970, by saying, 'Oh yes, I know exactly who you are, Mr Dalyell. You are the squadron sergeant major of the Awkward Squad in the eyes of the office.' It was not nastily meant. On the contrary, I had the feeling that this rather unorthodox diplomat had a soft spot for the Awkward Squad despite the fact that, at times, it could prove a huge nuisance. I wondered what in particular had triggered his reaction. The timing suggested my forays in the Indian Ocean. Alas, Lord Greenhill died prematurely and cannot reminisce.

A more careful participant in the world of British interests in the Indian Ocean was Sir James Dunnett. He was in the middle of what has to be an eight-year tenure (1966–74) as Permanent Secretary at the Ministry of Defence. Like me, he was the son of an Indian civil servant and, like me, he was an old boy of the Edinburgh Academy. Sir James, Miss Emery, Sir Alec Douglas-Home, Sir Denis Greenhill and most others involved have passed on. Most of the displaced Ilois are dead too. But some of them, and their descendants, remain in heart-rending conditions in Mauritius, unwelcome in the community. I judge that, if their claim had been properly understood by the House of Commons at the time I was raising concerns, the Ilois might have been treated more generously. The Civil Service advice was instrumental in denying Parliament that understanding. It is not fanciful to suggest that the plight of the Ilois is the responsibility of those who framed that advice and of the ministers who accepted and implemented it.

Nearly a decade later, on 29 April 1980, I wrote to Mrs Thatcher, concerned about reports of the use of Diego Garcia by an American task force and C14 aircraft. In particular I asked her to tell us the date and time when she first knew that Diego Garcia was being used by the United States in support of their operation in the Iranian desert to rescue hostages. It was abundantly clear that Washington did not care a tinker's cuss about possible British objection to the use of the territory, and a letter from Mr Speaker, George Thomas, of 1 May 1980 spoke volumes about Mrs Thatcher's views:

> There is of course no objection to Questions relating generally to the working of these bases, but the particular aspect which you wanted to raise, namely their use by the Americans' rescue force (if indeed they were so used) is one that has been effectively blocked by the Prime Minister's answer on Tuesday afternoon (Hansard col 1144).
>
> Where there is a blocking answer of this kind, the rules operate so as to prevent further Questions on this subject being tabled for at least three months. Much as I should like to help you, therefore, I am afraid I can see no way round this.

This was a classic example of governments being able to withhold key information which they didn't want to be exposed.

Mr Speaker Thomas, in my opinion, allowed himself to be pressurised by Mrs Thatcher. Everybody loved George – who insisted on becoming the Viscount Tonypandy – except me. The trouble between us, basically, was this. During the government of

Harold Wilson, he had been Minister of State at the Common-wealth Office, responsible for the BIOT, the Falklands and other areas about which I was being inquisitive. I thought that he could have put things right when he had the ministerial power to do so. Furthermore, George Thomas was no friend of the parliamentary dissenters. He did not call us, on occasion after occasion, when we could have been effective. Famously, a year after Thomas went to the Lords, his independent-minded successor, the Conservative Jack Weatherill, frustrated Mrs Thatcher by rigidly sticking to parliamentary rules and provoked her into mouthing aloud to colleagues on the front bench, 'Oh, what would George have done? How we miss George!'

In the 1980s and early 1990s, I was but one of a number of voices urging justice for the Ilois. Among many others who, in court case after court case, have kept the issue alive are: the solicitor Richard Gifford, who has tirelessly exposed the Ilois cause; the distinguished former Professor of Constitutional Law at the University of Edinburgh, Anthony Bradley QC; and Celia Whittaker, indomitable secretary of the Chagos Support Asso-ciation. This is not the place to chronicle the vicissitudes of the struggle in which I was but a bystander, after I retired. My reward from the leader of the Chagossians, Louis Olivier Bancoult, was that there should be named in the archipelago 'Dalyell Island', which proved to be little more than an obscure rocky outcrop, inaccessible other than by small boat. While the *Sun* newspaper emblazoned the story of 'Dalyell Island' on its front page, at least in the Scottish edition, wags among my constituents wanted to know if I would arrange a South Seas holiday for them there. I rather wonder what Captain Thomas Dalyell would have had to say on the matter.

I must mention a regret. One of the most strident voices in the middle and late 1980s was Robin Cook. As so often, however, Cook saw a problem through the prism of a proverbial stick with which to beat the government or, when it suited him, colleagues in the Labour Party. When, in 1997, Cook became Foreign Secretary and surely had it in his power to do something significant to help the Ilois, he did nothing for them. I suppose it was always thus with politicians – they raise hopes and expectations in opposition and then fail to deliver when they are in a position to do so. I sometimes wonder whether I would have been any different in their circumstances, much as I like to think I would.

*

I can pinpoint the moment at which I was assigned to the Awkward Squad by a majority of those in Wilson's government and the Parliamentary Labour Party. It was when the House of Commons returned from the summer recess in October 1965. If I reflect at some length on the circumstances, it is because they refer to an almost forgotten fragment of history but one which, had it not been for the fortuitous coup by the Indonesian Army, would have resulted in three quarters of a million deaths of Indonesian Communists (PKI) and could have become a British Vietnam in Northern Borneo.

My personal story began in March 1965 when I asked the Defence Secretary, Denis Healey, if I could go to Borneo to see at first hand the armed conflict that was destabilising the frontier between British Sarawak and Indonesian Kalimantan. 'Not enough helicopters to take you around,' was the gruff reply. Two months later I asked again, just before the Whitsun recess. Part of the reason I persisted was that, as Dick Crossman's PPS at the Housing Department, I was acutely aware of the shortfall in resources to carry out the housing pledges that Labour had made in opposition and the Confrontation was costing an inordinate amount of tax-payers' money. Overshadowing everything else in ministers' minds was the economic situation and the looming threats of possible devaluation.

Healey, with his deputy Fred Mulley, a charming and intelligent man who had been a German prisoner-of-war for six years, gave me a bollocking. On no account would he facilitate my meddling. However, in July, there took place the regular selection for MPs' visits abroad. This was in the patronage of the Whips. The Ministry of Defence was not consulted – and nor was any other ministry, for that matter. When I went to him about my desire to be put on the Far East delegation, Ted Short, the government's Chief Whip, looked at me benignly and said, 'My records show that, since October 1964 you have not missed a single vote in supporting the Labour government [its majority of five had been reduced in by-elections to one by the following year]. I've seen you in the middle of the night voting in your tracksuit in which you slept in a Library armchair. Tam, you will be rewarded!'

And so it came about that my equally assiduous kindred spirit, Brian O'Malley, the MP for Rotherham, sponsored by the Musicians' Union, and a possible leader of the Labour Party had he not died tragically young, were put on the September delegation to Singapore, Malaya and Sarawak led by John Cronin, a distinguished surgeon and the Labour MP for Loughborough. On arrival in Kuching, the capital of Sarawak, it was clear to us that the current government was widely believed to be corrupt and gave the impression of being supported by British arms. I was told both by an RAF officer and by a local journalist that parallels were being drawn between the taste for luxury of some of the current Sarawak leaders and the circle of the Emperor Bao-Dai, the Emperor of Vietnam, notorious for his extravagant lifestyle.

The concept of solemn obligations on the part of Britain to the peoples of Northern Borneo, which had been espoused by successive British governments ever since the nineteenth century at the time of Stamford Raffles seemed to me to be highly questionable in the context of 1965. I wrote down an exact quote from a British sergeant who had been upcountry in the jungle: 'Land Dayaks, Ibans and even more primitive peoples are mostly friendly and, at first, longhouse dwellers tend to make a fuss of strangers. Then they become less friendly. But the more civilised people are, the more anti-British they are. They tolerate us for what we spend and rob the boys of their money in the shops.' From a number of conversations, O'Malley and I were sure that the urban population of Kuching was distinctly hostile to the British presence in a military capacity. Visiting MPs were not really encouraged to venture beyond the perimeter of the officers' mess but O'Malley's trumpet-playing charm – yes, he did play the trumpet – and my acting a bit of the 'daft laddie' got round that hurdle.

In the countryside or jungle, the mass of the population could not have cared less who their rulers were. Life in remote longhouses would go on in the same way that it had done for thousands of years. Forms of government had far less relevance than the provision of elementary schools and basic medical supplies had. Ethnically and topographically, the frontier between British Sarawak and Indonesian Borneo (Kalimantan) was artificial. The political frontier meant little to Land Dayaks, Ibans, Kenyahs, Kayans and obscure tribes, like the Tagal Muruts, when it may take a fortnight's journey to reach them. These tribes owned land on both sides of the Sarawak–Kalimantan border and had relatives and friends over the whole tribal area.

Before setting out for the Far East and on Dick Crossman's introduction, I went to see Kingsley Martin, former editor of the *New Statesman* (for whom Dick had worked) and his partner, Dorothy Woodman, at their home at Carlisle Mansions near Victoria Station. At that time, the *New Statesman* was the holy gospel of many of the aspiring leaders in colonial situations. A letter from Dorothy Woodman was a passport for many of them. It was such an introduction that enabled me to meet not only interesting leaders of the Chinese community in Borneo but also Madame Tra Zander, spokesperson for and one of the leaders of the Sea Dayaks. She told me that it really was ludicrous to suppose that her people – or, indeed, any of the tribal people – would be greatly affected one way or another if the British Army were to go. I could not fathom the government's attitude that these supposedly 'poor, helpless, backward people' would be persecuted by Indonesians, with whom they bartered legally through points of border traffic or illegally more or less at will. As Madame Tra Zander put it to me, even at that time, 'It was becoming apparent that the real foes of tribal peoples were not the Indonesians across the Border, but greedy Western and Malayan logging companies.'

One of my abiding interests over a lifetime has been the

significance of the expatriate overseas Chinese community. As Kingsley Martin and Dorothy Woodman warned me, if the presence of British forces was largely irrelevant to the good of the primitive people, that presence was dangerous in relation to the hard-working Chinese population. One incident in particular made an impact on me. On Sunday, 29 June 1965, in a predominantly Chinese area, three policemen and four 'runner dogs' (informers) were tied up and brutally murdered. Yet all the children in the area had been warned by their parents not to go to the cinema that night, so most of the population must certainly have had an inkling of what was afoot. Why was this 'strike' by the left-wing organisation anticipated? It could just possibly have been that everyone was afraid of being beaten up and that our intelligence system was appalling. A much more likely explanation is that there was a great popular sympathy with the rebels. O'Malley and I ascertained that the response of the Sarawak government, applauded by the British commanders, was to set up a system of 'protected villages' where, at the real risk of being shot, the Chinese population had to return from their farms to observe a 7 p.m. to 6 a.m. curfew. Among the Chinese community leaders, to whom Kingsley Martin and Dorothy Woodman had given me an introduction, there was much talk of 'concentration camps'. I was told that ethnic Chinese men, most of whom were probably born and brought up in Sarawak, had taken to hiding in the jungle.

If they were not Communists already, there was every likelihood that they would join an underground organisation in this type of situation. Sitting on his verandah, overlooking the city, one of Kingsley Martin's friends pointed to the forest in the distance and said, matter-of-factly, 'That's where they go, when the police or British military are after them.' Away from reality of the situation the argument was used time and again: We were tough in Malaya. Templer's* methods were successful – this is what we must do to stand firm in Borneo.

---

* Field Marshal Sir Gerald Templer, British High Commissioner in Malaya 1952–54.

O'Malley and I concluded that, even if one accepted that there could be an analogy between Borneo in 1965 and Malaya in 1949, it would be dangerously misleading to say that tough measures à la Templer were an answer. Why was it, we wondered, that there was so much civil unrest among people for whose benefit the British military force was supposed to be in Borneo in the first place? Neither Madame Tra Zander nor the Chinese commercial establishment thought that, if British troops were to be withdrawn, Indonesians would walk in. They judged that *Konfrontasi* (confrontation) would simply fizzle out. Anyhow, as Madame Tra Zander put it to me, 'We are the same people, aren't we?' She was not in the least perturbed by the unlikely event of an Indonesian takeover. The consensus of opinion in commercial Kuching was that the colossal military expenditure represented an absurd waste of human skills. If the Dutch, arguably among the most hated of all colonialists, could return to Indonesia in significant numbers as managers, technicians and teachers – people doing a job, in other words – would the British not see their way to establishing a fruitful relationship with the Indonesians?

There was another problem – one with which I was all-too familiar as a trooper in the British Army of the Rhine. Across the spectrum of the Kuching community, there was vexation at the way in which a number of Dayak girls had been left as mothers by British soldiers who the authorities were unable to trace – and who, indeed, O'Malley and I suspected, they were not making much effort to trace. Among a people with a strict code of conduct for those of pre-marital status, the presence of unaccompanied young soldiers brought with it obvious problems. The unmarried mother in Sarawak caused far wider uproar than in a sophisticated society such as Western Germany.

The whole British information system seemed to vary from the corrupt to comedy farce. There was a system of informers in forward areas who were paid six Malay dollars (15 shillings in British currency at the time, which was twice as much as a Gurkha soldier's daily wage or several times that of a local worker) for merely observing their friends and neighbours. Some squaddies told me that they were of the opinion that many of the informers were in fact double agents and not averse to leading British soldiers into lethal traps.

'What,' I asked a senior officer, 'happens to these informers when the British positions change?'

There came the reply: 'The reaction is the typical Eastern shrugging of the shoulders, to the effect that "It was good while it lasted".'

This was naive rubbish. The clock could not be put back. The informers could not return to their paddy fields as if nothing had happened. This was especially true in situations where informers had abused trust in order to pay off old family scores. O'Malley and I felt that we were responsible for creating a sour relationship which could backfire on us.

Great play was made of the Hearts and Minds Campaign, run by the British forces, particularly by the commander-in-chief himself, Air Chief Marshal Sir John Grandy. Diligent enquiry in Borneo revealed to O'Malley and myself that few of the officers and even fewer of the soldiers knew much about the Hearts and Minds Campaign, which they were supposed to be conducting. Yes, it was certainly true that, in genuinely urgent cases, medical help was provided to longhouses near forward British Army positions.

'Of course,' I was told by one regimental CO, 'we must not do too much, for the understandable reason that we cannot employ our scarce helicopters transporting the sick for humane reasons when we have a military job to do.' Yes, it was also true that the British soldier was kind to Kenyah children but any sign of what might seriously be called a Hearts and Minds Campaign was absent in Borneo. Time and again, I got the coy reply from servicemen, 'Well, sir, I'm afraid I do not know very much about it personally!' I can hardly blame any soldier since, sitting next to the wife of the commander-in-chief of the navy in Singapore, an intelligent and otherwise well-informed lady, I asked her what she thought of Hearts and Minds and she replied, 'Oh, I haven't heard of that one – what does it do?'

Alas, in 1965, I became totally cynical about those who speech-ified about Hearts and Minds. It is a fig leaf. It is a delusion.

Predictably and predicted, foreseeable and foreseen, Hearts and Minds made no impact in the nine years of trying in Iraq. At the time of writing, the Hearts and Minds effort in Afghanistan speaks for itself. What my hostile attitude to Hearts and Minds did succeed in doing was to make an enemy of Sir John Grandy, shortly to be promoted to Chief of the Air Staff, who, I discovered later – and this was confirmed in the National Archives – complained bitterly to Harold Wilson about my behaviour, which was that of a well-mannered but serious critic of policy.

What really upset Grandy was my account in a newspaper of the answer to my question about the Hearts and Minds effort in Singapore itself, where the commander-in-chief's headquarters was based. I was taken to a youth club which I was told was given a great deal of help by Hearts and Minds. I could only report that this amounted to a British corporal giving some rather spasmodic boxing coaching to half a dozen youths, who clearly could not understand the instructions barked out in a heavy Geordie accent; some rather desultory games supervised by junior NCOs; one table-tennis table with much-abused bats; an absurd group of local 'vigilantes' and about a hundred screaming, bored kids. I then discovered that the total British contribution was £9,500 to cover 178 youth clubs and a good deal else. It was hardly surprising that the Singapore people did not take Hearts and Minds seriously.

*

It is not an exaggeration to say that, in my first years as an MP, the issue which most concerned me was that of the presence of British forces in the Far East, known at the time as the 'East of Suez question'. The air marshals and generals I met, though professionally able, seemed to be replete with platitudes on the larger issues and talked about the 'containment of Communism' – the then conventional wisdom following World War II when the Iron Curtain had descended between East and West. But, as senior officers are at a disadvantage in talking to a politician critical of the policy which they have to bolster, I did not want to embarrass them by probing too deeply as to why they thought

British Forces were in the Far East in the first place. To the junior officers, I said casually many times, 'What do you tell your men when they ask you why they are here?' Often the answer came back: 'They don't ask.' On the whole, the junior officers were as vague as they were loyal: 'As a simple soldier, I would say . . .' The NCOs and their men were far less inhibited. The truth was that, though they recognised that, by choice, they were professional soldiers, sailors or airmen, many were seething with discontent. This was much deeper than the usual service 'belly-aching' or 'dripping'.

The men I met were by no means as uncurious about being in the Far East as their officers thought. In a steamingly hot forward position under canvas, I vividly recollect being asked by a group of 'Jocks' what the hell a Labour government thought it was playing at by becoming more and more involved in what, to them, was a pointless conflict from the British perspective. One typical conversation, with a staff sergeant from Aberdeen, repeated with varying phraseology many times, was my saying, 'Why do you think the British are here?' and the staff sergeant replying, 'To protect British interests, tin, rubber and the like. It seems a bit daft when the Japanese, the French, the Germans, the lot, can trade without having to protect their interests.'

The fed-up-ness of the British soldiers was enhanced by strong persistent rumours that the Malay troops on the Sarawak–Kalimantan frontier had an understanding with the Indonesians the other side of the border under which they simply avoided attacking each other. Stories of Indonesians giving a sign and coming to the border for a chat and a 'brew-up drink' were rife. Some years later, at a reception at the Indonesian Embassy in Grosvenor Square, I was chatting to the military attaché. We got round to the subject of *Konfrontasi* and it emerged that he had served in Kalimantan.

'Were stories of Malay and Indonesian troops getting together, like the British and Germans at Christmas 1914 on the Western Front, true?' I asked him.

'Of course they were true,' he replied. 'It was not only at Christmas, it happened all the time. We used to laugh at the

British, pinch your weapons if we could and looked forward to the day when you'd be gone.'

At a reception given by the British High Commissioner in Singapore, I met a middle-ranking naval officer. He was fuming. The previous night, yet again, some of the Malayan patrol vessels in the Straits of Malacca had anchored at night when they were supposed to be on patrol. He had found out by chance that, on feast days, units of the Malay navy came to an arrangement with the Indonesians to avoid even the pretence of trouble. To make matters worse, this naval officer told me that his British sailors felt bitterly about successful efforts in apprehending smugglers, only to be told with a wicked smile by the Malay police that those whom the British Navy had caught 'had special permission' to barter.

Our final engagement of the delegation was a 16-course dinner, given to us by that astonishingly powerful, Cambridge-educated intellectual, Singapore's Prime Minister Lee Kuan Yew, and his equally sharp wife. As far as I was concerned, the occasion started inauspiciously. I ventured to say to LKY, as he was known to many, that we had been well received in Kuala Lumpur by the Tunku Abdul Rahman, the prime minister of Malaysia, and his deputy Tun Abdul Razak and that I had found them charming. To which LKY (in theory their partner at the time in the Malaysian Federation) replied acidly, 'Tunkus and Old Etonians are made for each other!' and passed on to another member of the delegation.

After a convivial dinner, at which I had restrained completely my desire for alcohol, I said, 'Prime Minister, could we have a serious conversation with you about "East of Suez"?' Now, in his early middle age, there was nothing that LKY enjoyed more than a rip-roaring argument; he adored verbal fisticuffs. Twelve hours later, on the plane going home, I made a lengthy note of the conversation of the night before.

Against the background of what I have described above, I thundered, 'Why are British soldiers being asked to risk their lives and health toiling through the second thickest jungle on earth in Borneo? Why are British sailors, cramped in to sweltering, often un-air-conditioned lower decks, required to risk their lives against mines and cunning booby traps? Why are helicopter pilots of the RAF asked to go out on missions into the Borneo night, navigating above some of the most treacherous landscapes in the world?'

LKY thundered back, to the approval of the Conservative members and, indeed, Labour members (other than Brian O'Malley, who kept out of it, for the valid reason that he wanted to talk to LKY about promoting music in Singapore), that I was a Little Englander of a pitiable kind. LKY was not pleased when I insinuated that his attitude was dictated by the financial advantage to his city-state. My colleagues, even O'Malley, were not pleased – I had been too acrimonious for a guest. In other words, I had been too bloody awkward.

*

Most junior ministers have little access to the British Prime Minister. But Harold Wilson, I found, was ever ready to see me and other backbenchers individually if he thought they had something to say. I went to his room in the Commons on the heels of a letter I had sent him, warning of a British Vietnam in Sarawak. He was most attentive. 'I hear what you say. I'll make enquiries and see you again.' He kept his word and sent for me 10 days later. 'George Wigg tells me you are wrong. So do some senior Foreign Office officials!' I pleaded my case and added that George Wigg was in a temper with me for going to see a member of a regiment, with whom he had served in India before the war, in Changi jail after he had been court-martialled. I explained to Wilson that I had done this at the behest of my friend and parliamentary neighbour, Malcolm MacPherson, MP for Stirling and Falkirk, whose constituents, the parents of the young soldier, had been to see their MP at his Grangemouth surgery. Wigg was angry that I had tried, as he thought, to infringe his beloved army regulations. Wilson listened to my explanation, removed the pipe from his mouth and drily observed, 'Tam, you should have learned that, in Labour politics, no good deed goes unpunished.'

The combination of Wigg and the Foreign Office had carried the day against me. As I suspected at the time and confirmed later from the National Archives, the War Office advice was altogether more ambivalent about the Borneo commitment. Just as I made for the Prime Minister's door, Wilson, an infinitely and touchingly courteous man, opened it himself.

Spotting my tie as that of my Cambridge college, he quizzed me, 'Tam, tell me, do you think you are a better democratic socialist than the most gifted alumnus of your university?'

This question triggered a volcanic response. 'That's it, Harold, you have been taken for a ride by that gifted, Westernised, Cambridge intellectual, Lee Kuan Yew!'

At breakfast the following morning, my boss, Dick Crossman, barked, 'What the hell did you say to the Prime Minster yesterday? Harold was quite put out. You really are very silly to think you can talk to the Prime Minister like that.'

Silly I may have been from my personal point of view, in that it gave Wilson the impression – probably correct – that I would have been a troublesome junior minister, but what is deeply true and altogether more significant is that the personal magnetism and driving intellect of Lee Kuan Yew had a mesmeric effect on Wilson and therefore on British foreign policy.

Only George Brown was remotely pleased by what he had heard about my encounter on the Labour Party bush telegraph: 'Black Tam – at it again – worse than I am with the PM!'

My impetuous response had blotted my copybook with the Prime Minister but not for long. Wilson made a habit of inviting a world figure such as Helmut Schmidt, the West German Chancellor, or Julius Nyerere, the Prime Minister of Tanzania, to address the Labour Party conference. In 1967, he chose Lee Kuan Yew, who held the conference in the palm of his hand. LKY was a rivetingly electric, commanding orator. On the Monday, he appeared on the BBC's *Panorama* and was inevitably questioned about the British 'East of Suez' commitment. I paraphrase part of LKY's interview: 'If Britain was governed by men like Tam Dalyell, then I would despair but Britain is fortunately governed by better men like Harold Wilson.'

My constituents in those days, watching the flagship *Panorama* in their thousands, wondered, 'What on earth has our Tam done?' The correct answer in this case was that I had been asking awkward but certainly legitimate questions about an overwhelmingly important government policy commitment. I told bemused constituents that my questioning had surely been part of an MP's role and this they appeared to accept. Over the years, believe it or not, I have letters signed 'Harry' (LKY's first name) to prove I retained friendly contact with LKY. No man was more uninhibited about bestowing advice on other people so I understand that the following story is not apocryphal. LKY goes on an official visit to China. In Beijing he proceeds to lecture Deng Xiaoping on how to run China, in the light of his own experience in Singapore. Deng Xiaoping listens politely and, at the end of LKY's tirade, says gently, 'Dr Lee, your thoughts will be very useful when I next run for the position of Mayor of Shanghai.' That, as the Scots would say, was to 'put his gas at a peep'.

*

In the spring of 1971, I began to 'suck up to' – I cannot think of a more accurate description of my approach – the legation head at the London fortress of the People's Republic of China, then in the throes of the Cultural Revolution. On the first occasion on which I was invited to lunch, I gingerly broached the possibility of a trade delegation from Scotland. It was 'noted' but clearly nothing was happening. That summer, Kathleen and I were invited to dinner. The occasion is etched in my memory on account of one happening. At the end of a delicious meal, the legation head's wife, Madame Pei, solemnly rose to address the half a dozen spouses. 'And now,' she said, 'we will go to the toilet.' Astonished but without demur, off they trooped to the spotless lavatory. Madame Pei, buttoned up to her chin in her dark-blue Maoist tunic, was a commanding lady, squat and powerful. Kathleen sensed Madame Pei eyeing with interest and rather wistfully the clothes of her Western lady guests and wondered if she would have liked to have been able to appear in a dress of traditional Chinese silk. But that would have been out of the question for her in 1971. In the meantime, I again raised shyly the possibility of a Scottish trade delegation. Nothing doing!

Fast forward to the fraught morning of 28 October 1971. It was the day of the crucial vote on whether Britain should enter the European Common Market (of which more in the next chapter). In this torrid atmosphere, I received a phone message in the Members' Lobby. It read, 'You will come to lunch today at 12.45.' and was signed Dr Pei, head of legation at the Chinese Embassy. Instinct told me to drop everything and that I should, without hesitation, accede. A wise man does not disobey the orders of imperial Peking! Arriving, somewhat breathless, in a taxi whose driver reassuringly chuckled, 'The last time I dropped a passenger here in Portland Place he told me to wait. Guv, I waited. After half an hour, he did not return, so I knocked on the door. The man who opened the door – no mean wrestler he looked, guv – told me that my passenger would not be coming back and asked what the fare was. After a brief phone call in Chinese, a man, who also looked as if he was familiar with the ring – boxing or wrestling – appeared with the fare and a generous tip. I drove off – better not to ask questions, guv!'

I entered the legation with a certain amount of trepidation. Just as we sat down at an immaculately set table, Madame Pei said, 'Your request has been granted by the officials of the Central Committee of the People's Republic of China. You will be in Guangzhou [Canton] for the trade fair on 11 November with your delegation.' I expressed delight but did not reveal that I had no delegation. What to do? As far as I knew, no one in the West, apart from Albania, had been 'invited' to send a trade delegation to China and only one British politician had been, some months earlier. This was Tony Benn, who had returned from China to tell an astonished leader of the Labour Party, Harold Wilson, and his deputy, the former Chancellor and Home Secretary, Roy Jenkins, that their role in life was to be that of 'advisers to the proletariat'. I fear this was not quite how Roy Jenkins saw himself.

I sensed the opportunity must not be squandered. I took up the telephone and mercifully got through immediately to my friend Dr Bill Robertson, a distinguished electrical engineer and chief executive of the Scottish Council for Development and Industry (SCDI). Quick as a flash, Robertson grasped the situation. He told me that, by chance, his chairman, Lord Ronald Clydesmuir, was in the office so I should phone back in ten minutes. This time I was put through to Lord Clydesmuir whose uncle, Sir Stephen Bilsland, had been a major industrialist, the driving force in the SCDI and a friend of my parents.

Lord Clydesmuir was quite clear: 'Yes, the SCDI would come to China.'

'Who,' I asked, 'would lead the delegation?'

'I will,' came back the decisive reply.

The experience was a revelation for me. I had been used to delegations of politicians, where punctuality was not a strong point. MPs would not be unduly bothered about keeping their colleagues waiting or cancelling visits at the last moment for no particularly good reason. In the world of SCDI businessmen, however, no one was ever late, on any occasion whatsoever. I discovered that it was infinitely more productive to be part of a trade delegation than simply to appear as a fact-finding politician, either on my own or on an official political delegation. Why the Scots were favoured became apparent on our then obligatory visit to a collective farm, not far from Peking. Striding through the muddy field, Lord Clydesmuir, sharing a sense of humour with the Maoist cadres, was in front. I was just behind, talking to a young agronomist, who had excellent English. The collective was the Sino-Albanian Friendship Commune. It transpired that the Chinese were under the impression that the Scots were a wretched, oppressed people, ill put upon by their neighbours, just like the Albanians.

What was interesting was their policy towards employment – ever so different from what is happening in China today. I record part of my official report to the SCDI:

The Chinese attitude is summarised by this cautionary tale. As a member of SCDI Trade Delegation to China and as Member of Parliament for West Lothian, where some 5,000 men work at the British Leyland Truck and Tractor Plant, Bathgate, I was naturally interested in the possibility of British sales of trucks to China. Observing, on our visit to the Capital Steel Works in Peking, a large number of heavy loads of metal being taken from point A in the factory to point

B by means of donkey and cart, I enquired whether it would not be more efficient for the loads to be taken by lorry. One question elicited another: 'If we had your lorries, what would happen to the donkeys?' 'Donkeys,' it was observed, 'did not use scarce petrol supplies and they did produce manure.' Pressed further, one of our Chinese hosts came out with the tart retort: 'Well, Mr Dalyell, if we took your lorries, what would we do with the donkey drivers?' This tale serves to illustrate a number of basic points. First of all, Chinese tradition, of over-riding importance in Chairman Mao's China, dictates that scarce resources shall be husbanded, that the best use shall be made of whatever materials are available. If there is a plenitude of donkey food and straw, and a shortage of petroleum, both processed and under the soil of China, then there is only one rational conclusion. Keep the donkeys, and use the petrol for the most modern jet airliners.

Chinese planning, which I suspect was often non-existent in a Western centralised sense and by no means perfect where it did exist, dictated the morality of making the best use of what one has got.

The Scottish–Albanian connection and the drifting apart of Cultural Revolution China from the West were encapsulated by the opening of my two-hour midnight interview with Jun Wen Chin, then head of the American and European section of the Chinese foreign office and trusted lieutenant of Prime Minister Zhou Enlai, in his office at the Chinese foreign ministry. 'Tell me about the policy of the Labour Party. As Leader Attlee was saying to us . . .' Seventeen years had passed by since Clement Attlee but, for Jun Wen Chin, it might have been just the other day.

At the beginning of November, I went to see Harold Wilson in the Leader of the Opposition's room in the House of Commons. 'Any chance of an introduction,' I asked, 'to your friend, Zhou Enlai?' With a twinkle – I knew he liked me, though I exasperated him on occasion – he told me that meeting Zhou was 'above my station in life'. But, he added enthusiastically, he would like me to meet some of the men of my own age who seemed to be 'running the Cultural Revolution', about which the West knew very little at the time. Good as his word, he did contact Zhou or his office on my behalf and thus it was that, when the SCDI delegation was in Shanghai, I suddenly got a call to get into a car, to go and see the mayor.

Never in all my life have I been treated so peremptorily. When I arrived at the mayor's headquarters, a secretary made it all too clear that the mayor was only seeing me because he had been asked to do so by Zhou Enlai and did not want to add to Shanghai's already strained relationship with Beijing and the prime minister. When I entered the mayor's room, Yao Wenyuan was sitting at his desk, an interpreter standing at his side. There was no question of me being asked to sit down, let alone be given a cup of tea, which would have been the normal etiquette. Within not minutes but seconds, the mayor launched into a tirade: the Opium Wars; the wickedness of the British East India Company; the Boxer Rebellion; the treatment of Chinese women, abused by foreigners. Then, unceremoniously, I was ordered out.

A third of a century later when I, as Rector of the University of Edinburgh, was helping Vice-Chancellor Tim O'Shea host the Chinese Minister of Education, I had at my lunch table the equivalent of the permanent secretary of that ministry. Learning that he was from Shanghai, I told him of my experience and encounter with Yao Wenyuan, one of the Gang of Four. The permanent secretary's comment was laconic. 'You,' he said, 'met the most wicked and brutal man in China of the twentieth century.'

CHAPTER EIGHT

The 1970s

MANY OF MY Labour Party contemporaries share my burning resentment of the oft-expressed attitude of Blair that no Labour government achieved much that was worthwhile before 1997. We find it outrageous. In 1924, Kathleen's great-uncle, John Wheatley, Minister of Housing and Health, pioneered council housing; between 1945 and 1951, the Attlee Cabinet of pensionable average age oversaw a radical recovery from war and the introduction of the National Health Service; and, between 1964 and 1970, the Wilson government kept Britain out of the Vietnam War, which many would recognise as some feat at a time of military involvement in Iraq, Afghanistan and Libya.

The Wilson administration had diverse achievements of which enlightened Home Office reform and the creation of the Open University were but two. In my opinion, it came to grief almost solely on account of the appointment of Mrs Barbara Castle as Ray Gunter's successor at the Ministry of Labour. If Gunter, gnarled veteran of many trade union battles as leader of the Transport Salaried Staffs' Association (TSSA), had been allowed to stay in post (and not moved, against his will, to the Ministry of Power, about which he knew little), the entire history of the 1964–70 government would have been different.

Mrs Castle produced a fractious policy document, 'In Place of Strife', which alienated the trade union movement. Gunter would have introduced legislation exactly along the lines of the senior Law Lord, Lord Donovan's, report in industrial relations which had been agreed as a modus vivendi by both the TUC and the

employers' organisations. Instead, Mrs Castle, flustered by un-
official strikes, in particular the action by 12 workers at the Girling
Brakes Factory which, absurdly, she thought would bring the
British motor industry to its knees, forged ahead with divisive
action, making the unions resentful and causing unexpected
electoral defeat in 1970.

Had Labour won in 1970, would I have become a minister? On
balance, I think not. Though, at that moment, I would have very
much liked to have gained ministerial experience but education,
health, home affairs and much else were covered by the Scottish
Office and Willie Ross would not have touched me with a barge
pole. It was not that he disliked me – on the contrary, we rather
liked each other – but he foresaw, as one of his deputies, I would
cause him problems and, in this, I cannot say that his instinct was
wrong.

When my friend Frank McElhone, a greengrocer from the
Gorbals, was appointed Under-Secretary for Education, he went
to Ross on day one and asked, 'What do you want me to do?'

'You'll do as you're tellt,' came the reply.

Willie Ross could not be sure that I would do as I was telt. My
views rendered me equally non-eligible for the Foreign Office
and Ministry of Defence. The department I yearned to be
appointed to was the Treasury but Roy Jenkins, then Chancellor,
had closer political friends in his circle.

So, after Labour's defeat in the 1970 General Election and no
longer an ever-present Parliamentary Private Secretary to a
Cabinet minister, I determined to use the opportunity to cultivate
the South American embassies in London. I developed a friendship with a number of ambassadors not only by accepting their
hospitality at embassy receptions but also by inviting them to
lunch or dinner in the House of Commons, which they greatly
appreciated as I made a point of inviting their wives. I also owe a
huge debt of gratitude to successive directors and staff of Canning
House, the equivalent of Chatham House, as a 'think tank' for
relations between Europe and Latin America.

It was at the request of the Brazilian Ambassador, Roberto
Campos, that Mr Speaker, Selwyn Lloyd, chose me to lead a

heavyweight group of nine MPs on the first Inter-Parliamentary Union (IPU) delegation to Brazil, from 23 April to 5 May 1976. On the first day, I went with Derek (later Sir Derek) Dodson and Robin Maxwell-Hyslop to San Jose dos Campos in a Bandeirante aircraft, designed and built in Brazil. How many people in Britain in 1976 knew that Brazil had an aircraft industry? I didn't. It was one of several surprises about the huge South American continent with its great natural wealth, vast impenetrable areas of rain forest and undiscovered resources.

These challenges were being tackled by a generation of energetic and gifted South Americans. Our first official call was on the governor of the state of São Paolo in his palace. Paulo Egídio Martins – I remember him vividly after 35 years – was a dynamic, optimistic go-getter in his early forties. I asked him, after two minutes of formalities (important Brazilians eschew small talk), what it was like to run a megalopolis of 16 million people. 'Not easy,' he said. 'Every male between 17 and 45 years of age seems to think he is Emerson Fittipaldi [then the world champion racing driver, who came from São Paolo].'

Our second visit was to the prefect of the city, with direct responsibility for water and drainage, Dr Setúbal, himself to be a future governor. Interestingly, he told us that his inspiration was Joseph Bazalgette who was almost single-handedly responsible for the magnificent sewers of Victorian London. We were given lunch by the Banco Hau, whose president, Deputado Herbert Levy, was also deputy speaker of the federal Camera dos Deputados, the Brazilian equivalent of the House of Commons. Levy, an anglophile and one of the most influential bankers/ politicians of the time in South America, invited us the following day to play tennis at his hacienda with his young grandsons who were, like most Brazilians, very competitive and worshipped Didi, Vava, Socrates, Tostao, the Santos brothers and Pelé.

After the game, Levy himself took over. He conducted us round that part of the hacienda where coffee and sorghum were growing with eucalyptus plantations, which mature in five years, visible in the distance. Levy's greatest interest, however, was his three prize Charolais bulls, which he had crossed with native cattle. He proudly said to me, 'At the fourth cross, the resultant cattle have twice the food conversion rate of the native cattle, while retaining the indiscriminate dietary habits of the native cattle.'

During our visit to Rio, we were taken to the directors' box of the Estádio Mário Filho – the Maracanã – which seats up to a quarter of a million souls, for a derby match in which the famous Fluminense were struggling against local rivals. I would have been terrified to be in the crowd, with firecrackers popping off in every direction. However, I had a great triumph. I secured the signature after the match of a sweaty Roberto Rivelino, one of the all-time greats of Brazilian football and possessor of a rocket-like shot at goal, which I have never seen bettered and equalled only perhaps by Stanley Mortensen in his heyday with Blackpool and England. The precious scrawl went down a treat with my then 11-year-old son Gordon.

The following day, at my request, I had a meeting with Dom Ivo Lorscheiter, secretary general of the National Conference of Brazilian Bishops and soon to be a cardinal archbishop of Rio de Janeiro. He outlined the position taken by the Roman Catholic Church in the political and economic environment current in Brazil. Declaring a personal interest in that my brother-in-law, Tony Wheatley (Kathleen's third brother), was a Jesuit priest, serving in Guyana and Mexico, I asked our host about Liberation Theology. He was ambivalent but not unsympathetic. The Church was of paramount importance in South America on account of its influence. It encapsulated the deepening conflicts between the Establishment on the one hand, with its power and wealth, and the needs of the poor on the other, between whom there was a huge gulf.

Before going on to Brasilia, we had dinner with the governor of Rio, Admiral Faria Lima. As leader of the delegation, I was seated beside him. For reasons that I adduce later in this book, our conversation on the Malvinas/Falklands was to have a pivotal effect on the future of my life in politics.

The plane journey from Rio to Brasilia was extraordinary. For hour upon hour, we flew over what seemed an empty land. Then,

suddenly, out of proverbial nowhere, there rose up the spectacular outline of a city of already 800,000 people. I sensed,
however, that at our first official meeting with the federal
government, the Foreign Minister, Antonio Azeredo da Silveira,
was less than enamoured about being catapulted out of the
gorgeous architecture in Rio de Janeiro. 'It is all very well for
Campos to dream up the excitement of a capital city in the centre
of the country, but . . .' It was the way he said 'Campos' that
indicated his rage about what had happened to him. Tone is
often more of an indication of feeling than actual words.

At dinner, we were the guests of the president of the Chamber
of Deputies and Señora Borja. I began my speech of thanks,
saying, 'Dining with the Borjas . . .' and made a jocular allusion,
God help me, to the effect that it was safer in Brasilia than in
Rome, 500 years ago, when the infamous Papacy-connected
family had no hesitation in poisoning those who crossed their
path. After dinner, our hostess sidled up to me and said, 'Señor
Dalyell, you made a very gracious and interesting speech. But
what can we do about our name? At the last five dinners we
have hosted for European guests, each has started with the
same theme allusion to the Borgias of Renaissance Rome. We
would change our name, only my husband's voters would be
confused!' Poor lady, she was sick of the reference. And I don't
blame her.

From Brasilia, it was on to Bahia/Salvador, where the lovely
sixteenth- and seventeenth-century churches brim with ecclesiastical gold. What St Francis of Assisi would think of the opulence
of the Franciscan church in Bahia, heaven knows! It was over-
powering and yet beautiful. Our final destination was Recife, the
capital of the state of Pernambuco. The governor hosted a formal
dinner in his beautiful palace, in which the furniture and objets
d'arts simply stunned us. From our brief, we knew that the
governor was a professor of medicine. Towards the end of the
meal, I asked him a somewhat direct question about prisons. He
started to reply and then interrupted himself by saying, 'Tomorrow, I will cancel your scheduled factory visits and take you
myself to the open prison at Itamaraca.'

This prison had been in existence for nearly 20 years. He explained that it took prisoners who were serving the final third or the last five years of their sentence and, according to their behaviour, they could become entitled to live with their wives and family in accommodation on the islands of Itamaraca where the prison was built. On the island, the governor showed us the school for the children. He told us that the prisoners were paid 70 per cent of the basic minimum wage for their labour and that they were allowed to farm plots of land on their own account. Through the interpretation of the excellent Señor Paolo Partes, an officer of the secretariat of the Brazilian IPU, I talked to prisoners in their cells, to which they had the key and could come and go as they pleased. The principal sanction was that of return to the normal prison accommodation for bad behaviour. I was amazed that, in the main assembly hall of the prison, there was painted, in large letters, a quotation in Portuguese from Winston Churchill: 'If you wish to judge what stage of civilization a society has reached, you should examine the way in which both the authorities and public opinion treat convicted prisoners.'

*

Please allow a digression. Looking back on 43 years in the House of Commons, I have more than a tinge of guilt that I displayed no personal parliamentary interest in prisons. I had various reasons or excuses. The big Central Scotland prison at Shotts in North Lanarkshire was not in my constituency but in that of Margaret Herbison and her successor John Smith, future leader of the Labour Party. Both knew a lot about and were more than capable of dealing with penal problems. Again, my father-in-law John Wheatley was a prominent appeal court judge and the last thing I wanted to do was to get entangled in his area of activity. Moreover, an MP is unwise to attempt to become a 'universal expert'. Instinctively, parliamentary colleagues do not listen to 'universal experts'. There were whole swathes of issues of huge political consequence on which it would not occur to me to open my mouth.

I had been an MP for more than 30 years before I first set foot in a prison. My duck was broken when I was invited by the governor of Saughton Prison in Edinburgh to give a talk to the nine lifers in his care, provided that the subject was neither religion nor politics. So I spoke on the Middle East and, in the course of questions – very intelligent questions – I mentioned the arms trade from Chile to Iraq. 'Oh,' piped up a swarthy, middle-aged prisoner, 'Mr Dalyell, I think I can help you with details.' It transpired that this prisoner had been the skipper of a vessel carrying arms, embargoed by the UN, from General Pinochet's port of Valparaiso, round Cape Horn, across the South Atlantic, into the Indian Ocean and up the Red Sea to a remote destination on the Saudi Coast, from which arms were spirited away to Saddam Hussein's Iraq. It was not for this that he had landed up in incarceration in Saughton but for skippering a boat that had been apprehended smuggling drugs on a huge scale.

*

One of the by-products of IPU delegations is that it creates the conditions for Westminster friendships between one's own colleagues and politicians of opposing parties. Those who have travelled together understand each other the better, whatever their opposing political views. Besides, good behaviour and courtesy to one another impressed foreign hosts, who were sometimes accustomed not just to hostility, but even to violence in politics. 'You British are so civilised,' we were often told by those awestruck by unlikely good relationships.

On 28 October 1971, Edward Heath, Conservative Prime Minister from 1970 to 1974, put the historic vote on British entry to the Common Market – his ambition for almost a decade – before the Commons. I was one of the minor ringleaders of the 69 Labour MPs who were to defy a three-line whip and join Heath and his government – although not all of his backbenchers – in the 'aye' Lobby. All hell in the political firmament had been let loose. Mrs Barbara Castle, by no means one of my enemies – she referred in her diaries to that 'nice Tam Dalyell' – had called me a 'traitor to the Labour Party' and opined that we were joining 'a capitalist conspiracy'. The former Secretary of State for Scotland and still very much the boss of the Labour Party in Scotland, Willie Ross, was huffing and puffing, growling and spluttering with rage. Others varied between the gently reproving and the bombastically sarcastic.

Allow me two postscripts. Five years later, after the incoming Prime Minister, Jim Callaghan, had sacked her from his Cabinet and with the advent of indirect elections to the European Parliament, the government decided to give Mrs Castle the consolation prize of leading the first group of Labour members elected to the new parliament in Strasbourg. Lo and behold, what did this erstwhile passionate anti-marketeer do? Not within months but within weeks, Mrs Castle was calling publicly for greater powers for the European Parliament. Why? Candidly, for no better reason than that our Barbara was there. It is in the nature of politicians to demand more powers for whatever institution to which they are currently attached. This can be clearly seen in the present Scottish Parliament – originally to be an assembly – where demands for greater powers come from all parties, not just the SNP.

The second postscript was that my pro-Common Market vote laid the foundation for my good relationship with Ted Heath. I found it easier to talk to him than most Conservative MPs did – because I wanted nothing from him that he could give me. I was greatly touched when I was invited along with Denis Healey, who had been at Balliol with him, Tony Benn, with whom he had worked closely on Iraq, and Jim Callaghan to the dinner which Madam Speaker Boothroyd hosted on the occasion of his 50 years as an MP, for which Sir Edward Heath KG, as he had become, chose the guest list. It was a nostalgic gathering of yesteryear. I reproduce the dinner table that night because, although I was to remain in the House for another five years, for me it was a farewell to the political firmament as I had known it.

IN HONOUR OF THE RT HON SIR EDWARD HEATH KG MBE MP

Thursday 2nd March 2000   7.30 for 8.00 p.m.

The Rt Hon Jeremy Thorpe   The Rt Hon Sir Anthony Kershaw

Sir David Madel MP	Lady Soames
The Rt Hon Lord Weatherill	The Rt Hon Sir Geoffrey Johnson Smith MP
The Rt Hon Michael Heseltine MP	The Rt Hon Lord Steel of Aikwood
The Rt Hon Lord Gilmour of Craigmillar	The Rt Hon Lord Thomas of Gwydir
The Rt Hon Sir John Morris MP	Lady Wilson of Rievaulx
The Countess of Avon	The Rt Hon John Major MP
The Rt Hon Lord Callaghan of Cardiff	The Rt Hon Lord Carrington
Madam Speaker	The Rt Hon Baroness Thatcher
The Rt Hon Sir Edward Heath	The Rt Hon Lord Hurd of Westwell
The Rt Hon Lord Thomson of Monifieth	The Rt Hon Tony Benn MP
The Rt Hon Kenneth Clarke MP	The Rt Hon Lord Carr of Hadley
The Rt Hon Lord Rawlinson of Ewell	The Rt Hon Lord Healey
The Rt Hon Sir Peter Emery MP	The Rt Hon Lord Prior
The Rt Hon Charles Kennedy MP	Mr Tam Dalyell MP
The Rt Hon Lord Pym	The Rt Hon John MacGregor MP
The Rt Hon John Gummer MP	Sir Patrick Cormack MP

Sir David Knox   Sir Timothy Kitson

In 1975, Harold Wilson (again Prime Minister following the two General Elections of 1974) decided to ask, in a UK-wide referendum, whether Britain should remain in the Common Market. This was typical Wilsonian sleight of hand and had been devised primarily to maintain a semblance of unity in the Labour Party and government, members of which were to have a free hand to campaign either for or against.

I held 'consultative' meetings in the constituency, in accordance with what we had been asked to do by Labour Party headquarters. At one such meeting, in a largish school hall in Bo'ness, precisely five people were present – my wife and I, two members of the public and the janitor, Jock Mackie, who had to be there to open and close the school and arrange the chairs.

After my spiel, I turned, earnestly, to the two members of the public, and said, 'What do you think?'

One of them, an elderly miner, relit his pipe, looked at me and said, 'Making difficult decisions, Tam, is what we pay you for.' He had a point – a good point.

It was not apathy about public meetings as such. It so happened that, a week earlier, I had been required to be on a platform at a public meeting, called to haul me over the coals for supporting an obscure Scottish measure, the Riparian Rights for Anglers No. 2 Bill, for which I had voted in the Commons – against my better judgement – out of loyalty to Labour Scottish Office ministers. Many of those present had been really agitated and the word 'traitor' was one of the less offensive epithets hurled at me. Compared to the ventilation of the supposed grievances of the anglers, relationship with Brussels was a calm affair in West Lothian. In Westminster, it had been a far from calm affair.

I am under few illusions as to why I was chosen as Michael Stewarts's deputy leader of the first Labour Party delegation to the European Assembly. It was not really on account of any entitlement as the current chairman of the Parliamentary Labour Party backbench Foreign Affairs Committee. Two other factors weighed more heavily with Harold Wilson and Foreign Secretary Callaghan in whose gift it was.

First, the long-serving German Ambassador in London, Karl-

Günther von Hase (1970–1977), asked for my inclusion in the delegation partly because I spoke German and partly because we had worked together in pro-European causes. Wilson, with good reason, wanted to oblige von Hase and his government. Wilson sidled up to me in the Lobby during a vote, recounting von Hase's request and adding, with a sly smile, 'Besides, Giscard d'Estaing has a soft spot for Old Etonians!' I also know that both EEC Commissioners, Christopher Soames and George Thomson, had asked for me. The second consideration was altogether less exalted. Callaghan thought that my anti-devolution views would create trouble for him and me and believed exiling me to Strasbourg was the answer. Little did he realise that it was far easier for me to speak and campaign against devolution if I was not in the Commons every working day and subject to the incessant pressure of parliamentary business.

*

The issue that dominated the 1970s, perhaps even more than Europe, was devolution for Scotland, though of course it had been around for some time. Undoubtedly, the election of Mrs Winifred Margaret Ewing as the SNP MP for Hamilton in 1967 was an important development, not least for the Nationalists and also Labour's response in terms of its devolution policy. On the first day of campaigning, I took three friends from the West Lothian Labour Party to canvas in Hamilton. By-elections have a political smell about them and the four of us agreed that, from our experience on the doorstep, we did not like this particular smell. I cannot say that those we called on were actively hostile – just sullen. And sullen electors are ominous. We trundled down each weekend and I became ever more alarmed as a result of our experience on the doorstep. When I suggested to Willie Ross that there could just be an SNP victory, his response to me was a gruff: 'Don't be silly!'

But my abiding memory was going with my friend, the late Professor John P. Mackintosh, to the council house home of the secretary of the Hamilton Old Age Pensioners' Association for a quick bite to eat at 5.30 p.m. before the final push for votes. In her kitchen, she said quietly to John and myself, 'Tom [Fraser] treated us as if we were that cloot!' [Cloot is the term for washing-up cloth or rag.] The Right Honourable Tom Fraser, Cabinet Minister of Transport, had been born in Lesmahagow, part of the Hamilton constituency, and had worked underground from 1925 until 1943, when he was elected as Hamilton's MP. He had been a wonderful senior colleague to me but, after Wilson eased him out of the Cabinet, the kind-hearted Prime Minister arranged for Tom to become Chairman of the Hydro-Electric Board in Scotland. Since this was a non-political post, in the mores of 1967, Tom felt he could not even have a party function to say goodbye after 24 years of being MP. The truth is that the electorate will wreak vengeance on a party where MPs leave mid-term for a supposed 'cushy number'. Death is excusable; causing a by-election for other reasons is not.

The victorious SNP candidate, Winnie Ewing, has forever complained that Scottish Labour MPs treated her abominably and, I feel, with some justice. They resented her victory in a traditional Labour citadel and their collective nose was out of joint. It was aggravated by the fact that, as Winnie Woodburn in her student years, she had been a prominent member of Glasgow University Labour Club. My own relations with her were, I think, friendly because the SNP had given me up as a bad job – this was confirmed by the fact that, much later, I was the one Scottish Labour MP who declined to sign the Claim of Right. I confess to a flicker of irritation when, having been elected to the Strasbourg European Assembly, Winnie pranced about as Madame Ecosse – a soubriquet bestowed upon her by that gallant Frenchman representing the Toulouse/Albi area, Georges Spénale, President of the European Parliament.

Please allow me to put my views on devolution in some historical context. The Dalyells have a family tree that takes us back into the mists of time but the first Dalyell about whom we know in detail is Thomas (1572–1632), burgess of the City of Edinburgh and butter merchant, trading largely in poor quality butter at the lower end of the market. In truth, he seems to have been the king of axle grease in Scotland and, in the seventeenth century, axle grease was a vital commodity for carriages, carts and canons. On 1 August 1601, in Culross Abbey, Thomas married Janet, daughter of Edward Bruce, Scottish Ambassador to the English Court. Bruce had gained the confidence of William Davidson, secretary to Sir Francis Walsingham, who was responsible for the day-to-day handling of the problem of Mary, Queen of Scots.

Bruce had become the negotiator with Sir Robert Cecil on the delicate issue of who was to succeed Elizabeth I of England. In the wake of the successful transition, Bruce was rewarded. He was taken to London in 1603 and made Master of the Rolls, more of a senior civil servant than a law officer. Bruce took his son-in-law, Thomas Dalyell, as Deputy Master of the Rolls. In nine years (during which he lived in Fetter Lane), he made enough money to come back to Scotland in 1612 and in the next 18 years build most of the house in which Kathleen and I now live.

How did he do it? In three words, 'Cash for honours'. By 1609, the 'hungrie Scots' – a mafia who did well out of the fact that a Scot had become King of England – had become deeply unpopular in London. Thomas saw the storm clouds and decided to return to Scotland with his fortune. The death of his father-in-law and patron, Edward Bruce (by 1611, Lord Kinloss), was no doubt a factor in his decision to return to Scotland to set himself up as a laird on a country estate (which he bought from his cousins, the Livingston family) where he could bring up his growing family.

When he was Minister of State responsible for guiding the 1978 Scotland Bill (which was to devolve a degree of power to Scotland) through the Committee Stage, John Smith came with his wife Elizabeth and their three daughters to lunch. Gazing up at the portrait of Thomas by the Aberdeen artist George Jamesone, Smith chuckled, 'So, he was the source of all the grief you are giving the government, in being so bloody awkward about the setting up of a Scottish Assembly.' He had a point. My ancestors had played a significant role in the 1603 Union of the Crowns and, throughout The Binns, decorative plasterwork and wood carving display thistles and roses as symbols of this Union. My parents, being staunch Unionists, were always very conscious of their commitment and duty to Great Britain. Inevitably, I imbibed some of this ethos.

Inextricably and in the public mind, I am linked with the 'West Lothian Question'. I, like every politician, am a man of some vanity but insufficient vanity to baptise an issue after myself. The circumstances of the birth of the 'WLQ' – as it has already been styled in examination papers – are as follows.

In 1978, during the passage of the Scotland Bill, on every clause, sub-clause and debatable amendment, I rose in my place and solemnly asked the same question with appropriate variation according to the issue under discussion: 'How can it be that I can vote on education in Accrington, Lancashire, but not in Armadale, West Lothian?'; 'How can I vote on health in Blackburn, Lancashire, but not in Blackburn, West Lothian?'; 'How can I vote on local government in Liverpool but not in Linlithgow, the county town of the area which sent me to the House of Commons?'; 'How can I vote on X, Y and Z in Whitburn, County Durham, but not Whitburn, West Lothian?' No doubt pompously and with a sniff of self-righteousness that Smith found insufferable, I would terminate my questions with the repetitive mantra: 'It cannot be asked too often.' Eventually, exasperated, Smith exploded from the front bench: 'Oh, yes, Tam, it bloody well can be asked too often.'

Then up rose the severe and saturnine figure of Enoch Powell. He said that the House had finally grasped what the honourable gentleman for West Lothian was on about (heavy irony). Both Powell and I had read Morley's *Life of Gladstone* and knew of the problems caused by the so-called 'Ins and Outs', which involved the prospect of nineteenth-century Irish MPs voting on English, Scottish and Welsh affairs even after Ireland had been granted Home Rule. 'To save time,' said Powell (the last thing he, as an anti-devolutionist, wanted to do was to curtail proceedings), 'let us call the gentleman's point the "West Lothian Question".' Some days before he died, suffering from cancer of the throat, I went to see Enoch at his home in Eaton Square. In a hoarse whisper, he hissed, 'I have bequeathed to you the "West Lothian Question".' And so he had.

My background was crucial in affording me a certain indefinable authority on devolution among my parliamentary colleagues – not least the fact that, by the mid 1970s, I had taken on the SNP and won no fewer than six times in West Lothian. The feeling developed: 'The fellow can chunter on and on, on the floor of the House, defying party policy, which would normally infuriate us and lead us to a call for his suspension from the Parliamentary Labour Party but hang on a moment – Tam is the fellow who has longest among us fought the SNP threat. And he has published a book on the subject, *Devolution: The End of Britain?* so just perhaps he has thought about it more than most of us!' I was given the benefit of the doubt. Tom Clarke, MP for Coatbridge, former Minister and Shadow Secretary of State for Scotland, viewing SNP success in 2011, with the dismay which was rife amongst Westminster MPs for Scotland, wrote to me on 20 May 2011, saying, 'You are right about these difficult times. I suspect that there will soon be a demand for a reprint of that famous book *Devolution: The End of the United Kingdom* [*sic*] by Tam Dalyell.'

A crucial crossroads in the Scotland Bill was the famous (or perhaps infamous) 'Cunningham amendment'. George Cunningham was the Dunfermline-born Labour MP for Islington South and Finsbury, although he later defected to the SDP. What we agreed on was this: 'Every MP knows that the Scotland and Wales Bills are unsatisfactory legislation. But they are justified by the fact that the overwhelming majority demand Scottish and Welsh Assemblies. We are entitled to challenge this so let us propose a 40 per cent hurdle. Most constitutions require this.' (This meant that 40 per cent of the *total* Scottish electorate, rather than those actually voting, had to vote 'yes' for the Scotland Act to become law.)

In a memorable speech, surprisingly well attended, George Cunningham launched his amendment in the Chamber. To the consternation of the Leader of the House, Michael Foot, and John Smith but not most members of James Callaghan's government, it passed. Since in the referendum, held on 1 March 1979, this condition was not met, the entire Bill fell and a General Election ensued. I did not get the flak from colleagues that I anticipated. Only Roy Hattersley tartly observed to my face: 'Tam, you do realise that, as a little side effect of your anti-devolution campaign, the Labour government fell and Margaret Thatcher became Prime Minister?' It was a comment that was grossly unfair – it was, in fact, the SNP voting with the Tories on a motion of confidence that brought the Labour government down, yet it contained just sufficient truth to make me blush.

With the benefit of hindsight – George Cunningham does not agree – I have come to believe that imposing a 40 per cent hurdle was a mistake. People in Scotland had been used to abiding by simple majorities. Unfortunately, from my point of view but, alas, understandably, the 40 per cent condition was seen as 'not quite cricket' by many and 'downright cheating' by others. Undoubtedly it cost the 'no' campaign votes. How many votes, none of us will ever know. But, in my opinion, it was enough to have given the 'no' campaign the probability of outright victory in the popular vote (the actual figures were 'yes': 1,230,937 and 'no': 1,153,500). Had there been an outright 'no', the issue of a Scottish Assembly might have been put to bed for a generation. But, as things turned out, pro-Assembly activists could resort to the emotive and ever-appealing mantra: 'We was robbed.'

But for the phoenix-like resurrection of the cause for a Scottish Assembly/Parliament there was an altogether more determinant factor than discontent over the Cunningham amendment. This can be encapsulated in just two words: Margaret Thatcher. Had there been a 'normal' Tory Prime Minister in the decade of the 1980s I doubt if the pro-Scottish Assembly bandwagon would have got back on the road. Given the passions that were unleashed by Thatcherite policies and given the anti-Scots attitude of some of her favourite ministers, in particular Nicholas Ridley, who had acted as a minister under Ted Heath to close down the Upper Clyde shipyards, it was hardly surprising that the pro-Assembly cause began to thrive again.

Of course, I knew Ridley very well. He had been my fag-master when I was a newish boy at Eton. As it turned out, my main duty was to go and hold his box of paints, while he was doing beautiful watercolours in Luxmoore's Garden on the

Thames at Eton. Our common art master, Wilfred Blunt, on hearing what I did, retorted, 'Ridley – more talented than his grandfather.' His grandfather was Sir Edwin Lutyens, architect of New Delhi and much else. But Ridley, a younger brother of a Northumbrian dynasty, could not conceal his impatience with the Scots, when he was Margaret Thatcher's Secretary of State for Industry. The North of England, he thought, had better claims to public finance and he railed against the nanny state. Later, when Ridley had an exhibition of his paintings in the upper waiting hall of the Commons, the acerbic Labour MP Peter Snape sidled up to me and expostulated into my ear, 'How is it that such a bastard can paint so beautifully?' Ridley told me that he rather enjoyed being called a bastard by Labour MPs and certainly enjoyed baiting his political adversaries.

I recount all this to try to convey the torrid atmosphere among Scots Labour Party members and its consequence of making it extremely difficult for those of us who were against an Assembly to raise our heads above the parapet. Unchallenged, devolution in the Labour Party gained momentum. Actually, had he become Prime Minister in 1992, I think that Neil Kinnock, whose Welsh sinews were anti-devolutionary, would have found ways of stopping the process or, at best, putting it on the proverbial back-burner. As it was, John Smith took over and, as he had been the minister responsible for trying to pilot through the 1978 Scotland Act, perhaps he could do little other than talk in terms of 'unfinished business'.

*De mortuis nil nisi bonum** but allow me a doubt about my friend John Smith. He was chosen by James Callaghan to do a lawyer's job in enabling the party policy to go through but whether he actually believed in a Scottish Assembly – as Donald Dewar and many others certainly sincerely did – is a matter of some doubt in my mind. He saw his job as a stepping stone to promotion – which, indeed, he achieved by becoming Secretary of State for Trade. On the morning of his tragic death in 1994, the *Independent* asked me to do a 3,000-word obituary for the following morning's paper. In my

* Say nothing bad about the dead.

haste, I cast blunt doubts about Smith's real belief in devolution. It was never contradicted by anyone. Furthermore, from the day of the failed referendum in March 1979, until 1994 when he died, Smith never gave his considerable mind to the logistics of devolution, or how it would actually work. Honourably, he was focused on achieving a Labour government of the United Kingdom.

My minority view on Smith was shared by my friend Jim Sillars, with whom I had done 18 debates up and down Scotland, on the pros and cons of devolution during the 1979 referendum campaign. Years later, I put the question to Jim Callaghan, by then Lord Callaghan of Cardiff, reminding him that, in 1976, when I was chairman of the Labour Party foreign affairs group, I used to go and see him, as Foreign Secretary, every Wednesday night. On a number of such occasions, I would say to him before I left, 'Jim, can I talk to you about the Scottish Assembly problem?' 'Oh Tam,' came the reply, 'don't bother me with that nonsense – tell me what the party is thinking about Cyprus.' Lord Callaghan, Delphic and cautious as ever, gave me to understand that he knew that Smith's heart was not in a Scottish Assembly, let alone a Scottish Parliament.

I returned to the House of Commons in 1979, to the opposition benches, with a majority of more than 20,000. The figures being:

Dalyell, T. (Lab)	36,713
Wolfe, W. C. (SNP)	16,603
Whyte, J. R. (Cons)	13,162
Sneddon, W. (Communist)	404
Majority	20,082

The Labour Party was so concerned that my obduracy to their devolution proposals would lose them the West Lothian seat that, unknown to me, they commissioned a polling firm to do a survey for them which forecast that I would narrowly lose West Lothian. The electorate thought otherwise and gave me a thumping endorsement. Frankly, I have discovered that voters rather like a politician who argues a case in which he obviously passionately believes, regardless of whether they themselves totally share those beliefs. And the West Lothian constituency, more than most, took the view that I might be a bugger but I was *their* bugger and no one would tell them – the electorate – what to do with me.

*

The best that I can say about Margaret Thatcher is that she appears to have been personally considerate to her staff, such as the Garden Girls – the secretaries in Number 10 Downing Street whose windows looked out on to the garden – and that, in Sir Denis Thatcher, she had the most discreet and cheerful of husbands, who was charming to me despite the fact that I provoked his wife. But Mrs Thatcher ruined Britain's industrial base, her behaviour during the miners' strike was shameful, she went to war in the Falklands to protect her position as leader of the Conservative Party, she was vindictive towards Cabinet colleagues and senior Conservatives who, to borrow Hugo Young's apt title, were not 'One of Us', and, as in the Westland Affair, she abused power and lied to the House of Commons. As readers will have gathered, I am not a tribal politician. I make no bones about having many Conservative friends. I had respect for Harold Macmillan, my first Prime Minister, for Sir Alec Douglas-Home, for Sir Edward Heath and for Sir John Major – but for Margaret Thatcher, no.

One of the realities of British politics is that a Member of Parliament is unwise to suppose that he or she can conduct more than one campaign simultaneously. Apart from the mundane considerations of finite time and energy, there is the weakness that flows from being dumped by a majority of colleagues into the category of the 'usual suspects'. So, during the 1970s, although I continued to write a weekly column for the *New Scientist*, I refrained from espousing scientific causes in a time-consuming and sustained way. In any case, I was immersed in the arguments about the future constitutional arrangements of the United Kingdom and the proposed establishment of an Assembly in Edinburgh. But, in the winter of 1979, there was one matter which niggled me ever increasingly.

At the time of writing in 2011, it is clear that hugely important and sensitive international considerations flow from the fact that Dr Abdul Qadeer Khan was not only the father of the Pakistani bomb but the purveyor of nuclear know-how to North Korea and Iran. It need not have been so. If I parade the detail, it is because I ask the reader to believe, not on account of the smug 'I told you so' syndrome, but to demonstrate something else – that governments increasingly pay less heed to what happens in the House of Commons.

Among the uncovenanted advantages of being a *New Scientist* weekly columnist was that I became the receptacle for information. One morning, I found in my bundle of mail in the House of Commons Post Office an anonymous letter with a Belgian postage stamp. Unsigned but clearly composed by the hand of someone familiar with nuclear physics and in perfect English was a concerned request that I should delve into the activities of a research student at the University of Brussels who, in his vacation time, had enlisted for low-level work at the German–British–Dutch Centrifuge Project at Almelo in the Netherlands.

The communication complained that security at Almelo was lax. High-profile 'issue' politicians like me attract a flood of anonymous letters and mail from cranks, but instinct told me that whoever wrote to me about Almelo was not a crank and had good reason to remain anonymous, for the sake of his job. I phoned friends on the staff of the *New Scientist*, Bernard Dixon, Dick Fifield, John Gribbin and Mike Kenward. They responded that the information that had come to me sounded all too plausible and, from their numerous contacts, they would find out what they could. I also phoned two Dutch friends and erstwhile colleagues in the European Parliament, Piet Dankert, later Dutch Minister of Foreign Affairs and President of the European Parliament, and Schelto Patijn, who had stayed at our home in Scotland during a pro-EEC Political Tour and was later to be Governor of South Holland and Mayor of Amsterdam. They both confirmed that there had been uneasy references in the Dutch press about the activities of this research student, whose name was Abdul Qadeer Khan.

On 29 October 1979, I put a detailed Question on security at Almelo to the Secretary of State for Energy, David Howell, asking for a statement and followed this with a Question to Mrs Thatcher on 28 and 29 November of the same year. And, on 6 December 1979, I had the following exchange with the Prime Minister:

Mr Dalyell: Will the Prime Minister undertake to ask the Dutch Prime Minister about a leak that was infinitely more far-reaching than any leak of Cabinet papers? I refer to the leak of crucial nuclear secrets from the Centrifuge Project at Almelo. Will the Right Hon. Lady ask the Dutch Prime Minister how the situation occurred, since it is arguably more damaging to peace in the world than anything done by the Rosenbergs or any other atom spies?

The Prime Minister: The Hon. Gentleman knows that we have already made protests about the matter, which involved a person who had been working at that plant of URENCO on enriched uranium and the centrifuge process and then went to work in Pakistan, where we are trying to see that there is not proliferation of production of nuclear materials or any nuclear weapons. The matter is not on the agenda, but I shall reinforce the protest that we have already made.

Twelve days later, as the Private Office at Number 10 Downing Street was vague when I enquired what had transpired as the result of the Prime Minister's Reply to my Question, I raised the issue on the Consolidated Fund, a traditional occasion when MPs lucky in the ballot can raise a topic of their own choosing. So it was at 5.12 a.m. I embarked on a detailed speech that lasted until 5.47 a.m., on the activities of the young Pakistani research student, A. Q. Khan, then research student at the Catholic University of Brussels under the distinguished nuclear physicist Professor Delaye.

Forgive me regurgitating my six opening sentences of a 35-minute speech but, from the vantage point of 32 years later, they seem sombrely prophetic.

Sentence One

Remembering Alan Nunn-May, Bruno Pontecorvo, the Rosenbergs, and even Klaus Fuchs, with his over-all grasp of the concept of the physics of the atom bomb, it is arguable whether any of them or, indeed, all of them together jeopardised world peace to a greater extent than the activities, in the second half of the 1970s, of Dr Abdul Qadeer Khan.

Sentence Two

Certainly, the effect of anything Anthony Blunt may have done pales into trivial insignificance compared with the probable result of Dr Khan's handiwork.

Sentence Three

We now have the real threat of regional confrontation in Asia or the Arab World, laying a powder trail to a possible world holocaust.

Sentence Four

The so-called vertical proliferation is one thing. More nuclear weapons in the same hands does not necessarily increase the likelihood of nuclear war.

Sentence Five

Horizontal proliferation – the acquisition of nuclear warheads by nations that previously had none at all – is quite a different matter.

Sentence Six

That is why even at ten minutes past five o'clock in the morning I do not apologise to an under-secretary, who has been very good-tempered and had to wait a long time for this Consolidated Fund Debate for keeping him out of his well-deserved bed and rest. [The under-secretary in question at the Department of Energy was the future Chancellor of the Exchequer, Norman Lamont.]

The guts of the case are that Dr Abdul Qadeer Khan came to Europe as a bona fide research student in metallurgy. At some point in the mid 1970s, he was persuaded to devote himself to gaining access to theoretical but, more importantly, industrial information that would allow his native Pakistan to build and operate a nuclear weapons capacity of its own. This came about as a result of mind-boggling inefficiency or naivety that was wholly uncharacteristic of the Dutch as a nation – in most things, they are among the most competent people on this planet – or connivance by people in key positions. Though I must make it clear that I have no evidence of connivance, clearly it is a question that has to be asked.

Manners and good sense are helpful on such occasions. I submitted my speech to the Department of Energy officials three days earlier on the grounds that it would be unreasonable to expect any minister to reply on so complex a subject to questions that were fired at him for the first time in the early hours of the morning. In February 2004, unprompted by me, the former Speaker, the late Lord Weatherill, who ass Deputy Speaker, had been in the chair at 5.12 a.m., sent me a copy of his letter to Tony Blair in which he referred to chairing a Consolidated Fund debate in December 1979:

> [A]t 5.12 a.m. . . . Tam Dalyell drew attention to the fact that Pakistan was in the process of acquiring nuclear know-how through the activities of Dr Khan. As usual, Tam had carefully researched his subject and the seriousness of this matter was accepted by Norman Lamont who was responding as Under Secretary of State for Energy. Thereafter the matter was, to my knowledge, not raised again, though I pray that it was not forgotten or overlooked by H.M.G.

On 20 October 2006, when Dr Abdul Qadeer Khan hit the headlines yet again, I wrote to the then Cabinet Secretary and the then Permanent Secretary at the Ministry of Defence. The reply from the former, Gus O'Donnell, can be not unfairly summarised as 'Before my time!' More revealing are the letters from my friends Robin Butler and the late Michael Quinlan, one of the most effective and able Permanent Secretaries ever to have been at the Ministry of Defence. My repeated parliamentary efforts to alert the government to the nightmare of a Pakistan/Islamic nuclear bomb had never filtered through to them.

*

At the beginning of each parliamentary session there is a ballot for Private Members' Bills. Virtually every non-governmental MP puts his or her name in the proverbial hat and the Speaker draws out 20 names in order. The lucky 20 then have several weeks to choose on what subject they would like to legislate and to produce a 'short title' of a bill. Only the first half dozen or so have any realistic chance of getting their name on the statute book. In the weeks before the submission of a short title, the lucky MPs are subjected to a barrage of letters, and approaches in other forms, from interest groups pleading for them to espouse their particular cause.

Thus it came about that the Northamptonshire MP Peter Fry, a supporter of the incoming Conservative government following the 1979 General Election, produced his application for a 'Protection of Animals (Scientific Purposes) Bill'. The scientific community began to be concerned. The position was encapsulated in an approach to me from the experimental pathologist, Professor Marion Hicks, backed by Sir Richard Doll, and the British Association for Cancer Research. I was curious about why Fry, who had no track record of interest in scientific research, had opted for this topic. The truth quickly emerged. A group of animal lovers in Wellingborough, in his constituency, had persuaded Fry that he would be hugely popular if he were to take up the parliamentary cudgels against vivisection. So he swallowed the prepared bill handed to him on a plate from the anti-vivisection lobby, with help from the League Against Cruel Sports.

I went to see the opposition Chief Whip, my former office room-mate, Michael Cocks, and said, 'Michael, could you have me nominated at the Committee of Selection to serve on the Wednesday morning Standing Committee on the Fry bill?'

'Certainly, old boy, delighted,' he replied. 'Constituents working at Bristol University have told me they are appalled by the consequences of such a measure passing into law. But no one wants to get across the animal lobby. As you wrecked the devolution bill – it was a nonsense – you are the very man to wreck the Fry bill!'

So I was duly chosen to serve. However, it was not to prevent proper care for animal welfare that motivated me, it was the importance of scientific research to mitigate human disease carried out in the disciplined and responsible way of so many within the scientific community. The benefits so many of us receive from modern medical technology are the direct result of properly conducted experimental research.

After the first session, it became abundantly clear, as I suspected, that Fry knew little about the briefs he was receiving from the anti-vivisectionists. I interrupted with a number of questions at intervals; substantive answer came there none. So I suggested to my friend Tim Biscoe, Professor of Experimental Physiology at University College, London (UCL), and his colleague Jim Pascoe to sit in the visitors' section of the committee room. On every amendment, when Fry spoke, Biscoe and Pascoe passed me notes and questions designed to torpedo Fry. At the end of the third Committee Stage, Fry referred to a seemingly horrendous experiment involving rabbits. When did it take place? Where? Fry said he would let me know, prior to the next meeting; he did not have the details.

At the beginning of the next session, I asked politely for the details of the experiment to which he referred – 'Well, actually, it was ten years ago. It was not in Britain but in the United States; and it was done with mice not rabbits.' So, at session number five, on a wet day, I smuggled a rabbit and a mouse, borrowed from the UCL laboratory, under my raincoat into the parliament precinct (anyone without a parliamentary pass would have been stringently searched). At the beginning of the Committee I held up these creatures, on a point of order, having warned the parliamentary press who had turned up in unaccustomed numbers at 10.30 a.m. 'Does Mr Fry know the difference between these two – a rabbit and a mouse?' I asked. All members of the Committee, including the chairman, laughed – except Mr Fry who was spluttering with embarrassment and anger. Fry's anger

was only excelled by the rage of the ladies from the anti-vivisection lobby in the public seats, who had been supporting him.
They fumed to the Lobby correspondents that Dalyell did not
even know how to hold a rabbit properly.

Since the ribaldry engendered led to Members of both political
sides saying they were not prepared to surrender their Wednesday mornings to a measure which had been exposed as deeply
flawed, the Fry Bill fell by the wayside. In vengeance, the anti-
vivisectionists organised their members, not to write to me, but to
my party leader, the now ex-Prime Minister James Callaghan, to
ask him how such a wicked, animal hating and, yes, 'evil' man,
could be a Labour Member of Parliament. I was summoned to
his office. Sadly shaking his head, Callaghan said, 'Not content
with wrecking the devolution bill, now you bring a hornets' nest
around my ears. What am I to say to all these letters?'

'Well,' I said unapologetically, 'it is quite simple – ask the letter
writers if they want the search for cures and palliative treatment
of cancer and other terrible diseases to go on?' That is the line his
office took but, to persuade him, I organised letters of support for
my actions, not only from Tim Biscoe, but also from a host of
other medical scientists. I am told the letter to Callaghan from Sir
Andrew Huxley, Master of Trinity and then president of the
Royal Society, stated that: 'Tam Dalyell has performed a service,
not only to the medical scientific community, but to the cause of
combating degenerative diseases by exposing the flaws in Mr
Fry's bill.' It was the first occasion on which the council of the
Royal Society asked their president to write a letter of support to a
party leader for the actions of an individual MP.

It was not the only occasion on which I was involved with
agricultural artefacts in the House of Commons. I was on my
hind legs, making an innocuous and constructive speech on
education in support of the Secretary of State for Scotland from
the third row on the Government benches, when a load of horse
manure, hurled from the gallery above, struck me, and splattered
the benches round about. There was a commotion among those
in the visitors' section of the gallery. With a stiff upper lip, I
continued my speech, concluding my remarks some five minutes

later, pretending to be unperturbed. After I sat down I went to my friend, the duty badge messenger (the attendants are called badge messengers), a tall, mustachioed former Corporal of Horse in the Royal Horse Guards.

'Who on earth did that?' I asked.

'Well, apparently, sir, my colleagues in the Gallery have ascertained that it was Miss Mintoff, daughter of Dom Mintoff, former prime minister of Malta. She told them that she was angry about the British government's treatment of Maltese people – nothing to do with Scottish education.'

'Where on earth did she get the horse manure?'

'Not ours, sir – too loose!'

As cavalrymen, one to another, we laughed.

CHAPTER NINE

The 1980s

IN MY OPINION, James Callaghan was the best presenter of a case from the Commons Despatch Box during my 43 years in the House of Commons. He treated civil servants with respect and got the best out of them; his 'special advisors' were his friends, Denis Healey, Chancellor of the Exchequer, and Merlyn Rees, Home Secretary. After I had been one of his leadership supporters in 1976 following Wilson's resignation, he said to us with a chuckle, 'You will be astonished at my ingratitude!' And yet it was said so nicely that I laughed.

When Jim resigned as Labour leader in 1980, I voted for Michael Foot as his successor. As I wrote in my contribution to his obituary in the *Independent*, had he got into Downing Street Foot would have been a successful Prime Minister. He basked in the affections of the Labour Party and was a good delegator and chooser of people – and not simply because he chose me as his science spokesman!

This was a front-bench position. The trouble from my point of view was that there was no Minister of Science to shadow. Michael Foot told me that I would have had opportunities from time to time to speak from the opposition front bench in industrial, trade, health and education debates. If there was rivalry between ministers over opportunities to appear at the Commons Despatch Box, it is as nothing compared to the rivalry among shadow ministers for opportunities, squabbling like Kilkenny cats in a sack. Result? I appeared on one obscure occasion towards the end of business on a Parliamentary Order on a one-line whip. But I was not unduly upset, since my mind was on my role as a member of Denis Howell's team, dealing with an issue close to my heart.

Protection of habitats such as that of corncrake was a central issue in the legislation brought forward in 1980 by the new Conservative government with the Wildlife and Countryside Bill. Hedgerows, wetlands and other important habitats were disappearing. In Marion Shoard's seminal book, *The Theft of the Countryside*, she powerfully argued the folly of replacing oaks and other ancient woodlands, which were home to so many species and provided sources of food for others with serried ranks of conifers. The 1980/81 bill, eventually an act, was the first serious parliamentary attempt to address the problem of the changing nature of farming production and land use.

Most committee stages of bills are ephemeral. Old battles are quickly forgotten and should not be regurgitated but the 100 hours spent in committee on the 1980/81 act was altogether different. First of all, the legislation had been a long time in the cooking. A lot of preparatory work had been done in Whitehall departments during the previous Labour government. Secondly, the Cabinet minister in overall charge was Michael Heseltine, the creator in his Northamptonshire home of one of the most remarkable arboretums of the twentieth century. (Years later, when I was among his guests, as a member of the All-Party Gardens Committee of the House of Commons, Heseltine said to us, 'In 150 years' time, who will care a fig for what the Deputy Prime Minister from 1992 to 1997 has achieved in the hurly-burly of politics? But in 150 years' time, they may remember who created this arboretum.' And they certainly will ask about the vast metal statue of Lenin, which Heseltine purchased for his garden as the Soviet Union disintegrated!)

Under Heseltine was Tom King, later a long-serving Defence Secretary, who had a great constituency (Bridgewater) interest in and knowledge of the unique habitat of the Somerset Levels. The minister-in-charge, meanwhile, was my Scottish friend Hector, later Sir Hector, Munro, a former RAF pilot and go-ahead Dumfriesshire farmer who cared deeply about the countryside.

In overall charge for the opposition was the Shadow Secretary of State for the Environment, Gerald, later Sir Gerald, Kaufman, an astute politician with a huge intellectual background, steeped in knowledge of artistic and cultural worlds. His contribution to the passage of the bill was benign oversight but, on one occasion, he took me aside to say, 'Tam, are you quite sure that you are not being a pawn in the hands of the National Trust for Scotland?' Kaufman had become – understandably so – slightly uneasy about the number of amendments I was putting down, inspired by (Sir) Jamie Stormonth-Darling and colleagues on the council of the National Trust for Scotland, of which I was then a member, and access to the Trust's lawyers, with a view to putting into law some of the Trust's policies. Overall, while committed to the principles of the Trust in Scotland and England, I don't think it would recognise me – or, indeed, any of my family – as their pawn.

In immediate charge of the opposition team was the one and only Denis Howell, the most remembered sports minister of all time and as tough and straight-talking a Birmingham politician as they came. Ted Graham (now Lord Graham of Edmonton) was his deputy and, as leader of the Co-operative Party, knew a great deal about agricultural marketing, without a knowledge of which there can be little informed discussion on habitat. Other members were Andrew Bennett, an ardent rambler and hill walker who cared about wilderness areas, and Peter Hardy, who had written a book on badgers.

When Hector Monro was finding it difficult to persuade his ministerial colleagues to accept our amendments for the creation of marine nature reserves, Hardy and I took up the last hour and a half of a session talking, not filibustering, and in order, speaking about the Halvergate Marshes in Norfolk. The government – not wishing to use the 'guillotine' procedure – finally caved in and designated five Marine Nature Reserves (MNR), ranging from the Scilly Isles (very successful); to Lundy (successful); Skoma in Anglesey (not very successful); and Loch Sween in Argyll (downright unsuccessful). This was an example of the use of parliamentary procedures, later to be described as 'arcane', to achieve worthwhile objectives in the 'real world'. Some years later, when I went as Kathleen's paying spouse on the Royal Commission on the Ancient and Historical Monuments of Scotland (RCAHMS) annual tour, we asked the locals at Loch Sween, latish at night at the RCAHMS board dinner, why they had been so opposed to an MNR. The truth emerged. They thought MNRs would involve the coming of inspectors – tax inspectors; no welcome visitors in the West Highlands.

The 1981 Wildlife and Countryside Act brought non-governmental organisations together for the first time in a legislative environment. We used to meet at 4.30 p.m., break for dinner between 7 and 8.30 p.m., and then go on until midnight. To be effective, opposition MPs need to be able to talk to experts immediately if they are to dent ministerial arguments. Friends of the Earth was represented by the young Charles Secrett, later to be their director; the Royal Society for the Protection of Birds by Stuart Housden, later to be director in their all-important Scottish region; the World Wildlife Fund by Simon Counsel, later to be a key figure in the Rainforest Foundation; and the Council for the Protection of Rural England by the very young Fiona Reynolds, now the Director-General of the National Trust.

Shortly after she became the boss at Heelis House, the headquarters of the National Trust, I said to her, 'Fiona, Denis Howell must have been a bit of a shock to your system then.' She smiled and said, 'You can say that again, he certainly was.' Then she added rather sweetly: 'You rough lot educated me on public affairs – and perhaps I owe my new position in the Trust to your schooling.' The 100 hours of the committee stage, devoid of cheap or indeed any yah-boo politicking, was an educative event for politicians and non-politicians alike.

In the wake of my being immersed in the Wildlife and Countryside Act I also wrote a book, at the request of the publishers Longman, called *A Science Policy for Britain*. Since it only reached the bookshops after an unanticipated early call for a General Election in 1983, it can be guessed how many were remaindered. Who would want to read the thoughts of an ex-science spokesman of a defeated political party? Nonetheless, I contend that extended, often gruelling, committee stages of bills did educate politicians in scientific issues, as well as scientists and NGO officers in rudimentary politics, or what R. A. Butler gave as the title of the best-written memoir by a politician, *The Art of the Possible*.

My most remembered episode of my months covering science was a visit which I asked to make to the Freshwater Biological Research Station on Lake Windermere, near where we were to spend our Easter family holiday. The director, greeting us, said, 'We knew we had to welcome your visit as the official opposition science spokesman but my colleagues and I are really delighted to welcome you, Mr and Mrs Dalyell, since we have specimens of the flat worm Dalyeliidae.' This was the name assigned to an unprepossessing creature (albeit one of great interest to marine biologists) in recognition of the work done on this species of the marine littoral by my ancestor John Graham Dalyell (see Chapter 1).

*

Often it is said to a politician, 'Did you do any single thing to change the course of events – events which, had you acted differently, would not have happened?' In one instance, I claim that the answer is a clear-cut 'yes'. Without my raucous challenge to the conventional wisdom of the time that the British Olympic team should not participate in the 1980 Olympiad in Moscow, they would not have gone. I galvanised important parliamentary colleagues, particularly the ex-sports minister Denis Howell, to offer public support for going. And, I put spine into the British Olympic Association (BOA) to defy governmental and political meddling in what was rightly their decision – theirs alone and not that of the British state.

My personal story in this matter goes back to a parliamentary visit to the United Nations in New York for which I was selected as chairman of the Parliamentary Labour Party Foreign Affairs Group. Our host was Tony (Sir Anthony) Parsons, the UK United Nations representative and future special foreign affairs adviser to Margaret Thatcher. I told him of my deep antagonism, based on my father's family history over a century and a half, towards Mrs Thatcher's policy of supporting the Mujahideen against Russian occupation. Parsons said that, as the loyal representative of Her Majesty's Government, he could not possibly say that he agreed with me but added, 'Since you are obviously sincere and serious about the situation in Afghanistan I will arrange, if you wish, for my friend and colleague Oleg Troyanovsky, the Soviet ambassador to the United Nations, to see you. It might not be a bad thing if the Russians were to know that points of view such as yours were held by some MPs in Britain!'

I jumped at the offer. Off I trundled early next morning to the fortress-like building in New York which served as the Russian embassy to the United Nations. I was offered a very strong coffee, which I was told came from the Caucasus. On a sofa sat Troyanovsky and his friend Anatoly Dobrynin, Soviet Ambassador in Washington for an unprecedented quarter of a century and rightly credited as the one man responsible above all for defusing the Cuban Missile Crisis in 1962. They were coldly and contemptuously angry with Mrs Thatcher for supporting the Mujahideen and told me no good would come of British and American support for these guerrillas. 'Do you have any idea what these people are like?' they asked. 'And does she?' Obviously not. She just wanted to cause trouble for Moscow. Would I like to get what they were saying from a first-hand witness, who happened to be in New York for the General Assembly, Madame Tarastakova, deputy prime minister of the Kyrgyz Soviet Republic? The following day, I returned to the fortress. There she was, this six-foot tall, pale-faced, Chinese-looking lady who could have easily passed for one of the 8 million granddaughters, many times removed, of Genghis and Kubla Khan. In slow but nearly perfect English, she asked me if I knew that her country, Kyrgyzstan, grew the tastiest apricots in the world? She also told me about her goats, on land to the north of Bishkek. We discussed honey from mountain flowers and various methods of keeping bees at high altitude. Then she came to the point and asked if I knew that the guerrillas of the Pashtun and some other Afghan tribes were so barbaric that they cut off the penises of captured Russian soldiers? 'What does your Mrs Thatcher think she is doing giving encouragement to such people?' she added. Half successfully, I explained that she was not 'my Mrs Thatcher'.

I left New York with the firm belief that British help to the Mujahideen was folly and on no account should this unwise policy, designed to embarrass the Russians, be used as a reason for making it impossible for the British team to participate in the Olympic Games.

So I returned from New York determined to do everything possible to oppose Mrs Thatcher's attempt to have the British team withdrawn from Moscow. It was not going to be easy. Albeit a number of Conservative MPs were personally reluctant to follow their Prime Minister's lead but it was equally the case that some prominent members of the opposition front bench and a substantial number of my Labour parliamentary colleagues were of the same mind as the Prime Minister. Furthermore, there were respected voices outside Westminster who advocated withdrawal of the sportsmen and -women. 'Bad as I felt it to be that our athletes, under the banner of Olympic ideals, should lend prestige to the Nazi regime,' thundered the distinguished theologian Professor Thomas Torrance, a former Moderator of the General Assembly of the Church of Scotland, 'I am sure no athletes of my generation, other than quislings, would ever have attended Olympic Games after the invasion of Czechoslovakia or Poland.' A very few athletes themselves endorsed this view, including Ian Weir, a well-known wrestler, and Christopher Stewart, a long-distance runner. Even more significant was the decision by the British Equestrian Federation, the Royal Yachting Association and the Great Britain Archery Board not to participate. Members of all three told me years later that they regretted their stance, and that they had not fully understood the true nature of the situation which existed in Afghanistan but were being patriotic.

Denis Howell and I identified the key point – the decision to go or not to go rested not with Mrs Thatcher or her government but with the members of the BOA.

They were dithering and understandably so – after all, when a British government tells citizens of the United Kingdom that their proposed actions are against the national interest, their instinct is to comply. The BOA was composed for the most part of deeply patriotic and normally supportive people. The only hope was to persuade large sections of the public that there were two sides to the Afghan story and that consequently the BOA would have a lot of support in the country should they decide to go to Moscow.

I asked this question repeatedly and, as a campaigner, I was oblivious to being labelled as a repetitive bore. If the Moscow of 1980 really was a rerun of Berlin in 1936; if the Afghanistan of 1979 was comparable with Austria in 1937 or even Hungary in 1956; if Amin (leader of the Mujahideen) was Alexander Dubcek; if Leonid Brezhnev and Alexei Kosygin were Adolf Hitler and Herman Goering, then opponents of British participation in the Moscow Games would be justified. But with increasing publicity I was able to argue that no such correlation existed. We should pause before condemning the Soviets. Why, in Heaven's name, should the cautious elderly men in the Kremlin decide to dispatch troops into what they knew would be the thankless mountains of Afghanistan? For Middle Eastern oil? Hardly – they had massive untapped oil of their own and, anyway, the Southern Caucasus region was an easier approach to the Middle East and Iranian oilfields than through Afghanistan. For world domination? Afghanistan would be an odd place to start. No, what Moscow did not want – just as it had not wanted in General Tam Dalyell's time in the seventeenth century – was chaotic, militant irredentist Islam on its southern borders. Did Moscow go into Afghanistan because it did not fancy the Chinese or the Americans going in? Partly. Because, in Afghanistan, a mad Pol Pot-type slaughter was beginning? Partly. But none of the later reasons it trumpeted constituted a reason for wrecking the Olympic Movement. Besides, if the British government really wanted the Red Army out of Afghanistan, boycotting the Olympics was a counter-productive policy.

I asked press and public to ponder the following facts. First, the Russian government only went into Afghanistan with extreme reluctance, after refusing no fewer than 14 official requests from the legitimate government of their oldest ally to help. There was a bloodbath of 55,000 deaths, many of them women and children, before the first unit of the Red Army arrived. As late as 1978, the Russian 'stooge president', Karmal, was the most popular figure in Afghanistan. His rival, Amin, an unscrupulous warlord, had, officially or unofficially, enlisted the help of the American CIA in his personal cause. For the Russians, this was the last straw. Second, I had cleared my position with the office of Indira Gandhi of India, who had hosted Colin Jackson MP, my wife Kathleen and me at her official residence in Delhi some 15 years earlier, and with Benazir Bhutto of Pakistan, who had invited me some years earlier to speak at the Cambridge Union during her presidency. I did not know of a single Asian leader who supported Mrs Thatcher and Ronald Reagan over Afghanistan.

When the BOA sensed that these arguments were striking a chord with swathes of the British public, their resolve to go to Moscow was strengthened. As one of them said to me, 'You put spine into us.' The less important consequence was that Alan Wells of Scotland triumphed in the 100 metres and that Sebastian Coe and Steve Ovett preformed memorable feats and broke records over the middle distances. The more important consequences were that the Olympic movement was saved. If Britain had followed America in opting out, there is a genuine question to be asked about what exactly the future of the Movement would have been. One of my most treasured possessions is a card, in the handwriting of Dick Palmer, General Secretary of the British Olympic Association, dated 1 May 1985, sending me a complimentary report on the Los Angeles Games. 'With my personal thanks,' it read, 'for helping to keep the show on the road in 1980.' The truth was that the show very nearly did come off the road.

One of the questions, which I believe swung public sympathy in my direction, was why an athlete or an athletics body should feel guilty about going to Moscow at a time when the German government had just signed a new 25-year economic agreement with the Soviet Union. If it were legitimate for Krupp, and a host of other firms in chemicals, electrical machinery, and general engineering, to trade with the Russians, how could they suggest that it was wrong for Coe, Ovett, Wells, and fellow athletes to attend the games? What was sauce for the commercial goose was also sauce for the sporting gander. On first reflection, it may be thought that compared with many other momentous issues of peace and war, prosperity and poverty, sport is not all that important. But in the context of the early 1980s, sporting issues were inextricably linked, if not with the immediate issues of peace and war, with those of acceptable *modus vivendi* international relationships.

*

There was one aspect of my interest in and relations with the Russians that I did not grasp until 26 December 2004, Kathleen's and my forty-first wedding anniversary. Our son Gordon and his wife, Pamela, turned up with a present for Kathleen in one hand and for me, with a smirking quizzical smile, a copy of the *Scotland on Sunday* newspaper. 'You'd better see this,' they told me. Over the byline of Murdo MacLeod, a seriously good journalist, stood out a large headline: 'Tinker, tailor, soldier, politician: why Kremlin failed to woo Dalyell'. I regurgitate the opening four paragraphs of MacLeod's article:

> Looking back, he had all the right credentials: an education at Eton and Cambridge, strong left-wing leanings, and an even stronger maverick streak. Kremlin spooks certainly believed he could help further the cause of international socialism.
>
> And so it was that Tam Dalyell – Father of the House of Commons and MP for Linlithgow – was targeted by the KGB as a promising recruit to their cause.
>
> *Scotland on Sunday* can today reveal the remarkable story of how the Soviet secret service attempted during the early 1980s to woo Dalyell, but ultimately failed because the veteran parliamentarian had 'too many principles'.*

---

* In fact I doubt I would have been worth recruiting at any time in my life! Twenty years or so after I had come down from King's College, Cambridge, Kathleen read in the *Observer* that my respected senior tutor, Patrick Wilkinson, had been a recruiter for MI5 and MI6. When he and his wife, Sydney, came to supper not long after, Kathleen could not resist asking him why he had not recruited her Tam. 'Not the right material, my dear,' he replied with a smile. Needless to say, it was the answer she expected.

The revelations come from Soviet defector Oleg Gordievsky, who has told *Scotland on Sunday* that Russian intelligence believed Scottish MPs were more susceptible to KGB overtures than their counterparts south of the Border.

Until then, I had no notion that I had a walk-on part in Gordievsky's autobiography, *Next Stop Execution*, which I had not got round to reading.

Looking back, certain 'incidents' suddenly slotted into place. On 16 September 1981, Glasgow Rangers Football Club was drawn against Dukla Prague, actually the Czech army team, in a late round of the European Cup. Rather unexpectedly, I had received an invitation to go to Prague from the Czechoslovak embassy, all expenses paid. Since the first question that any MP returning from a foreign visit receives from parliamentary colleagues is (and always was), 'Who paid for you?', I said I was tempted to accept their offer, would love to see Prague and was a great fan of Scottish football but I would pay my own hotel bill and try to hitch a lift on the Rangers team plane. No luck there. The secretary of the club, a friend of my in-laws, phoned to say, 'No. If we take you on our plane, we would have to find room for every Scottish MP who wanted to come – and that would be 30 or 40 more!' I was uncomfortable about accepting the free place on Czechoslovak Airlines, so I politely declined.

At around this time, I became suspicious that my phone was being interfered with. So, I went to see the Home Secretary Roy Jenkins in his room in the House by reluctant appointment. He did not like being bothered after his dinner, although he had to be available in the House for late votes. Though he had been our guest at The Binns, he received me coldly and told me that he would neither confirm nor deny that the security services were interested in me. When I told him about the Czech football invitation, he said, 'Just as well – I am thankful that you did not go.' Later, I discovered that, very often, the Czechs carried out intelligence work at the request of the Russian KGB.

But what really aroused Gordievsky's anger was my friendship – yes friendship – with a 35-year-old Russian journalist called

Mikhail Bogdanov, ostensibly representing the newspaper *Socialist Industry* in London. He was the son of a prominent musician in the magical Leningrad Philharmonic Orchestra. His manners were charming. From the second time he came to see me, I had not the slightest doubt that he worked for the Soviet state – how else was he in a position to invite me to the Soviet Ambassador's reception in Kensington Palace Gardens?

Nevertheless, in Gordievsky's memoirs, he is less than flattering about me:

> For sheer naivety, we all agreed that no one could touch Tam Dalyell, the Old Etonian left-winger with a castle in Scotland. Although never classified as a confidential contact, he became useful to the KGB's propaganda initiative because of his obsession about the sinking of the Argentinian cruiser *Belgrano* during the Falklands War . . . It was Bogdanov who courted Dalyell: he met him frequently in London, and stayed at his castle . . . Whether or not Dalyell realized he had been dealing with a secret intelligence officer is another matter: I doubt it . . . In the London section station's annual report to the Centre for 1983 (which I compiled), there was a section on Tam Dalyell, saying how helpful to us Tam's obsession [with the *Belgrano*] had been. Unfortunately when I submitted the report to Guk [his superior] for clearance, he in his ignorance changed 'Tam' to 'Tom' without asking me so that the document went off to Moscow with a glaring mistake in it, much to Bogdanov's disgust.

I discussed Bogdanov with Alex Kitson, the trade unionist and future chairman of the Labour Party. Kitson had started his working life in Edinburgh delivering milk from horse and cart; it was a two-boy job and his regular mate in this venture was another young Edinburgh lad by the name of Sean Connery – wags would ask whatever became of the horse! Kitson was very left wing and streetwise but he was no Communist and no feminist. 'Jack Jones and I know Mikail well,' he told me. 'Of course he's bloody well KGB. But if you and I talk only to Russians who are pure and have no connections with the KGB, we are simply wasting our time. Such people do not matter.'

Jones, Kitson, others on the left and I simply thought that the Russians should be talked to and, besides, we had no secrets, had not signed the Official Secrets Act and had no opinions which could not have found an airing in the *Guardian* and other newspapers. Kathleen and I had no hesitation about inviting Bogdanov, his wife Natasha (Khrushchev's frequent interpreter, whom we were not surprised to learn held the rank of colonel in the KGB) and their nine-year-old daughter, Anastasia, to stay with us for a couple of nights at The Binns. Of course, we let the Foreign Office know and complied with the procedures then in place for Russians travelling out of London. They had to inform the police of their car and route details and report every day to the nearest local police station. When, as a matter of courtesy, I contacted the police superintendent from the Lothian and Borders force, he retorted, 'Frankly, I am more concerned about the drunken brawl in Whitburn on Saturday night than with the KGB in West Lothian.'

At about this time, in 1981, I was approached by the British security services asking if I would be prepared to help them in relation to one of my constituents, a Mrs Nessie Currie of Blackridge, whom they thought could be dangerous. My curiosity overcame me. Mrs Currie would not mind my describing her as 'politically scatty'. At one moment she was Communist, next moment she was Tory and, in phases, she joined the SNP and the Labour Party. Her politics went with the phases of the moon. Her husband, Sandy Currie, an excellent and well-respected pharmacist by then in his late fifties, lived in fear of being apprehended by the French Foreign Legion to which he had once been fleetingly connected. The idea that Mrs Currie constituted any threat to the British state was simply preposterous, much as she would have liked it to have been thought so. I guessed – rightly as I now know – that it was me and not Mrs Currie that the spooks wanted to see. I had no high opinion at that time of British intelligence as a whole, although there were outstanding and sensible individuals such as Tony

Cavendish, who would invite me to the Cavalry Cub in Piccadilly for free-ranging discussions.

In 1982, I kept my Russian connection at the political level through the embassy in repair. Learning that he would visit Scotland, Kathleen and I invited Leonid Zamyatin, the Soviet Ambassador to the Court of St James, and his wife to lunch at The Binns. Their present to us of an elegant Tula porcelain cup and saucer reignited our memories. Zamyatin had been Nikita Khrushchev's official spokesman and he, and we, had no inkling of the impending break-up of the Soviet Union.

The first time I had any idea that the USSR could break up was when I sat next to Gary Kasparov at a dinner in the House of Commons when he had beaten seven clerks of the House, seven members of the House of Lords and seven members of the House of Commons in a simultaneous match. Kasparov, with all the confidence of a chess grand master in foreseeing future scenarios, was adamantly certain that the Soviet republics would go their own way.

I was chosen to sit next to him because I was the last out, playing as carefully as I knew how the classic Nizmovitch variation on the Karo Kann Defence, a match duly reported by Raymond Keane, the chess correspondent of *The Times*, rebuking me for having moved a pawn one move too far after 16 moves. Kathleen says of the encounter with Kasparov that the reason I did so well comparatively was that my thought processes are different from other people. It's also why she can, on occasions, beat me. I have to say that on a subsequent occasion when Kasparov came to London he took on nine teams at once, including the Bank of England, the Stock Exchange, *The Times* newspaper, Lloyds Insurance and the House of Commons. Next to me was the youth team, where a nine-year-old was spilling his popcorn and noisily drinking his Coke. The lad was Luke McShane, a future Grand Master, and he was giving Kasparov more of a challenge than the rest of us put together.

Increasingly more important to Kathleen and me was our developing friendship with Dmitry Fedosov. Dr Fedosov, when we first knew him, was the senior research fellow of the Institute of General History at the Russian Academy of Sciences, and had originally come to The Binns at the suggestion of Professor Paul Dukes of the University of Aberdeen, as he was translating the diaries of Patrick Gordon, who had succeeded General Tam Dalyell as general of the Scots Greys and who features in the diaries. Dmitry's father had been a diplomat in London and, for some years, served the great Soviet Ambassador to the United States, Anatoly Dobrynin, in Washington. Dmitry's command of English is impeccable and his knowledge of Scottish history – in particular, the history of Scottish families who had connections with Russia – is encyclopaedic. It was he who put the flesh on the bones of what we knew about General Tam's time in Russia and gave us a lot of new information, in particular revealing how lucky he had been to get out in 1666 when the tsar, who had granted him permission to leave, changed his mind and sent troops after him and they just failed to stop him leaving Riga with the 12 wagonloads of treasure gifted to him by a grateful tsar. Alas, we know not what became of the treasure.

*

In the light of conversations in Brazil in 1976, I was profoundly unhappy about any military solution to the situation of the Falklands/Malvinas. At the onset of the crisis, I was one of two MPs to interrupt Mrs Thatcher during her speech to the Commons on the fateful morning of Saturday, 3 April 1982. My question was hostile: 'What country in South America would be sympathetic to British military action?' And on every parliamentary day, I found some means or another to question the policy as the Task Force moved inexorably south.

But I did not at that stage question the sinking of the *Belgrano*. I accepted Defence Secretary John Nott's explanation that it had been because it was threatening the Task Force and the commander of the submarine HMS *Conqueror* had taken action to protect the fleet. Two months later, when hostilities were over, I read an article under the byline of Eric Mackenzie, a reliable reporter, that Commander Christopher Wreford-Brown, had replied to the question, 'Why did you sink the *Belgrano*?', to the effect that he was a first-time submarine commander and that he did not do it off his own bat 'but on orders from Fleet Headquarters, Northwood'. This was very different from what parliament, the press and the people had been led to believe. Small inconsistencies tend to be part of larger inconsistencies; smaller lies part of larger lies.

With some rudimentary knowledge gleaned from my experience on the *Dunera*, I began to delve. It emerged from my relentless Parliamentary Questions that, at the time she was sunk, the *Belgrano* was on a 270 course bearing north north-west – in other words, sailing away from the Task Force. Further, it emerged that the *Belgrano* had been, unknown to the captain, at the mercy of HMS *Conqueror* during the time that she was 'ragging' or re-fuelling. If the *Belgrano* really was a threat, why wait until she was on her way back to Argentina?

What had altered the situation – and the need to sink the *Belgrano* had little to do with military considerations – was the emergence of the Peruvian Peace Proposals, which would have denied Mrs Thatcher the military victory that had, by that time, become essential for her political survival as leader of the Conservative Party and Prime Minister. I could never forgive her for using war as an instrument of domestic politics. As a result of my campaign for the truth about the sinking of the *Belgrano*, I wrote two books for the small but brave publishers, Cecil and Jean Woolf. *One Man's Falklands*, a hastily produced diatribe against Mrs Thatcher's adventures in the South Atlantic, was published in 1982, and *Thatcher's Torpedo*, which set out the details of the former cruiser USS *Savannah* renamed the *General Belgrano*, appeared in 1984

One of the unforgotten moments of the 1983 General Election was when Mrs Diana Gould, a housewife from Cirencester, demanded to know – on prime-time television – of Mrs Thatcher why she had sunk the *Belgrano*. It was an electric moment – Mrs Gould flustered Mrs Thatcher, perhaps for the only time during the decade of the 1980s. Two days earlier Mrs Gould, whom I did not know, had phoned me asking for a briefing on the *Belgrano*. Never was I so delighted.

The upshot of my opposition to Mrs Thatcher's war in the Falklands was that, in the *Spectator* awards of 1984, I was told I was the first winner of the category 'Troublemaker of the Year', for which the prize was a flagon of Scotch whisky. Pompously, I declined to attend saying I did not see my opposition to the Falklands War as troublemaking, and that such an award debased me as a serious politician. When, rather preening myself with my virtue, I reported this to the monthly meeting of my constituency Labour Party, Allister Mackie, the chairman, reacted by saying, 'Most of the executive would nominate you, Tam, as parliamentary git of the year for not accepting the whisky!'

There is a beguiling temptation for politicians to succumb to dilating at length on the theme of 'how right I was, what foresight I displayed!' In relation to the trial of Clive Ponting, it is for others to judge how right or wrong I was and the validity of my foresight. My claim is that my behaviour was impeccable.

Ponting's was one of the cases of the century. It confronted parliament with deep issues of truth and the position of a civil servant who knows that his 'political masters' are deceiving the House of Commons. Much has appeared in print and in law books on the Ponting case so allow me simply to tell my side of the story.

Campaigning MPs are the receptacle for myriad people hoping that their particular cause will be espoused in parliament. I fear that, eventually, many missives went into my wastepaper basket after I had sent a courteous acknowledgement, either declining to help or suggesting a parliamentary colleague who had more expertise in the field in which the letter writer was concerned. But one typed postcard I received in July 1984 was altogether different – it could only have been written by someone with detailed inside knowledge of the circumstances in which the submarine HMS *Conqueror* had sunk the Argentine cruiser the *Belgrano*. And it was addressed to me in the (correct) expectation that I was about the one and only MP who would understand the import of the information. Most other MPs would not have cottoned on since they did not have the advantage of being handed, as I had been, the diaries of Lieutenant Narendra Sethia,

the supplies officer of the *Conqueror* – another example of un-
solicited information that had been sent to me a few months
earlier by a concerned member of the Task Force that had gone
to the South Atlantic.

In short, the postcard revealed that the *Belgrano* had been
sighted a day earlier than officially reported, was steaming away
from the Royal Navy Task Force and was outside the exclusion
zone when the cruiser was attacked and sunk. I surmised that
whoever had constructed the postcard anticipated that I would go
running to the press, waving the communication as further proof
of the need to establish the truth about the sinking of the *Belgrano*.
Running to one or more of my friends in the press would have
laid me open to the charge of treacherous behaviour and incurred
the contempt of my more discerning parliamentary colleagues.
So I went to see Kenneth Bradshaw, Clerk Assistant, later
distinguished Clerk, of the House, on an informal basis.

'Should I read the postcard in an adjournment debate which
would take time and luck, in the weekly ballot?' I asked.

Bradshaw advised, 'Whatever you decide to do, Mr Dalyell, for
Heaven's sake, keep it as "Proceedings in Parliament".'

This conferred 'absolute privilege', meaning that anything I
said was unassailable in the courts. This was of great importance
at a time when Mrs Thatcher's ministers were predatory in
finding fault with me, as they sought to protect their 'crown
jewels' on the sinking of the *Belgrano*.

Then a possible avenue occurred to me. The Select Committee
on Foreign Affairs had recently heard from witnesses and published an interim report on the Falklands War. The chairman of
that committee was Sir Anthony Kershaw, an ever-loyal supporter of Ted Heath and no particular friend of Margaret
Thatcher. I anticipated that Kershaw, an honourable gentleman
and friendly to me, as the father-in-law of one of my best friends
at Eton, Bobby Nicolle, would be incandescent that the truth had
been withheld from the Select Committee. Just as Ponting had
miscalculated about my reaction, so I miscalculated about Kershaw's reaction. Kershaw, far from being angry that a Select
Committee of the House of Commons which he chaired had

been deceived, did what I should have guessed any officer who went through 1940–45 with the 16th/5th Lancers would do and asked the Ministry of Defence for their comment.

On a Saturday morning at 7 a.m., with my razor and shaving brush in hand, I nearly cut myself badly when the first item on the BBC news was that a civil servant had been arrested following contact with a Labour MP about the Falklands War. I realised with a thud that that 'Labour MP' could only have been me. What on earth should I do? My first instinct was to phone Tommy (later Sir Thomas) Brimelow, who had been Permanent Under-Secretary at the Foreign Office and Head of the diplomatic service, and was now a Labour peer. But, given that, at that time, I thought my phone was bugged, the last thing I wanted to do was to land Tommy Brimelow in an awkward situation.

I was at home so I went to my surgery in Bathgate. When I got to the community hall early, there were a dozen constituents in the queue, waiting to have their social security, pensions and other problems attended to, together with the Scottish press corps' finest, dispatched by their offices to interrogate me since someone in Whitehall, I know not whom, had identified me as the MP in question. Rather stupidly I mounted my high horse and told the press 'no comment', at least until I had carried out my surgery obligations to my constituents. That lasted two and a half hours. The journalists stomped off, furious with me for having been the cause of their interrupted Saturday morning, and those with connections with Sunday newspapers were mortified at having to phone their expectant news editors that they were unable to get anything from Dalyell. The one junior reporter who was dispatched to stay until I had seen the last of my constituents fumed in a rage that he had a ticket for either Rangers at Ibrox or Celtic at Parkhead and, delayed 30 miles away in Bathgate by me, was going to miss the start of the match. I was hardly astonished to be the recipient of a volley of unflattering press crucifixion in Sunday's and Monday's papers.

It emerged that the author of the postcard had been Clive Ponting, a senior civil servant at the Ministry of Defence. He was arrested and dispatched for trial at the Old Bailey, charged with a criminal offence under Section 2 of the Official Secrets Act of 1911. His defence, although he admitted the charge, was that the matter was in the public interest and its disclosure to a Member of Parliament was protected by Parliamentary Privilege. Wisely, he chose Bindman's as his solicitors, where Geoffrey Bindman detailed the brilliant Brian Raymond (who was to die tragically young) to handle Ponting's public interest defence. Appalled that I might be the instrument of a long prison sentence – and had he been found guilty, it would have been a long sentence – I turned up each morning of the 11-day trial at the Old Bailey.

Over the first few days, matters progressed inauspiciously for us – 'us' being the entourage of Ponting's defence. Roy Amlot QC, the extremely effective Crown prosecuting counsel, seemed to be carrying all before him. Then all of us in court pricked up our ears. Michael Heseltine decided not to come to the court himself as Secretary of State for Defence but had sent his private secretary, the young Richard Mottram, destined 20 years later to be Permanent Secretary at the Department of Work and Pensions.

Now, I will never know whether he did it on purpose because he was appalled by the deception of parliament or to try to help his beleaguered friend Ponting or simply by mistake, but what Mottram casually revealed was something quite extraordinary. He said that details about the sighting of the *Belgrano* had been altered, on purpose, in Admiral Sir John Fieldhouse's official report of the war behind the Admiral's back. Fieldhouse's anger at being treated in this way made the alert but rather bewildered jury wonder if there was not a purpose in altering, in a most significant way in relation to the truth about the sinking of the *Belgrano*, behind his back. If so, what was that purpose?

Mottram had spilt the beans. Shortly afterwards in the trial, Brian Raymond produced a tall, softly spoken elderly man, with slightly ill-fitting clothes, as a witness for the defence. Bruce Laughland, Ponting's able QC, asked him about some points of law. The judge, Sir Anthony McCowan, known to be a hard-liner and ambitious, barked at the witness, 'Are you trying to teach me my law?' Since our witness was Sir William Wade, an author of many significant legal texts, the jury thought Sir Anthony's treatment of him, as if he were some miscreant off the street, was ill judged. They, therefore, drew the conclusion that the judge was biased against Ponting from the start. Rather quickly, they rejected his summing-up and produced a verdict of 'not guilty'. The nation was astonished and public interest law was never to be the same again.

Given the huge amount of time and effort I devoted to the Falklands issue between 1982 and 1986, it might be supposed that the country in South America that I was most likely to have visited was Argentina. Indeed, throughout the 1980s, I received numerous invitations to go, not least from members of the Anglo-Argentine community, 100,000-strong in Buenos Aires. I would have loved to accept them. But, and it was a huge 'but', I thought it would play into the hands of my 'enemies', a large and distinguished slice of the British population and press at that time. If I were to go to Argentina I ran the risk of being feted as a hero, possibly with pictures of me garlanded with flowers and feted by adoring Argentine girls appearing in the *Daily Express* and generally being branded as a traitor to 'our boys' in Port Stanley. And, of course, it would be an opportunity for the Argentineans to use me as political propaganda against my own country and therefore would not have done my cause – my belief that the Falklands War was wrong – any good at all.

Politicians, who have argued against what is seen (often wrongly) as a patriotic British case, can be fatally damaged by accepting hospitality from and being lauded by the people who are seen as Britain's enemies. Wisely, I avoided going to Argentina until I received an invitation from a source which I thought would be seen as impeccably bulletproof. David, 2nd Viscount Montgomery of Alamein, son of the Field Marshal, had worked for Shell International between 1954 and 1962, mostly in South America. An extremely active Member of the House of Lords, he probably had more contacts throughout South America than any other British parliamentarian. With his close links to the Anglo-Argentine community, he had been horrified at how we drifted into war in 1982. He took the initiative in setting up a conference of Argentineans, Brits and Falkland Islanders in the beautiful hill town of Salta in northern Argentina. In these congenial surroundings, it did seem as though the Falkland Island councillors might reach a modus vivendi with Argentina on the long-term future of the Islands, which would not require a significant British military capability.

Alas, predictable and predicted, foreseeable and foreseen by Montgomery, a number of the Argentinean participants, including the president's brother, Eduardo Menem, and me, the impetus for change fizzled out when the Falkland Islanders returned to Port Stanley and their intransigent neighbours and no doubt their supporters within the British government. On going back to Buenos Aires, en route for London, Montgomery took me to meet some of his friends in the Anglo-Argentine community, a number of whom had fought with the British Army in World War II. Yet again I was left to ponder how on earth the Falklands situation had erupted into war. One memory is encrusted in my mind. Curiosity prompted me early one morning to take a taxi to the cemetery where Eva Peron is buried. Her tomb had become a shrine. A 50-something-year old man sidled up to me and asked, 'Británico?'

'Yes,' I replied. Then, in English, he explained that, as a conscript, he had been sent to the Malvinas. Yes, he had been better treated as 'a prisoner' of the British than by his own officers as a conscript. He respected British servicemen. But, he warned me, without rancour, that one day there would be another conflict and that Argentina would win. 'If an accommodation is not reached between Britain and Argentina,' he told me, 'I fear for the future.' So do I. In June 2011, President Kirschner was once again sounding the trumpets of discord over the Malvinas.

*

I am told by historically minded scholars among the clerks of the House of Commons that I hold the record – not one that I am proud of – for being chucked out of the Chamber and the Commons precincts on four occasions, twice over the sinking of the *Belgrano* and twice over the Westland Affair, of which more anon. Each time there was no shouting, there was no display of bad temper – on every occasion, I was scrupulously polite in my exchanges with the Speakers.* But, on each occasion, it was for using the forbidden word 'lie' in relation to the Prime Minister. I never contended or, indeed, thought that Mrs Thatcher was a habitual liar but, on two occasions, I believed she had told a particularly crucial lie. The first was that she claimed not to have known of the Peruvian peace proposals before she gave the orders to sink the *Belgrano* during the Falklands War.

The second occasion was during the Westland Affair, when I was the MP who named Colette Bowe, spokeswoman at the Department of Trade working directly to Leon Brittan, the Secretary of State, as the source of information about the selectively leaked law officers' letter. Mrs Thatcher was quoted accurately by the *Sunday Times* as saying to colleagues, 'I may not be Prime Minister at six o'clock tonight' and was saved by a wind-baggingly silly speech by Neil Kinnock, as Leader of the Opposition, who over-egged every pudding he could think of. All Kinnock needed to do was say, 'Before the House can make up its mind, Prime Minister, we require an answer to these questions.' And there were at least four obvious, potentially lethal questions. Some parliamentary colleagues and journalists – truthful people themselves – have opined to me that I am over-obsessed with lying. Maybe. But I simply do not think that our democracy works properly if those at the pinnacle of power get away with deliberately lying to the House of Commons to deflect accountability. Perhaps my extreme attitude has something to do with the circumstances prevailing at the period of my first months as a Member of Parliament. It was the time of the Profumo Affair. Profumo had left office and was disgraced not because he had

---

* Robert Rogers, Clerk Assistant in the House of Commons, in his excellent book *Order! Order!: A Parliamentary Miscellany*, records, 'Members named by the Chair since 1945 include: Dame Irene Ward, Bessie Braddock, Tam Dalyell (on four occasions), Ken Livingstone, Dennis Skinner (on three occasions), Ian Paisley, George Galloway and Alex Salmond.'

betrayed his actress wife, Valerie Hobson, not on account of Christine Keeler or Mandy Rice-Davies but because he had lied to the Attorney General and his ministerial colleagues (he later redeemed himself by his charitable work in the East End).

My expulsion from the Commons, meanwhile, provided no answer to the allegations that the Prime Minister had lied over the *Belgrano*. The strange situation was that I had been arguing publicly at meetings round the country that Mrs Thatcher lied to the Commons about events leading up to the sinking of the *Belgrano*. I was most specific about the Peruvian peace proposals, having been to see the former Prime Minister of Peru, Manuel Ulloa Elias, at his home in Lima, where he typed out the proposals, and the former President of Peru, Fernando Belaúnde Terry. Mrs Thatcher made no attempt to take me, or the papers that reported me, to court.

Is it not strange that an MP, who is supposed to be privileged in the House of Commons but not outside, can make more allegations against the Prime Minister at public meetings with effective impunity but be silenced for trying to make the same points in the Chamber to which the Prime Minister is supposedly accountable? How could I have said in the House that she did not lie and withdraw the charge? For the Speaker to invoke what is effectively a rule of etiquette to prevent the ventilation of an unpalatable but substantial allegation was really to reduce the Commons to the status of a genteel debating society. I repeatedly called for a judicial inquiry and, rather than silence the messenger, parliament should have responded. They did not and never have. Nor, when I was proved right, was there any apology, let alone a refund of the pay docked during the period of my suspension. I was disinclined to circumvent trouble as Churchill had done by wrapping up lies as 'terminological inexactitudes'!

*

One of the duties and, indeed, pleasures of being an MP are factory visits in the constituency. I made many such visits over my time as an MP, and it was distressing to witness the decline of industry in the area during the 1980s. Usually, I developed a relationship and, in many cases, friendships with both managers and representatives of the workers. One such was with Cameron Iron Works in Livingston. From its title, one might have supposed it was a nineteenth-century leftover. On the contrary, it had the biggest and most modern forge in Western Europe and made components for the North Sea oil industry. Cameron's parent (and only other) plant was in Houston, Texas.

Why had they decided to make an investment in Livingston? It was partly because a geologically suitable green-field site was available 15 miles from Edinburgh Airport, but I discovered another reason. The all-powerful president of the Cameron Iron Works was Herb Allen, who had 180 metallurgic alloy-related patents to his name and was a world authority on 30-foot-long stainless-steel extruder piping and how active ingots could become an electrode. Herb had had a Scottish grandfather, who had been a shale miner at the Deans Pit near Livingston. Sweetly, this successful and powerful Texan said to me, 'I guess it appealed to me to be honouring my granddad!' The link between the shale-oil industry and that of Pennsylvania for a short period was a pattern to be followed by many more than old man Allen.

His vice-president, the six-foot-eight Texan Jerry Brougher, was a pioneer in the development of propulsion machinery for underwater craft and metallurgical components for jet aircraft. Being taken out by Jerry in his two-seater car 'personally designed for a man of my height at my request by the Commendatore Enzo Ferrari' at 135 mph from Houston on the motorway to Cameron's plant was breathtaking. What Scottish industry did learn from the Americans was the need to get parts on time. They complained that lead time was a year longer in Europe than in the United States.

For a quarter of a century, the British Leyland plant at Bathgate and its ever-recurring problems were at the epicentre of my existence. At its peak in the 1970s, it was the largest concentration of machine tools under one roof in Europe. As the factory was plum in the middle of my constituency and as my parliamentary neighbours, like John Smith, had other fish to fry and others were reluctant to get involved in the complicated, time-consuming practices of the motor industry, I, unusually, was solely responsible for all that pertained to British Leyland, Bathgate and parliament.

The background was as follows. In 1958/59 not, I think, for reasons related to electoral advantage, Harold Macmillan and his Cabinet decided that something had to be done for an area where the shale oil industry was being put out of business by the cheap and plentiful oil from the Middle East. Every year from 1955 until 1961, my predecessor as the MP for West Lothian, John Taylor, a good man, deputy opposition Chief Whip and not without influence in the Commons, would move an amendment to the Finance Bill, urging the relaxation of duty tax on shale oil and shale oil-related products such as industrial wax. The Treasury under Derick Heathcoat-Amory and Selwyn Lloyd would have none of it. The result was that, albeit three shale mines were near exhaustion and would have had to close anyway, other mines, particularly the productive Deans and Philpstoun, were forced to close prematurely, while there were ample reserves. Once a padlock is put on the pit entrance, likely flooding and dangerous air pockets make it impossible to re-open.

A lot of men in the area of Broxburn, Pumpherston, Seafield and Uphall, in their forties and fifties, found themselves confined to the scrap heap. Although in retrospect it was against the economic interest of Britain that the shale oil industry should be forced to close down, I confess I was not angry. As a teenager, I had been taken down the Whitequarries Pit and had to crawl through a long passage, which the miners were obliged to negotiate every working day. By its nature, shale is a very jagged mineral and serious cuts to the skin and knees could be debilitating in the long term – industrial injury was common. At the West Lothian selection conference in 1962, I was given the vote of the shale miners in the first ballot and right the way through the balloting process.

Some years later I asked Joe Heaney, the last General Secretary of the National Union of Shale Miners, why, unexpectedly, he had supported my candidature. 'It was quite simple,' he told me. 'The executive members of the union and I said to each other that we could not be sure of Tam Dalyell's politics but, on due consideration [a favourite trade union phrase], we concluded that Dalyell, aged 29, would be the most likely man to take a continuing interest in our members' benefit claims, long after the Shale Union had ceased to exist.' Indeed, for 30 years, I regarded it as my priority and sacred duty as an MP to get to the bottom of the complexities of individual retired shale miners' compensation cases.

At the time the decision to cajole the motor industry into coming to Bathgate was made, the situation in the coal industry was somewhat different. It was anticipated that the British coal industry would go on forever. Certainly, there were regular closures as pits were exhausted. The rich anthracite mine at Woodend, Armadale, closed in the autumn of 1962, for example. Willie Collins of Blackridge, the Communist pit delegate, invited me to go down his pit with him 'because I want you, as a Labour MP, to know the conditions in which we won anthracite, vital for the foundry industry in Armadale, Bathgate and Falkirk'. The daily hardship faced by those working at Woodend left an indelible impression. Of course, it was good that Willie Colllins and others should be able to work in the better conditions of the motor industry.

This was the background against which Westminster and Whitehall decided that part of the British Motor Corporation (BMC) – a panacea at that time for creating jobs – should come to Scotland. Shortly after I was selected as the Labour candidate, three friends of mine, intelligent, far-sighted officials of West Lothian County Council, took me aside and said, 'We are very uneasy. Of course we welcome BMC but the real employment lies in the ancillary industries which support the motor industry and, if they don't come, sooner or later BMC will return to the Midlands. The supply lines are too long to be economically sustainable.' They were to be proved right.

Within weeks of being elected, early in the summer recess, I went to Birmingham to see the major suppliers of the day – Wilmot Breeden, Rubery Owen, Hardy Spicer, and Lucas, the electrical equipment giant. As my parliamentary friend, the

Welshman Cyril Bence, a motor engineer as well as an MP, had warned me, I made not the slightest impact on the kindly disposed management. The problem was best encapsulated by a relatively small firm that made steering wheels. 'Do you realise, Mr Dalyell,' said the manager, 'that we make enough steering wheels in three weeks to supply your Bathgate and your Linwood for a whole year?'

On the last day of my visit, Sir George Harriman, the crusty old boss of Austin at Longbridge, invited me to lunch in his plush official dining room. With him was Alec Issigonis, the genius designer of the Mini, and George Turnbull, who, having been passed over for the top job at Austin, was soon to go off to Korea and lay the foundations for their spectacularly successful motor industry. I shall never forget what Harriman said to me, as I was leaving at the end of the lunch: 'Dalyell, I am an old man and you are a young man. Before you come to retire as MP for West Lothian, I fear that the Bathgate move will end in tears. When this happens, please bear in mind that we never wanted to go to Scotland in the first place – we were pressurised and encouraged by the Cabinet to do so.'

Harriman was right – it did end in tears. But that is not to say that forcing the motor industry to come to Central Scotland was not worth doing. For a quarter of a century, BMC Bathgate provided good jobs which we would not otherwise have had so, in the context of the time, government direction of industry was far from stupid. What did strike me was that assembly lines, while financially and health-wise of much greater benefit to the work-force, were also monotonous and, for many, a poor substitute for the interest and challenges of their previous work. I remember vividly going to a prize-giving for apprentices at the Atlas steel works in Armadale, famous for having produced the heavy armour for most of the battleships at Jutland during World War I. When I asked the winner if he was looking forward to becoming a fully fledged pattern maker, he said, a little asham-edly, that he had decided to go to BMC to work on the assembly line.

Hindsight is a wonderful thing. Reflecting on decisions after half a century, there were a number of gratuitous mistakes. The first manager of the plant when it opened was Keith Sinnott. He was a well-intentioned man but very southern English, whose expertise, on which his career had been built, was marketing. Day-to-day decisions were left to the plant manager, a tough, rough-and-ready Midlands engineer. He did not like Scotland or the Scots and came reluctantly as a career stepping stone; he did not like the full-time union officials he had to deal with; he did not like the joint shop stewards; and he certainly did not like me. Within months, he sacked my friend John Boyle, ostensibly for bad timekeeping. This was to be calamitous for the future of the plant. Mr Boyle, brother of the future West Lothian County convener, James Boyle, was a coal miner and had been the respected pit delegate at the huge Whitrigg Colliery. He carried a great deal of weight with the newcomers to the motor industry and had a record of being against strike action. In vain, did I plead Boyle's case. Sinnott felt he had to back his plant manager but the sacking of the very man, who could and would have tempered or avoided strike action, led to adversarial industrial relations in the plant. Bathgate got a bad reputation, aggravated by the Scottish press, often more ignorant and certainly less calm than the *Birmingham Post and Mail*, the *Coventry Express* or the *Leicester Mercury*. In the public mind, Bathgate and strikes were closely associated. In my opinion, this was unfair but damaging.

More damaging in the eyes of BMC's most senior management was the disappointingly slow productivity of the Scottish work force. There was the sad story of the Communist convener of shop stewards at Longbridge, Dick Etheridge, on his fraternal visit to the other Scots vehicle plant at Linwood in Renfrewshire, brought there under government direction by Lord Rootes. Etheridge said to the senior shop stewards, 'Why are you guys going slow? What is the dispute?' They looked blank. 'Um, going slow?' Alas, it was their normal pace. The basic truth for Linwood and Bathgate was awkward. The Scots had a deserved international reputation as engineers but high-speed repetitive work on assembly lines was in the blood of those brought up in Coventry and Birmingham but it was not in the blood of the ex-coalminers and ex-shale miners in their late thirties, forties or fifties. Through no fault of their own, many Scots tended to be less productive than their English counterparts. This played into the hands of those members of BMC management, who had homes, wives, children, schools and mortgages in the West Midlands. They wanted to get back and their lack of enthusiasm for the Scottish operation manifested itself.

Stories began to circulate about indiscipline in the plant. I went to one among several mass meetings, confronting a couple of thousand or more workers with the uncomfortable prospect of withdrawal and closure. I now think that I was a bit naive in swallowing the threats and blandishments of management too easily. I provoked huge resentment in the joint shop stewards' committee by saying over the microphone to one of many hecklers, 'If workers regularly go to sleep on the nightshift, what do you bloody well expect BMC to do but to move south?' In the previous week, the *Scottish Daily Express*, then in its heyday as a well-read newspaper, had, it claimed, discovered a group of BMC employees sleeping on the nightshift. I was wrong to snap out in public on the basis of an *Express* story.

My relations with the extremely able shop stewards, Stan McKeown, Chris Bett, Bill Schroeder and Jim Swan and their colleagues were mended in 1977 when I took my guest, the powerful Danish European Commissioner, then responsible for industry, Finn Olav Gundelach, to meet with them for an hour. When BMC was nationalised and became British Leyland in 1975, Sir Donald Stokes, head of the hugely successful Leyland Motors in Lancashire, gave Bathgate a fillip and the long-term position looked brighter. Public perception of the quality of trucks and tractors improved.

The manager during the best years of BMC/British Leyland was Jack Smart, an engineer, brought in from Rootes of Coventry, who earned the respect of both managers and the workforce. He had good relations with the leaders of the two key unions, the Transport and General Workers' Union (TGWU) and the Amalgamated Engineering and Electrical Union, whom he rightly treated with respect, but all was far from well. Moss

Evans, then responsible for the motor industry within the TGWU, later its general secretary, came to lunch with me in the House of Commons. He was frank with me – just as Sir John Boyd of the AUEW had been years before. The Trade Union General Secretaries, given they had to prioritise the conflicts into which they were prepared to enter lock, stock and barrel, did not see maintaining the motor industry in Scotland as one of them.

With the industrial problems of the early 1980s, the writing was on the wall for Bathgate. Sales were disappointing and the supply lines for parts were for ever becoming increasingly expensive. In 1984, I went to the Secretary of State for Scotland, George Younger, to plead for government help. He gave me the impression he was right behind the Bathgate case but, in fact, he did little. Truth to tell, there was perhaps little he could do. As Sir George Harriman had predicted to me, 22 years previously, it was to end in tears.

Jim Swan and a small group of his shop steward colleagues made a valiant attempt by various means to save the plant. Resistance crumbled. There was no appetite for industrial action. It was made clear to me that most of the men were happy to collect their redundancy money and not brew tea outside gates in the cold on the picket lines. I learned that it was fruitless taking up cudgels on behalf of employees who, probably sensibly, had little stomach for it.

Women in such situations can sometimes be feistier. Ironically, at the time of the closure of British Leyland, the Plessey factory nearby in Bathgate was also closing. The ladies, for such they most certainly were, led by the charismatic Ina Scott, decided to have a round-the-clock continuous sit-in. I deemed they had a respectable commercial case against closure and, when not in the House of Commons, would visit them before they curled up in their sleeping bags at around midnight. One evening, a rumour spread round the grapevine that the police were coming to evict the women in the Plessey factory. I phoned the superintendent of police, a friend of mine, who was off duty. He said icily, 'Do you, Mr Dalyell, think that Lothians and Borders constabulary would do anything so silly and probably illegal as to turf these ladies out of the factory in the middle of the night in their nighties? Please do not be daft. We have to live with them – some are mothers of my constables – for many years.'

Eventually, the day came for court action. Scotland was entranced by pictures on the front page of every newspaper of the respectable females of Bathgate dressed in their best, fur coats and all, trooping out of the bus taking them to the hearing of their case in the High Court. Despite the granting of an injunction giving them a breathing space, the factory eventually closed down a few months later. They too had to succumb to the economic climate. The Age of Thatcher had dawned.

A young solicitor called Kenny MacAskill secured the injunction. He was my most strident and vituperative SNP opponent at any election but I supported him publicly on his very controversial decision to allow Abdelbaset al-Megrahi to return to Libya in 2009.

*

In 1986, a political 'explosion' – yes, it was no less – occurred, triggered by a technical report on the disposal of nuclear waste. The arm of the government concerned was not long out of their political cradle and thought that the optimum sites, which they identified, would be in the heavy clay of southern England. These were densely populated areas of countryside, boasting many fiercely articulate electors. Naivety was compounded by the fact that the site most preferred for waste disposal was in the Essex constituency of John Wakeham, at that time the government Chief Whip.

All hell was let loose. Everyone identified was a 'Nimby' ('Not in my back yard') so the reckless Dalyell opined in the Commons that the necessary decision should be made on grounds of geology and local acceptability, pointing out a two so-called 'nuclear communities', who knew about the nuclear industry and knew that waste was in fact a properly engineered product that had to be stored safely and monitored. West Cumbria and Caithness had good, if not the very best, geological conditions and would willingly welcome the work involved to keep their young people in the area. I then added that if the geological conditions proved right, I would happily support a nuclear waste facility in my own West Lothian constituency. I was not a Nimby.

Cue much chortling in parliament and in the press. There was also a little unreported support from those who knew that the phrase 'dumping of nuclear waste' was entirely inappropriate and that what we should be talking about was the storage in stable geological conditions of carefully engineered material encased by vitrified glass. The least bothered people were the majority of my constituents, who were prepared to listen to my proposal, which would bring the skilled and well-rewarded jobs that Nirex (the government body responsible) might offer to the area. And they had for years suffered from the ill effects that the coal industry had on their health.

At the 1987 General Election, my SNP opponent was my erstwhile Labour colleague and friend Jim Sillars, with whom I have remained on excellent personal terms ever since. The SNP hit on the idea of producing a cheap, one-sided election communication to be put through the door of every household in the constituency. They started with the mining area in the south of the county, telling them that 'Tam Dalyell would put the nuclear waste of Britain, Europe and the United States down the mineshaft at the abandoned Polkemmet pit', with the implication that deadly toxic material would find its way into the water supply and poison the electorate. A couple of days later a similar missive appeared on the doorsteps of central areas of the county: 'Tam Dalyell would put the nuclear waste of Britain, Europe, and the United States beneath the National Park area in the Bathgate Hills.' It was designed to scare the proverbial shit out of the electors of Bathgate, Armadale and Torphichen. I heard that one SNP speaker at a meeting actually pinpointed my supposedly favoured spot for nuclear waste as Cairnpapple in the Bathgate Hills – in the view of Historic Scotland, this is the most significant Bronze Age site on the Scottish mainland. The last batch of leaflets was to be directed at the electorate of Linlithgow and South Queensferry, where our children, Gordon and Moira, attended local schools to the north of the constituency. An additional after-thought had also been dreamt up – 'Tam Dalyell would put the nuclear waste of Britain, Europe, the United States *and* Japan under his own House of The Binns'. Fortunately, the electorate laughed with and not at me and I recorded a comfortable majority.

*

In 1987 I had an invitation from Charles Secrett, the very committed director of Friends of the Earth, to go with him (at my own expense!) to the rally of the Amer-Indians which was to take place at Altamira on the Xingu River in Brazil. My friendship with Secrett was kindled during the long hours of the 1980/81 Wildlife and Countryside Bill, when he was Friends of the Earth's Parliamentary Officer. I took our son, Gordon, who had just finished his law degree at the University of Edinburgh, with me, partly in case I incurred health problems (we had to have a cacophony of inoculations against various tropical diseases) and partly so that he could experience staying in the rainforest – a magical experience, particularly at night – and assess its global importance to the planet for himself, as one of the generation that would have to cope with any climate change.

I was appalled by what we found – kilometre after kilometre of scrub, the result of logging and burning on a huge scale. Secrett and I were enormously moved by an elderly indigenous man who, through a translator, said, 'For thousands of years the rains came and watered the forest. We fed ourselves and were happy. Now, look at this!' The driving force behind this first-ever coming together of the tribes from all over Brazil was the group of charismatic leaders of the Kayapo – Megaron, Riuni and Paikan. The chief guest and star attraction was the rock star Sting, who had an impressive record of campaigning for both the rights of native peoples and the rainforest. It is not an exaggeration to say that the publicity engendered by the Altamira rally and the pictures of the representatives of so many of the Amazonian tribes in their colourful attire and feathers did propel the rainforest issue on to the world stage.

Following the rally, I flew to Brasilia, where friendships forged a decade earlier enabled me to have an interview with Fernando César Mesquita, then minister for the north in the Brazilian government. When I asked him why he could not be more effective in preventing illegal destruction of the rainforest, Mesquita sighed, 'In your constituency – I have been in Edinburgh – you, as an MP, would soon know if anyone was to build an airstrip. The Amazonian region is so vast that airstrips and helicopter pads can spring up without my knowing about their establishment, even with attempts at putting planning permission laws in place.' That encapsulated the problem of protecting the forest from gangs, often armed and willing to use those arms.

On account of my connections with the Scots Greys, a regiment with whom in the British Army of the Rhine he had had a happy relationship, the military attaché at the British embassy asked me to a party he was giving that night in his house. This gave me the opportunity, not usually accorded to a foreign politician, to meet some of the military top brass, who, de facto, were in charge of Brazil at the time. They were not thugs but seemed to me intelligent, patriotic men who had enlisted in the army, as it was the gateway to influence and status.

But one of them verbally assaulted me: 'What was a socialist politician from Europe doing meddling in the Amazon? It was Brazil's Amazon.' This was General Leônidas Pires Gonçalves, chief of staff.

I turned the other cheek. 'General Leônidas,' I replied, 'you may think poorly about me but I think most highly of you. When President Tancredo Neves died, you had the power and opportunity to impose military rule in Brazil. You chose not to do so, preferring to maintain civilian rule and democracy. For that decision, I salute you.' It may have sounded like flattery but it was no more than the truth.

He mellowed. A very sensible conversational dialogue ensued, in which he contended that, if Europe really thought the Amazonian rainforest was the 'lung of the world' with a global impact, then the world had a duty to contribute towards its preservation. This was the argument which was to be accepted 30 years later by the oil-rich government of Norway, who then contributed substantial funds to protect the Amazonian 'lung', and a principle for which I argued in several Commons adjournment debates.

Subsequently, and unwittingly, I was to render an ill service to Brazil. The Latin-American department of the Foreign Office phoned me and asked if I could help them out (at their expense) by giving lunch *à deux* to the governor of a small state in Brazil, a no-hope candidate for the presidency of Brazil, Fernando Collor de Mello. I obliged as I often did when they had government or British Council guests from South America. We got on well. I enthused about Altamira, and particularly about the participation of the visionary scientist José Lutzenberger, from the southern province of Brazil next to the Uruguayan border, Rio Grande do Sul. His theme was that, with the destruction of the Amazon rainforest, the air currents meeting the high Andes and reverberating back, eastwards, across northern Brazil, carrying moisture, would no longer maintain the conditions of the Gulf Stream. This would mean that Northern Europe, including Britain, would soon acquire the climate of Labrador. I sang his praises and the 'no-hope' governor de Mello became president of Brazil in 1990, contrary to expectations.

He appointed Lutzenberger as the minister in charge of the environment. I was horrified. De Mello had not asked me whether Lutzenberger would be a good minister; that was quite different from being a wonderful teacher on climate problems and a charismatic rainforest champion. My darkest forebodings were fulfilled. Lutzenberger was counter-productive to the causes he was so ardently committed to and was eventually eased out of the government. The moral of this is that there are horses for courses and Lutzenberger was not cut out to be an administrator.

The following year Paikan, Megaron and Riuni came to Britain, sponsored by a number of non-governmental organisations. I arranged to have them to lunch at the House of Commons and invited the distinguished Amazonian botanist Ghillean Prance, Director of Kew Gardens, to be with us. As the host I was flustered when they did not turn up at the appointed hour in the Central Lobby of the House of Commons. Ghillean Prance was totally relaxed and reminded me this was central London and not the Amazonian rainforest – the rhythms were entirely different. When they arrived 45 minutes later, not in their traditional garb but in suits, probably wisely and sensibly for weather reasons, but about which I was a bit sad, all eyes turned to Megaron who, of course, had his tribal ring in his mouth.

Paikan's opening words were 'I smell food' and he led us, unerringly, in the direction of the cafeteria. Never fazed, the imperturbable Ghillean Prance gently commentated to me, 'Par for the course.' I then took them to see Mr Speaker Weatherill, who was brilliant and charming, as he always was to MPs' guests from all over the world. Gazing out of the windows of Speaker's House, Paikan surveyed the tall buildings of Shell-Mex and the City and mused to Prance and myself, 'You have seen us at home in our forest. What do men at the top of tall buildings over there, making decisions, know about us in our Amazonian home?' What indeed! What struck me in my relationship with these impressive men was not just the importance of the preservation of the rainforest as their natural habitat but the intelligence and age-old experience with which they organised themselves and made their case for living in harmony with nature. Perhaps unintentionally they alerted us, in the modern technological world, to the essential values that need to be preserved to ensure this planet survives as an environment that nourishes and provides for its peoples.

*

For more than 22 years, I have been immersed in the issue that has come to be known simply as 'Lockerbie', the blowing-up of Pan Am's *Clipper Maid of the Seas*, in which 270 lost their lives – the biggest mass murder in British legal history. I am one of what has been called the 'professors of Lockerbie studies'. If asked to write about all the relevant aspects of Lockerbie of which I know, it would occupy not one volume but two. So I confine myself here to my personal involvement. But, put simply, I believe Lockerbie is about the Americans.

Strangely enough, I was in the House of Commons, participating in an ill-attended debate on Scottish affairs on 21

December 1988, when Jim Sillars sidled up to me and said that there had been a dreadful air crash in the south of Scotland. It was I who interrupted the proceedings to ask for a ministerial statement at 10 p.m., at the end of business. Little could I have dreamt that this dreadful incident would be with me for the next quarter of a century.

As so often, the acorn from which great oaks grew came from my role as a constituency MP. I received a phone message, which said, 'Mr Dalyell, I would normally come to your weekend surgery, but seven days a week, in daylight hours, I am going to the crash site at Lockerbie. In the circumstances, could I come to see you at your house?' 'Come tonight,' I replied. It was Hogmanay 1988 – New Year's Eve – which we as a family did not keep in the traditional Scottish manner. I knew my constituent by reputation as a well-respected police sergeant, who lived in South Queensferry.

On arrival, he told me he was a fingerprint specialist. He was sincere and deeply troubled. 'Dumfries and Galloway Constabulary are the smallest stand-alone police force in Britain,' he told me. 'So we, from Lothian and Borders Police, are bussed down daily to help them. What bothers me as a police officer is that there are all these Yanks milling around among the evidence, in a way which would not be acceptable in any Scottish murder investigation. These guys have been flown in from the United States and we have no control over them, where they go and what they do.'

My first reaction to him was rather negative. 'After all, the majority of those who perished were American citizens,' I reasoned, 'and we Scots cannot, in conscience, deny American investigators.'

Doubtful, my police friend left me saying he had to get home to bed, as he had an early start for Lockerbie in the morning.

Two months went by. I brooded. Then, in March, the Minister of Transport, Paul Channon, told six journalists in the Garrick Club that the perpetrators of Lockerbie would be identified and brought to book within weeks, if not days. Now, Channon was a political opponent (and the son of 'Chips' Channon, the most

THE 1980S 235

entertaining political diarist of the inter-war years) but also my parliamentary 'pair'. He was not a liar; he was not a fantasist. Those particular seasoned Lobby correspondent journalists would in no way have misunderstood him. I concluded that he meant what he said and honestly believed that the perpetrators would be apprehended. It was Iran and Syria who were in the frame. Then, out of the blue, Channon was dismissed from the government. He told me, 'One day, I will tell you exactly what happened – but not yet!' Alas, Channon died before he felt released to talk to me – party loyalty was of great importance to him.

What became clear to me was that, for some reason or another, the government of the United States did not fancy any thorough investigation by the British into the disaster. From March 1989, my burning curiosity was aroused. The scenario began to unravel in my mind. In the summer of 1988, the USS *Vincennes* had shot down an Iranian airliner carrying pilgrims to Mecca. No apology. The captain of the *Vincennes*, on the contrary, had been decorated. The Iranian minister of the interior at the time was Ali Akbar Mohtashamipur. He vowed vengeance; blood would rain from the skies; ten American airliners would be destroyed. Gradually, I came to conclude that a Faustian agreement had been reached whereby the Americans would, tit-for-tat, connive at one airliner being destroyed. Far-fetched? A ridiculous conspiracy theory? Well, I did not think so. Crucially, from 1982 to 1986, Mostashamipur had been the Iranian Ambassador in Damascus. He had contacts with the terrorist gangs of Beirut and the Bekaa Valley, particularly those led by Ahmed Jibril and Abu Nidal. My school friend Stephen Egerton, who had been Ambassador in Baghdad, Riyadh and Rome, knew Mohtashamipur personally and told me he was quite capable of organising the destruction of an airliner.

Thanks to the work of a remarkable documentary journalist, Allan Francovich, and his assistant John Ashton, who were to become close friends of mine, it emerged that a notice had gone up in the American embassy in Moscow, telling diplomats and their families not to travel on Pan Am flights from Frankfurt.

Service people in the American Army of the Rhine were pulled off the flight. So were the South Africans, whom Washington liked, including P. K. Botha, the foreign minister, and Rusty Evans, confidant of Nelson Mandela. But Bernt Carlsson, the United Nations negotiator on Namibia, for whom Washington had a distaste, was allowed to stay on the Flight 103 passenger list.

It was pre-Christmas. The planes were eagerly taken up by students and young people making last-minute plans – Martin Cadman's son, Pamela Dix's brother, Rev. John Mosey's daughter, Dr Jim Swire's daughter and others. The British bereaved were profoundly unhappy about the Fatal Accident Inquiry and made an appointment with Channon's successor as the 'responsible' minister, Cecil Parkinson. He received the relatives sympathetically and promised a public inquiry. Just as they were going out of the room, Parkinson stopped them at the door by calling out, 'Of course, I'd better clear the public inquiry with colleagues, and make sure they agree.' A fortnight later, a sheepish Parkinson told them that his 'colleagues did not agree to a public inquiry'.

It was when Dr Jim Swire revealed to me how he and his group had been denied a public inquiry that I was galvanised into 15 years of parliamentary activity, which included 16 adjournment debates, four times as many, I was told by the clerks, as any MP had ever had in the Commons on the same subject. Only one colleague, I surmised, could possibly have told the politically powerful Parkinson what to do or what not to do, in his own department, and that was the Prime Minister, Mrs Thatcher.

More than a decade later when, as chairman of the All-Party Latin-American Group, I had hosted a morning meeting with the then president-elect of Colombia, Dr Álvaro Uribe, Victor Ricardo, the Colombian Ambassador, invited me to dinner at his residence, as Uribe wanted to continue a conversation with me which had been truncated in the morning session. Now the South Americans are very formal. A man takes a lady into dinner so Uribe had with him the daughter of President Virgilio Barco Vargas, who was to be his foreign minister, and the Colombian Ambassador in Paris, who was to be his defence minister. To make up numbers, he invited 'a little old lady' from two doors up.

Since he lived at 76 Chester Square and she at No. 74, this was Margaret Thatcher. Guess who was invited to take her into dinner? Me! I had not spoken to her in private for 17 years – before that we had been friends – since I suggested, twice on Westland and twice on the Falklands, that she had lied to the House. I decided to behave myself and opened the conversation by saying, 'Margaret, I'm sorry your head was damaged!' (A few weeks previously, a deranged man had taken a hammer to her marble bust, on exhibition at London's Guildhall.) Mrs Thatcher replied, graciously, that she was not sorry for herself but that she was indeed sorry for the sculptor.

As we sat down to dinner, I ventured, 'Margaret, just tell me one thing. Why is it that in 800 pages . . .'

She purred, 'Have you read my autobiography?' She was obviously immensely pleased.

'Yes, Margaret, I have read it extremely carefully. Why is it that you did not mention Lockerbie once?'

'Because I did not know about it,' came her astonishing reply.

'But you, rightly, as Prime Minister, hurried up to Lockerbie and were photographed looking into the eyes of the first officer, Captain Wagner, dead in the cockpit!'

'Yes,' she said, 'but I do not know what really happened and I do not write about things that I do not know about!'

I think that Mrs Thatcher was telling the truth. She did not know. What I am entitled to conclude is that she countermanded Parkinson's offer of a public inquiry to the relatives for no other reason than that she was told by Washington that on no account were the British to delve too deeply into what had happened. Had it been revealed that the highest echelons of the American government knew sufficient to pull off VIPs but let youngsters go to their deaths, what would have been the effect on public opinion in the US? They would have exploded with anger. The tragedy happened in the crucial handover period between Reagan and George Bush, Sr.

In the spring of 1991, I was invited to Libya on an Afro-Asian delegation led by my friend Bernie Grant, the black MP for Tottenham and his wife, Councillor Sharon Lawrence. Allow me a not altogether irrelevant digression, as it gives a flavour of this remarkable colleague. There is a Burns Club in Bathgate, West Lothian, which calls itself the 'Jolly Beggars'. Each year, one of my priority duties as the constituency MP was to find a prominent MP who would, and could, deliver the 'Immortal Memory'. Herbert Morrison had done it successfully; John Smith had been brilliant; others had fallen flat on their face. I invited Grant and he was outstanding. His theme was Burns and slavery. The chairman, Allister Mackie, a considerable and erudite Burns scholar and enthusiast, acknowledged that everything Grant said about Burns – who had very nearly gone to Jamaica and dabbled in the slave trade – was true. Grant held his audience in the palm of his hand and concluded, 'My name is Grant. Some of you are probably called Grant.' Indeed they were. 'The difference be-tween us is that your grandfathers were slave owners and my grandfather and great-grandfather were slaves in the sugar plantations, along the Demerara River in British Guyana. You see there was a system by which the slave owner bestowed his own name on the slave.' The Bathgate audience gulped. 'And,' continued Bernie Grant. 'My mother's name was Blair, where the same system applied.' The audience, mostly dyed-in-the-wool socialists who were not enamoured by New Labour policies and Tony Blair, chuckled with delight and exploded with merriment when Grant put his hand to his beard and said, dead-pan, 'Come to think of it, I should get a DNA test done to see what relation I am to the Prime Minister!'

On account of his humour and charm, Bernie Grant was well in with the Libyans. I was to think that had the Libyans had anything to do with Lockerbie, we would have got some inkling about it. Imagine, therefore, my astonishment when immediately on our return, an announcement was made that the Libyans were to be charged with the Lockerbie crime. A meeting with the Foreign Office Minister, Douglas Hogg, was cancelled ('Surely you will not want to come to discuss Anglo-Libyan friendship!'). We got the meeting re-instated. Hogg's story about a Maltese connection seemed implausible from the beginning (this hypoth-esis involved a bomb being put on a Frankfurt-bound plane at

Luca airport, then being transferred in London onto PanAm 103). In truncated form, my view was then and is now that in 1991 Libya was made a scapegoat. The Americans, who wanted to go to war with Iraq, did not want at that moment to further antagonise Iran and Syria, whose citizens were the real perpetrators of the Lockerbie crime.

Since this is an autobiography and not a Lockerbie anthology, may I just make some personal points?

Firstly, Lockerbie would have faded into history had it not been for the determination of a truly remarkable group of British relatives to maintain the search for truth and justice. But, on behalf of the relatives, Dr Jim Swire told me that they could not have kept going without the unswerving support that I gave them in the adjournment debates.

Secondly, it was on my word, along with that of Jim Swire, John Mosey and Professor Robert Black QC, that the Libyan government were persuaded to surrender their nationals for trial at Camp Zeist in the first place. And it was we who persuaded Nelson Mandela to use his influence with Colonel Gaddafi to go ahead and allow Libyan nationals to submit themselves for trial under Scottish law.

Thirdly, I visited Mr Megrahi in prison, both at Barlinnie in Glasgow and at HM Prison Greenock. It confirmed my certainty that this intelligent and charming engineer had been a sanctions buster for the Libyan oil industry and Libyan Arab Airlines, which is totally different from being a mass murderer.

Fourthly, in March 2001, I led the Inter-Parliamentary Union delegation to Libya and saw Colonel Gaddafi in his tent outside Sirte. If I could have read his mind, it would have said, 'Libya and Mr Megrahi had nothing to do with Lockerbie. But I have got to, for the sake of the Libyan economy, get Libya back into the international trading community, so it would be worth paying $2 billion in compensation.' To this day, Libya has not admitted guilt although the compensation would seem to admit this to the world.

In the light of the Libyan civil war of 2011, the easy and shallow retort in various quarters has been, 'So, Tam Dalyell was wrong about Lockerbie.' Gleefully, it has been suggested that I should consume a considerable menu of humble pie. I fear I will do nothing of the kind for a host of reasons. Three things are clear to me: 1) that Mr Megrahi is not guilty as charged; 2) that no 'device' went by air from Malta to Frankfurt; and 3), as I have contended for 20 years and more, that the main perpetrators of the crime were the Abu Nidal and Ahmed Jibril groups associated with the Popular Front for the Liberation of Palestine.

CHAPTER TEN

The 1990s and the New Millennium

ONE OF THE uncovenanted benefits of being Parliamentary Private Secretary to an exciting Cabinet minister is that a young MP gets to meet a range of interesting people he would not otherwise come into contact with. One such was the small, dark-moustached, soft-spoken Arthur Gavshon. South African by birth, he was a veteran correspondent for Associated Press in London. He told me that 'Kinshasa is no place for those with health problems; you should take any opportunity to go to Zaire (as we must now call the Congo) while you are young and fit. Britain has a role there: the Belgians were by far the worst colonialists, worse by far than either the British, Dutch, French or Portuguese, and they are thoroughly discredited.' Gavshon had sown a seed.

In November 1990, by which time I was in my late 50s, the opportunity came. The Inter-Parliamentary Union (IPU) received an invitation, the first one from the parliament of Zaire, to send a delegation of MPs. Mr Speaker Weatherill, in my opinion one of the considerable Speakers of the House of Commons, decided I should lead it. The visit turned out to be truncated and dogged by ill luck. On the only occasion in my life when it has happened to me, my bag in the hold went missing, having been misdirected back to Schiphol Amsterdam. The lesser consequence of this was that I had to borrow a change of underpants from my friend John Cummings, the MP for Easington, a cheerful former miner who smiled and said, 'Down the pit, we were always sharing!' The altogether graver consequence was that, as leader of the delegation, I had been entrusted by the IPU with carrying the customary presents – fine china for our chief host and President Mobutu, down to Westminster mementoes for lesser hosts. Alas, they turned up in Kinshasa after we had departed.

And we departed prematurely. Four days into the visit, we had gone to the Eastern Congo. Contrary to my advice, the Conservative MP for Ealing North, Harry Greenway, a friend and political opponent in that order, phoned the British embassy in Kinshasa on some trivial matter only to be told that there was an urgent demand from Labour and Conservative whips that we return forthwith for a crucial vote. I thought it absurd since we were paired, two Labour and two Tory, and so cancelled each other out. I was prepared to defy the whips but the others, fearing retribution in Westminster, were unwilling to defy and explain later. There is much to be said for the blissful ignorance of being out of contact, deep in the African rainforest. But, there is another reflection. Time and again, British MPs have been hauled back from valuable exchanges abroad – junketing, contrary to the beliefs of some newspapers, was rare – for some macho-posturing by government and opposition business managers. There seemed little realisation of the effect that such priorities had on our host countries who had gone to trouble and expense preparing for the visit. We were on the brink of establishing a continuing dialogue with Zaire, which could have been hugely beneficial, when it was summarily brought to an end for ephemeral domestic party-political reasons. Whether or not the four MPs did or did not return from Zaire made not a whit of difference to the vote which would decide Margaret Thatcher's fate at that point.

Within a few days of our arrival in Zaire, we picked up that there were two sides to the Zaire story, as there are to every issue. On the one hand, the all-powerful provincial governors were personally chosen and appointed by Mobutu. Of democracy there was no sign. But, in my view, the men – and they were all men – he had chosen were highly capable and doing their best to create order and prosperity. On the other hand, there were ominous signs of impending civil war, which would break out in 1997 and cost the lives of some five million people. On our last night in Lubumbashi, formerly Elizabethville, capital of the fabulously rich Province of Katanga, there was a gentle knock on my bedroom door. It was an official who had been present at our meeting with the muscular governor and had not been called upon to speak. After a furtive entrance, he told me that he thought I had an honest face and asked if he could have a word with me. Patrice Lumumba had been his friend and hero. Lumumba, he said, had been brutally assassinated here in Katanga. The Belgians had been in on the foul deed up to the hilt. The official confided in me that, though he thought the governor was personally an able and, on the whole, decent man, I should not be 'taken in' that everything was going wonderfully well.

My visitor had come because he did not want the outside world to be taken in. Life was dangerous – very dangerous indeed – in Zaire. There were many violations of human rights and trouble was brewing. Each governor Mobutu appointed was always from a different province from that over which they governed. This meant that they were supposedly above the factions and tribal rivalries which beset Zaire. They may have been above the factions but they were in no position to snuff them out. As for Mobutu, my visitor had admired him when he was Lumumba's chief of staff. But my visitor used colourful French language to explain to me – Francophile Africans can be marvellously eloquent – something which boiled down to meaning that nowadays his president could not see the difference 'between public funds and his own pocket'. Mobutu, he conceded, at least held the country together. Civil war was to explode seven years later in 1997, and the riches that should have come from cobalt and copper were squandered.

When we arrived back, I fear there was scant interest in Zaire's situation. The buzz was all about the exit of Mrs Thatcher from No. 10. Oceans of film and learned articles have been devoted to the departure from Downing Street. May I be allowed an aside? In pivotal positions, in what should have been her Praetorian

Guard, she had fortuitously placed two old Etonians. Tim Renton, my exact contemporary and close school friend, was clever, thoughtful and charming – but his loyalty was to his party and I surmised from the opposition benches that he was less bothered about a change of leader. (I suspect, but do not know, that his preferred choice was his fellow Eton scholar, three years senior to us, Douglas Hurd, whose junior minister he had been in the Foreign Office.) Not disloyal, Tim Renton was not going to exert himself as Government Chief Whip for Margaret Thatcher personally. No less importantly, her PPS, who should have been her eyes and ears, was the lazy and complacent Peter Morrison – he was a friend of mine and would forgive me for this description. Had she had a beaver of an assiduous PPS like Ian Gow, she probably would not have left No. 10 until 1992. With her leading the party, the Conservatives are likely to have been defeated in that year's General Election. Gow, who had served her so effectively in her first years in Downing Street, was murdered by the IRA in 1990.

In my opinion, Neil Kinnock lost the 1992 General Election, which Labour was expected to win, at the rally in Sheffield, when he behaved like a triumphant Welsh boyo. Yes, I am sorry for him. He was late for a meeting at which he was later to make one of his best speeches. Unhappily, the evening TV news schedules could only take his entry to the packed hall of supporters. His opening greeting was accompanied by a wave of the arms which would have been acceptable at Cardiff Arms Park at a rugby international but not at a political rally. It was clearly a case of triumphalism before the triumph. When I saw it later on TV my heart sank. John Major, a palpably decent man on his soapbox, was going to win.

Neil Kinnock really did care about the Labour Party and deemed it best that he should give way to a new leader. His exit was one of exemplary dignity. The choice was between a clever lawyer and an even cleverer lawyer. Bryan Gould, who had won a seat in Southampton, was a brilliant academic and superb on television but he was a New Zealander. John Smith, a famously sharp debater, was handpicked by the shrewd Dick Stewart,

Convener of Strathclyde Council and Margaret Herbison's trusted election agent, to be anointed successor in the impregnable seat of North Lanark. Smith, albeit a right-winger, was Labour through and through and had the respect of the left, Dennis Skinner and all. He had the great capacity to banter with good humour with those who disagreed with the policy he was espousing. He would cause much mirth in mimicking Dalyell and Skinner – and others.

I voted for Smith as leader with enthusiasm, despite the fact that we held diametrically opposed views on matters of devolution. Smith would have won the election; the majority for Labour in 1997 would not have been as large as Blair's but this would, in my opinion, have been a good thing. I am a Pymite. Francis Pym, Chief Whip, Defence Secretary and Foreign Secretary opined, to Mrs Thatcher's consternation, that 'in British politics majorities over 50 are unhealthy'. Pym was right.

I shall never forget the dreadful day John Smith died. I was shattered. Ten minutes after hearing the appalling tidings, I got an urgent telephone message to call James Fergusson, the pioneering and scholarly obituaries writer of the *Independent*.

'Would you do an obituary for John Smith for tomorrow's paper?' he asked.

'Five hundred words top-up?' I offered, assuming there was already a draft obituary on file.

'No, the cupboard is bare. Three thousand words,' he said.

I have never worked so hard since my university finals – and missed the tributes on the floor of the House.

But, alas, it was forever thus. 'The King is dead – long live the King.' A successor had to be found – immediately. Any consideration of my voting for Tony Blair was snuffed out by the actions of the Blair people promoting their candidate – indecently, in my opinion – before John Smith was cold. I found their jumping of the leadership gun nauseating. So, I suspect, did Gordon Brown, for whom, at that stage, I might have voted and who was certainly the choice of Allister Mackie, Brian Fairley and other key members of the Linlithgow Constituency Labour Party.

Margaret Beckett was another candidate who had been a very

effective stand-in leader in the interregnum and was to be an excellent departmental Cabinet Minister. I have, however, too active a memory and an underdeveloped 'forgettery'! As Margaret Jackson, a rampant left-winger, before she married my friend Leo Beckett, she had eagerly accepted Joan Lestor's place in government when Joan had resigned her education portfolio on a matter of left-wing principle, indicating to me that ambition had priority over left-wing political belief. I thought it was *de trop*. In retrospect, I judge that Margaret would have won the 1997 election and would have been a far better prime minister than Blair.

In the event, I voted for John Prescott. I think he would probably have won the election – just. What I am more sure about is that he would have turned out to be a good prime minister. In the European Parliament, I had seen at close quarters how he could win the loyalty of officials. With the Downing Street machine behind him and with civil servants of the calibre of Robin Butler (now Lord Butler of Brockwell) looking after him, there would have been none of the nonsense which was later to dog him. I don't think I was daft in supporting Prescott. And Pauline Prescott is a remarkably sensible and nice lady.

Why was I so cool about Blair? Partly because, as a member of the National Executive of the Labour Party, I had been told that he had won the last-minute nomination by being anti-EEC, to the extent of pulling out of Europe and suggesting that he was extreme CND, ending British nuclear weapons. Very different from New Labour. It was also partly because a friend of mine, a teacher at Fettes, had told me, 'Be careful of Blair – he's a superb actor, he's good at getting others into trouble but avoiding it himself. In fact, he's a shit and, take it from me, your Labour Party will come to regret it if you choose him.'

Blair's premiership became inextricably linked to military action in the Balkans and the Middle East, an area of particular interest to me on account of my family background (see Chapter 1). It was my father's reminiscences of his period on the North-west Frontier in the years immediately before and immediately after World War I and the fact that some of my ancestors had met their ends in the First, Second and Third Afghan Wars which generated my vehement hostility towards Mrs Thatcher in the summer of 1987 when she offered her help to the Mujahideen.* The issue had also been used as the basis of her opposition to the 1980 Olympic Games. To be fair to her, she did not consign it immediately to her bucket. I knew this because in mid July I bumped into Willie Whitelaw at an evening reception in the Dean of Westminster's garden and, with his own rather unusual kind of wink, he boomed at me, 'Saw your epistle to the Prime Minister. Margaret showed it to me. At least she did not say to me, as she often does, that one page of foolscap is enough. But, don't think you'll get anywhere with her in advancing your views on Afghanistan. You won't.'

*

Iraq was another issue that dominated my last decade and a half in the House of Commons. My first contact with Iraq, however, came shortly after I was first elected. I was invited to Iraq on a freebie by John Stonehouse, the MP for Wednesbury, who had been to Iraq twice and claimed to have 'good friends there' (I am not entirely sure but one of the 'friends' might have been a young

---

* On 17 June 1987 in the *Independent*, I was riveted to read under the byline of Mark Urban, Defence Correspondent, 'MI6 and CIA supply rebels with British missiles – UK and US in covert Afghan arms trade'. Basically, it was about giving surface-to-air missiles called Blowpipes to 'rebels' – i.e. the Mujahideen – to be used against Russian helicopters. I wrote to Mrs Thatcher and she replied on 29 June, asking what it was that disturbed me about the article – whether it was 'the fact that the Afghan resistance are reported to be in possession of modern weapons to defend their country against the Soviet occupation'?
  I replied, quoting Mark Urban's article: ' "The supply of missiles organized by the CIA and MI6, exploited gaps in British controls on arms exports. The missiles are made by the Government-owned Belfast company, Shorts." Is this wise?' There followed 35 handwritten pages asking if MI6 was indulging in unauthorised decision making, why she was 'frit' to come to the Commons and make a statement about the supply of Blowpipe missiles to the Mujahideen, why she saw Afghans in black-and-white terms of goodies and baddies, and going in to great detail as to what I had learned in New York from Oleg Troyanovsky and Anatoly Dobrynin, the Russian Ambassadors to the UN and USA.

Saddam Hussein). I was tempted to accept but I had just started working for Dick Crossman, who strongly advised me not to go with Stonehouse. He was still to become an important middle-ranking member of the Labour government elected in 1964 and no one foresaw his disappearance more than a decade later or those clothes left on a beach in Australia.

In retrospect, I wish I had gone. Along with colleagues, I had questioned the supply of arms to both Iraq and Iran during that horrible eight-year war between them (1980–88). But I fear that I and others rather succumbed to the argument that 'if the UK does not supply them, then France, Czechoslovakia and Russia certainly will. Only international control of the arms export trade will be effective in covering all nations.' But there was no more useless system than the fig leaf of End Users Certificates. Once sold, the reality was that the seller did not know the uses to which the arms would be put or, indeed, whose hands they may fall into.

The world was outraged by the Iraqi attack on Kuwait in August 1990. I too was horrified, even though I'd inherited my father's prejudice against Kuwaitis, without knowing quite why he held them in such distaste. I did know something of the history. Kuwait, like Iraq/Mesopotamia, had been part of the Ottoman Empire. On the creation of Iraq, a process led by the British, the state of Kuwait had been hived off, partly at the instance of, and benefit of, the Anglo-Persian Oil Company, as it was, long before it metamorphosed into British Petroleum or BP. I judged, therefore, that Baghdad's claims were not entirely bogus. Later I was to find in Baghdad, even among sensible officials, the belief that Kuwait ought to be the nineteenth province of Iraq. I was also aware of the very recent tensions between Iraq and Kuwait when the Iraqis, at the end of the war with Iran, asked the Kuwaitis for financial help on the grounds, not altogether spurious, that Iraq had protected Kuwait from the militant Islam of Ayatollah Khomeini. The ruling elite and Sheikly family, however, replied with disdain. In particular, they suggested that Saddam Hussein should go back to the drains where his mother was a whore and that they would reduce the value of the Iraq currency, the dinar, to the value of lavatory paper. This infuriated the pathologically proud Saddam Hussein.

There was one other matter that inhibited me from going along with the outraged herd, and gave me confidence in opposing the war. The Iraqi embassy in London assured me that the US ambassador in Baghdad, a senior career diplomat called April Glaspie, had given the Iraqi leadership tacit assurance that the Americans would acquiesce and take no military action, given Washington's appalling relations with Teheran. Later, there was talk of the folly of appointing a woman as ambassador to a Muslim state. This was nonsense. Saddam's regime was secular, quite unlike that in Riyadh. Furthermore, Glaspie was able and competent. I thought it was inconceivable that she should have conveyed such an impression without a green light from senior State Department figures, particularly Lawrence Eagleburger, back in Washington.

My views were very unpopular in the Parliamentary Labour Party, bolstered by the pride of place given at the Labour conference to an attractive young Kuwaiti woman who, from the platform, produced a tear-jerking, harrowing tale of the ravages inflicted on Kuwait. Now, it is the case that some Iraqi soldiers behaved as soldiers the world over do, and some looting did, indeed, take place. But there was one incident, above all others, that galvanised the American public into supporting a full-scale operation to go to war with Iraq. This was the appearance on coast-to-coast American television of a distraught Kuwaiti woman, who had claimed to be a nurse in the paediatric ward of the Kuwait hospital and who had seen with her own eyes Kuwaiti babies being thrown out of their incubators by thuggish Iraqi invaders.

It was difficult to exaggerate the impact on American viewers. Some months later, it happened that two Filipino nurses, who worked in the babies' section of the hospital, saw a video repeat of the heart-rending appeal. 'Funny,' they said, 'we worked in those wards and no babies were thrown out of any incubators. What's more, we thought we knew all the nurses who worked with us in the wards. We do not recognise the nurse who appeared on

American television.' On further investigation, it transpired that she was not a nurse at all. She turned out to be the actress daughter of the Kuwaiti Ambassador in Washington and her appearance had been arranged by Doulton's, the public relations firm. When challenged about why they had done it, their lame reply was that 'all's fair in love and war'.

A few years later in 1995, on the sixtieth anniversary of my father's founding of the Bahrain-Awali Caledonian Society, Kathleen and I were invited to the St Andrew's Night Dinner. The oil community put us up at their guesthouse and told us that they had arranged a courtesy visit to the current Sheikh of Bahrain. Well, what do you take as a suitable present for Croesus or any man as wealthy as the Sheikh of Bahrain? We had the answer. We collected together a large number of films of Bahrain taken between 1932 and 1937 by my mother on her brittle cine-camera films, expertly restored by Janet McBain of the Scottish Film Archive based in Glasgow. These were of dhows and pearl diving and domestic scenes. Hers were the first 'moving pictures' ever filmed in Bahrain. We also had a collection of portraits and photographs of people living and working in Bahrain during that period – some of which we could identify and others not – many including the Sheikh family. Since she had learned Arabic, my mother had been invited to places and into homes where European women almost never went.

When we were summoned to meet the Sheikh and his younger brother, the Prime Minister, we took these items as our presents in the hope that they might see fit to place them in the Bahrain Museum. Our audience was extended well beyond the allotted time as the brothers looked at each photograph, purring to each other: 'But that must be Great Uncle so and so'; 'Who could that be?'; Yes, it might'; 'No, probably it is.' They were delighted to have images of 60 years ago that they had never seen and did not know existed. As we were leaving, the Sheikh presented Kathleen and me with a Rolex watch each. However tempted, the rules for such generous gifts from foreign hosts is quite clear and we handed them over to the British Ambassador in Bahrain, who said that Kenneth Clarke, the then Chancellor of the Exchequer, would be glad to have them. I have often wondered to whom the relevant arm of the Treasury sold them.

After the pleasantries were over and presents were exchanged, we made to leave. I said that I had just one question on which I would value their opinion – Iraq. They immediately invited me to resume my seat and called for more coffee. They were very worried. The impression had been created in Britain and the United States that the Gulf Sheikhdoms and Emirates were thankful to the West for having protected them from Saddam Hussein. This was not the case. Kuwait was a special case, and had brought a lot of the trouble on themselves. Saddam had many admirers in the bazaars of the Sheikhdoms. There was mounting antagonism to the use of Bahrain as a base against fellow Arabs. The Sheikh nodded his agreement when his brother said that the Iraqi/Kuwaiti problem could have been sorted out at a specially convened conference of the Arab states in Cairo.

Six years later, I learned that the bombing of Baghdad in 2003 absolutely appalled them. To the Gulf Arabs, Baghdad was a special place. And, for them, the damage to the ancient sites of Iraq was an insult and injury to Arab cultural heritage and history. Had they lived to see it, both my father and mother would also have been appalled by what became the Second Gulf War. If I was dismayed by the need for the military response at the time of the First Gulf War, I was vehemently and stridently opposed to the Second. And, never at any time did I agree with those who contended: 'We ought to have finished the job and pushed on the whole way to Baghdad.'

I remember Field Marshal Sir Gerald Templer at the time of Suez, saying: 'Yes, of course we can push on to Cairo – but what I want to know is what the bloody hell we do when we get there?' The situation with Baghdad was identical. Besides, I was told later by an officer, then retired, of the lead British armoured regiment on the Kuwait–Iraq border, the Royal Scots Dragoon Guards, that they had little ammunition left and only two days' fuel supply for an advance that certainly would have met resistance in those cities that my father knew so well: Basra, Karbala, Kut and Najaf. However, I confess that after the ceasefire, I, like others throughout the world who had never been to Iraq, thought the regime of Saddam Hussein would implode. After visiting Iraq in 1993, it was clear that my judgment and that of almost everyone else in the West was mistaken. Saddam was impregnable, not only through terror, but because he had a lot more popular support than Western leaders and the media had thought possible.

I owe readers an explanation as to how my visit to Iraq in 1993 came about. As a *New Scientist* columnist, I had a certain report sent to me. The report was produced by the University of Harvard Medical School and it looked at the conditions which a group of doctors, sponsored by Harvard, had found among the children of Iraq. I was utterly appalled by their conclusions. A country that had been famous for its medicine – and Baghdad had recently been voted the cleanest city in the Middle East – had been reduced to a chronic shortage of drugs and sanctions were hitting the vulnerable, young and old. I had struck up a friendship with a Basra-born engineer and oil trader, Riad el-Taher, who, now a UK passport holder and living in Esher, was a natural source to ask about the report. To my question, 'Do the Harvard team exaggerate the gravity of the medical situation?', Riad's reply was, 'Come and see for yourself. I can arrange it.' Indeed, he was one of the comparatively few individuals in Britain who *could* arrange it. Most Iraqis living in Britain had fled from the Baathist regime of Saddam Hussein and were bitterly opposed to it. I had made enquiries and Riad was in a rather different position. He had friends among the technocrats who ran the oil ministry in Iraq and also in the foreign service, one of whom was Tariq Aziz.

Though I was told that Riad had no close links with the Tikriti gang who surrounded Saddam, I understood that my visit had to be personally approved by the president. This was made easier by the strange coincidence which was brought to his attention. A friend and constituent of mine, Brian Cadzow of Glendevon Farm, near Winchburgh in West Lothian, a pioneer sheep farmer and breeder, had been invited to Iraq in the early 1990s when Saddam was vice-president and responsible for improving Iraqi agriculture production. Mercifully, the rams he sold had done their stuff to the satisfaction of Saddam and his ewes, and my association with Cadzow seems to have been a plus so the visit, at our own expense, went ahead.

George Galloway, then the young MP for Glasgow Hillhead, asked if he could come with me, and I said, 'Certainly,' though it was with some hesitation that the Iraqis agreed since George, out of all the British MPs, had been the most outspoken in denouncing the abuse of human rights in Iraq. So we flew to Amman and stayed in a hotel overnight so we could set off on the obligatory 15-hour journey across the desert in a well-worn taxi to Baghdad the following morning. Waiting for us, all geared for earnest dialogue, were 18 members – all Iraqis – of the British Iraqi Friendship Society. After the first hour of discussion, George prefaced his remarks on the third topic which they had prepared by stating, 'I seem to be the only one here in this room who has not been to a British university!' Sure enough, there were graduates from the universities of Aberdeen, Birmingham, Cambridge, Dundee, Edinburgh, Imperial, Leeds, Loughborough, the LSE and Strathclyde. Some of them regarded London as their second home.

A programme had been arranged. First on the list was a visit to the Saddam Children's Hospital in Baghdad. I was absolutely shocked. What had before the First Gulf War been a model hospital, closely connected with doctors working on Great Ormond Street at the frontiers of infant and child medicine, had become bedlam – overcrowded and short of drugs and, in particular, dealing with very young children born with terrible malformations attributed, in large part, to the use of radioactive, armour-piercing shells during the First Gulf War. In the afternoon of that first day, passing the grave of Gertrude Bell, I went to the Iraqi Museum. A tearful deputy director showed us the first floor, which was stuffed with the memorabilia of the current Baathist regime. The treasures of ancient Iraq, the 'Cradle of Civilisation', were stowed away in basements. Before the First Gulf War, I had been to see Douglas Hurd who was not only Foreign Secretary but also a scholar of the ancient world from his time at Eton. I asked Hurd to warn the Americans about the effects of their indiscriminate bombing. As well as the destruction of these ancient sites, particularly the Ziggurat of Ur, there was the collateral damage that could be inflicted on the civilian population. I know Hurd did his utmost to try to stop the bombing but the damage to important archaeological sites in the valleys of the Tigris and the Euphrates has been appalling and one can only applaud the efforts of those led by Dr Harriet Crawford (Lady Peter Swinnerton-Dyer) to mitigate the catastrophe.

Our second day in Baghdad was taken up by doing the rounds of Saddam Hussein's senior ministers. They were not members of the Revolutionary Council but were perhaps more like civil servants than politicians. They gave me the impression of being extremely able people. Nor were they chosen on ethnic grounds, or exclusively from the Sunni power brokers. One absolutely key position, that of minister of health, was headed by a Kurd, Dr Mubarak from Sulaimaniya. The ethos was secular. George Galloway and I were invited to address a session of the Iraqi parliament, which I felt to be less of a rubber stamp organisation than was portrayed in the West. Yet again, George proved that he is one of the very best orators in Britain and I thought his content sensible, candid and, indeed, brave.

My memory is also of the reception laid on for us after the formalities. Both at the parliamentary session and the reception there were numerous women in headscarves, indistinguishable from those one might encounter in the streets of Athens or of Rome. One quarter of the members of the Iraqi parliament were women and, when I asked one of them about the handling of Kurdish issues and reports of discontent in the oil-rich cities of Kirkuk and Mosul, where a significant majority of the population was Kurdish, she replied, 'We Kurds are rather like the Irish and I read that you British have problems in the north of the island of Ireland.' It was often Kurd against Kurd – some, like Dr Mubarak, supporting Saddam, others bitterly opposed to him. Mohammed-al-Adhami, the chairman of the foreign affairs committee, asked us to his apartment for supper. George Gallo-

way, Riad and I were touched by the goodness of the meal – fish
from the Tigris – cooked for us when food, even for the elite (at
least those outside Saddam's inner Tikriti circle) was so scarce.

After saying goodbye to our host, Mohammed-al-Adhami, and
before turning in for the night, we went for a stroll through the
bustling streets of Baghdad in the cool of the evening. As rather
obvious Westerners, I felt safer at that time in the streets of
Saddam Hussein's Baghdad than in the streets surrounding
Westminster and Horseferry Road, where I had a pied-à-terre.
My friend Norman Buchan (the MP and former boxer) had been
badly mugged there and later I myself had endured the disagreeable beginnings of a mugging before being saved by a quick-
witted passing motorist.

We then hired a car and a (government-approved) driver to
take us to Basra in the south. I thought of my dad as we drove
through Kut, where he and his generation had been hugely
exercised by the massacre of British forces in 1917 and, when we
stopped at Amara, we were reminded of what the RAF had done,
dropping bombs and killing civilians not in the recent First Gulf
War but during World War I. Then it was on to the Marshes and
Qurna, where the great river Tigris meets the Euphrates, at that
point reduced to little more than a trickle by the dams being
constructed by Turkey and Syria, just below the melting snows of
its headwaters. At the provincial border, we were met by a local
councillor of the Baath Party.

As we passed, I asked if we could go and see the inside of one of
the Marsh village houses. We decided to go back half a kilometre
to a settlement picked at random by me. The locals made us
welcome instantaneously, which was not unusual for country folk
in my land when strangers descend on them. What did strike me
was the warm goodwill towards the Iraqi Baathist councillor,
whom self-evidently they regarded as a friend in the same way
that a popular local councillor would be received in West
Lothian. Much has been made of the alleged persecution of
the Marsh Arabs by the Saddam regime and, indeed, of the
draining of the Marshes. Doubtless the programme was an
ecological disaster and robbed some people of a way of life that

their ancestors had 'enjoyed', if that is quite the right word for such a hard existence, for millennia. But the uncomfortable fact for me was that the detailed plans for drainage had been drawn up by a distinguished firm of consulting engineers in Glasgow. I thought that the plight of some Marsh Arabs had more to do with a mistaken idea about economic progress than political vengeance and persecution.

In Basra, which my parents had found to be a truly lovely city, we visited some of Riad's hospitable and charming extended family, who could trace their ancestry back with certainty for 800 years – twice the time since my ancestor Thomas Dalyell had first settled at The Binns. We were received by the Governor of Basra, Latif Mahal Hamoud, which was the nearest I ever got to Saddam Hussein's innermost group. Governors of major cities and provinces were men (they were all men) of huge power, personally handpicked by the president himself. They were always from a part of Iraq that was far from the area over which they governed – thus the governor of Basra came from Mosul, in the north, while the governor of Mosul came from the south.

The devastating effect of sanctions was brought home to us by a visit to the hospital at Umm Qasr on the Iraq–Kuwait border. The chief superintendent, trained at Imperial College Medical School, in London, opened his nearly bare cupboards, which, before sanctions, had been well stocked with medicines produced by the great pharmaceutical companies of the world. The bitterness being bred amongst a population that once looked to Britain made me very sad and angry at the folly of sanctions.

On returning to Baghdad, we had a meeting with the Iraqi Foreign Minister, Tariq Aziz, the international spokesman for the regime but, interestingly, a Chaldean Christian. Communities of Chaldean Christians had existed in Iraq since time immemorial. The first thing Aziz said to us was, 'You were dining us and we were dining you – and then all this happened.' The 'all this' he referred to was, of course, the First Gulf War. He was deeply hurt, personally. Like many Iraqis, by no means all sympathetic to the regime, Aziz passionately believed that the West ought to be grateful to Iraq for having been its shield against militant Islam in the form of Ayatollah Khomeini.

I returned to Britain believing that the policy of sanctions against Iraq was both immoral – because those who suffered most grievously were the children and old people – and unwise – because it engendered burning resentment against Britain and the United States, not only among the friends of the Iraqi regime, but in swathes of the Arab world, which did not like to see an Arab country humiliated. George Galloway and I did the rounds of both ministers and Shadow Cabinet ministers to endeavour to persuade them that sanctions should be lifted. Impact made we little: distaste for Saddam prevailed. One Shadow Cabinet member insulted me by suggesting that I was one of Lenin's 'useful idiots' (a reference to idealists who had espoused the Russian revolutionary cause in 1917–20).

There was a lacuna of understanding about the Arab world. Also I detected a feeling among ministers and shadow ministers that, gratuitously, they did not want to irritate the many friends of Israel by being too lenient towards Iraq. Where I detected this, I reminded them that there was an ancient, if small, Jewish community, allowed all the rights of Iraqi citizens, in Baghdad. Tariq Aziz was only one of those who observed correctly, 'We do not think that your friends in Saudi Arabia tolerate, let alone make welcome, a Jewish community and it was in Riyadh, not this city of Baghdad, that a princess was dragged through the streets to the scaffold for being found to be an adulteress!'

*

When, with the advent of a Labour government in 1997, it became clear that my incessant nagging of parliamentary colleagues was achieving little, Riad suggested that I join a group of Irish politicians, for whom he had arranged a visit to Iraq. They were to be led by Albert Reynolds, the former Taoiseach and famous as the father of the peace process. Once again, no planes being allowed into Baghdad Airport, we made that horrendous journey from Amman across the desert. Reynolds and I shared one huge quality that is useful for any politician – the ability to go to sleep at will in the most uncomfortable of places. For 12 out of the 15 hours it took, the former Irish prime minister was curled up in the back of a truck. Facing difficulties with sleepy and surly immigration officials at the Jordan/Iraq frontier in the early hours of the morning, I was exposed to the persuasive charm of the Irish. Indeed, part of the reason I was so pleased to go with Irish colleagues was that I reckoned they would cut more ice with the American leadership than any of my British Labour friends, who might have been willing to come to Baghdad. Reynolds, in particular, had excellent contacts on Capitol Hill.

We deemed it sensible not to ask to see Saddam himself. Had he taken the initiative, we could not have refused to see the president of a country to which we had gone. Years later, when George Galloway went to Iraq and was given an interview with Saddam, he received a pasting from the British press that was counter-productive to our cause. After visiting again, in my case, the Saddam Children's Hospital, where conditions, through no fault of exasperated (mostly British-trained) doctors and nurses, conditions had deteriorated to become even more appalling than five years earlier, we saw a succession of ministers. And then we were due to see Tariq Aziz for half an hour. It was cancelled early in the morning, on the grounds that Mr Aziz wanted to talk to us properly and, with that in mind, we were to go to his house for an evening meal.

Instead of a half-hour meeting in an office, we spent five and half hours in his home. In view of all that has been written, doubtless accurately, about Saddam's palaces and sundry extra-vagances, I should record that Tariq's home was a pleasant but modest stand-alone house, in a well-ordered residential area of modern Baghdad. Our meal was cooked by Mrs Aziz, who seemed to be helped by just one young woman working in the kitchen, and was a delightful and simple Iraqi meal of Tigris fish that we all enjoyed. Saddam's sons may have earned a dreadful reputation for excess but there was little to suggest that his ministers led a 'high life'. Indeed, there were a number of indications that the president's son, Uday, was the source of considerable complaints by officials.

Most of our evening was naturally devoted to discussion of the current relations between Iraq and the West and, in particular, to the comings and goings at the United Nations in New York, a city Tariq Aziz knew well. I was moved and I acquit myself of naivety, by Tariq's pleas to Reynolds to use his friendships with Irish-American politicians to gain their understanding of Iraq's position in the US Congress. Tariq Aziz obviously did feel fervently about a renewed threat from Iran, answering my question about the gassing of the Kurds at Halabja by saying, 'Dreadful things were done by both sides in the eight-year Iran/Iraq war. But the fact, substantiated by a report in the *Wall Street Journal*, was that the toxic subjects which caused the deaths were only possessed by Iran; Iraq had none of that particular awful weaponry. What could very well have happened was that Iraqi gunfire led to the explosion of chemical weapons in the possession of Iran.' The Irish and, I later concluded, our hosts genuinely believed this explanation.

Telling Tariq Aziz about my father working in Mesopotamia for Sir Percy Cox and Gertrude Bell (the subject of an extremely interesting book by the late H. V. F. Winstone) uncorked a fascinating reminiscence of his own childhood, teenage years and early adulthood. His parents had opposed the Ottoman Turks and he had opposed the British and the French. He is, above all else, an Arab Nationalist, with a vast knowledge of modern Middle Eastern and, indeed, European history – a decent man who wanted peace.

On my return, I asked to see Tony Blair about the sanctions and why they should be lifted, taking with me kindred spirits, Alice Mahon, MP for Halifax, and Robert Marshall-Andrews, the MP for Medway. Coming out of the sofa discussion in the Prime Minister's room, we said to each other that we had had a courteous enough hearing but that there had been no meeting of minds. One curious, well-meant jocular remark illuminated what we saw as Tony Blair's lack of understanding of the situation in the Middle East at that early moment of his premiership. When I referred to my father's experience of working with Arabs in the Gulf, he quipped, 'So all this trouble in Iraq is your fault, Tam!'

At one level, it was a harmless enough remark but at another level, Alice, Bob and I thought it betrayed a basically flippant attitude and encapsulated a dangerously cavalier approach to the situation in the region.

Blair was in what the philosopher John Stuart Mill picturesquely called 'the deep slumber of a decided opinion'. Interviewed on his *Desert Island Discs* on 13 December 2010, I was interested that Robert Harris, the former political editor of the *Observer* and distinguished author, told listeners that, at Blair's invitation, he had spent a lot of time shadowing him and had come to realise how readily Blair was prepared to engage in war.

*

There is a temptation in memoirs to expand at length on how right and prescient one was and how wrong and deluded those who took a different opinion were. Should a scholar or historian be sufficiently interested in the detailed blow-by-blow account of my barrage of letters, Parliamentary Questions and contributions to debates in the House of Commons on Iraq from 1998 until my retirement in 2005, they will have to go to consult the superb archive at Churchill College, Cambridge, who – do not smile – asked for my papers as Mrs Thatcher's papers are also lodged with them and the Master of the College, Sir David Wallace, and the archivist Dr Allen Packwood, deemed that researchers in years to come might find it convenient to have the papers of the arch-critic easily available nearby.

But – inevitably there is a 'but' – time and again, Downing Street, ministers and parliamentary colleagues, many personal friends of mine among them, have reiterated the refrain, 'Why does Tam Dalyell suppose that he knows better than the rest of us about Iraq, and the threat it poses to the world?' The answer was, I thought, quite simple – because I had been to Iraq twice, had studied the situation and talked deeply and at length to Iraqis and those who knew about the issue. What I knew and what others did not appreciate was that little information of value was likely to emerge from Western intelligence agents in Iraq because, in that society, they would almost inevitably be exposed as 'spies' and put to death in excruciatingly painful ways. Such information as was available to London and Washington came overwhelmingly from Iraqi exiles who had fled Saddam, loathed his regime and were happy to goad Britain and the United States into hostility and armed conflict, with a view to restoring their own positions within Iraq.

Repeatedly, I asked the Prime Minister and others whether they were sure their information came from untainted sources. Equally repeatedly and perhaps understandably, they declined to reveal their sources – least of all to me. My criticism of Blair is that he did not ask probing questions as to how exactly crucial information on which possible military action would be based had been obtained and from whom. And this criticism applies equally to members of his Cabinet who were also in a position to ask questions – had Cabinet ministers delved deeper, I doubt if Britain would have been complicit in the bombing of Baghdad. This begs the question of *why* they didn't delve deeper. I thought there was a simple answer – that to meddle in any subject outside a minister's own portfolio was, to put it mildly, frowned upon by Downing Street, while to question the Prime Minister's judgement on Iraq was to invite dismissal from the Cabinet, however senior one was.

My own view on Cabinet government is that a minister, indeed, has a duty to his own portfolio and perhaps that is his main duty but government policy is the responsibility of the whole Cabinet and each member should contribute their own opinion on the important policy decisions of the day – unlike the Duke of Wellington, in his secure Waterloo mindset, who said, 'I tell the Cabinet what to do and they do it.'

Several times I went to see the Chancellor of the Exchequer, Gordon Brown, my parliamentary neighbour across the Forth. I had known him since he was a student leader and rector of the University of Edinburgh. I would come out of his office convinced that he was deeply unhappy with Blair's belligerent attitude on Iraq, not least on account of the consequences for the Exchequer. However, what I felt was – he was too cautious to explicitly say so – that he placed his relations with the Prime Minister higher in his priorities than an objective assessment of action against Iraq. Indeed, I am pretty sure that he judged that, if he kicked over the proverbial traces over Iraq, Blair would sack him or demote him from the Treasury. In this, he may not have been wrong. And, if Brown felt vulnerable, no other Cabinet minister, other than John Prescott, the elected deputy leader of the Labour Party and Deputy Prime Minister, could imagine that they were secure.

As Father of the House from 2001 to 2005, I had a long, first-hand memory. In the Labour government of 1964–1970 there were a number of Cabinet ministers who had their own power bases in the party – in other words, they were members of Labour's National Executive Committee (NEC). Harold Wilson knew that, if he were to sack Callaghan, Castle, Crossman, Gunter or Greenwood, he would have to go along to Transport House, then the Labour Party headquarters, and meet them at the Wednesday morning NEC meeting, at which, in those days, there were vital votes. Blair had, on account of repeated electoral defeats, partially ascribed to factional fighting within the party, been allowed to dismantle the NEC as the guiding authority of the party, with unhappy consequences in my opinion. As a result, Downing Street had accumulated more power than ever before. Of course, Cabinet ministers could choose to resign but usually didn't until it was too late.

Robin Cook's resignation speech in March 2003 earned him cheers and plaudits – it will be a remembered parliamentary event. But if he and Clare Short, who was also later to leave the government, joined those of us who, on a technical motion, *de facto* had voted against war a month earlier (as we begged them to do), I have no doubt that 50 more Labour MPs would have voted against war and Blair would not have been able to forge ahead. I am afraid, *de mortuis nil nisi bonum*, that Cook, had he not become Blair's creature on sufferance due to events in his private life, would have by 2002 become leader of the Labour Party. He resigned when he did because he foresaw that he was about to be sacked and decided to leave the government in spectacular fashion on a high moral tone. I could not quite forget that, when I asked to see him in Livingston, once part of my constituency, about Iraq after my return from Baghdad in 1998, he curtly responded that I could make an appointment with a junior minister in London, as he did not have time to give me the 10 minutes for which I asked during the long summer recess.

One of my regrets is that my American contacts, so useful in the 1960s, were out of office and out of power. General Colin Powell did come to a packed Commons committee room and cut an impressive figure. As the world now knows, the dossier, a document compiled on the instructions of Bush and Blair as a justification for going to war with Iraq, distorted such facts as there were emanating from intelligence sources, largely unattributed. I, along with a few others, notably, Robert Marshall-Andrews, Alice Mahon and John McDonnell, the MP for Hayes and Harlington, challenged it vociferously. The real tragedy of the British government's co-operation in attacking Iraq was brought home to me when, in 2004, on a visit to the Truman Library at Independence, Missouri, I was told, 'When we heard that a British Labour Prime Minister – a Labour Prime Minister – was enthusiastic for military action, we thought that the Bush administration must have a good case.' They doubted – and so did many others – whether even Bush would actually have embarked on the Second Gulf War if America had been alone.

*

A backbench MP cannot be and should not try to be a universal expert. If one does utter an opinion in public on every conceivable topic, each opinion is understandably devalued in the eyes of colleagues. This, then, was my excuse for being a 'Johnny come lately' to the momentous issues involved in the break-up of Yugoslavia. And, it was a chance invitation for an extraneous reason which catapulted me into Yugoslav affairs.

At a summer party Kathleen and I gave for Scots Greys officers at The Binns in 1998, they said to me that, as an MP who spoke much in the Commons on defence matters, I really should come and see them – not at Redford Barracks in Edinburgh, where they were then stationed, but in the field on their next tour of duty. So, at the invitation of their commanding officer, Lieutenant-Colonel Simon Allen, and facilitated by the invitation of a lift in his plane from John Reid, the Minister of State for Defence (and justifiably popular with service personnel), I was dropped off for four days with the Scots Dragoon Guards (as we must now call the Greys after their successful amalgamation with the Carboniers).

During the visit, the scales fell from my eyes. The brutalities and the carnage in Bosnia had been truly horrific – families who had co-existed amicably for centuries turned on one another savagely. A squadron sergeant major put it graphically: 'My lads cannot tell a Muslim from a Christian – and, I bet, neither can you, Tam!' I couldn't. The truth was that the Bosnian Muslims by origin were no more Turk/Arab Middle Eastern than the sergeant major or myself. They were the great-grandchildren of those Slavs who had decided, in the days of the Ottoman Empire, that their bread was better buttered and that minor promotions were more likely by adopting the religion and practices of the Turkish invaders.

I left Bosnia wondering how it could come about that human beings, who had once lived together, could wreak such havoc and destruction in the lives of their once-upon-a-time friends. Not before time, the global significance of the situation in Yugoslavia dawned on me. Through my parliamentary friends Alice Mahon, MP for Halifax, and Robert Wareing, MP for Liverpool Liverpool West Derby, who had espoused an understanding of the Serbian cause, I came to know Radomir Putnikovich, the champion of the Serb case in London, who marched with us in demonstrations against the First Gulf War. He convinced me that Bosnia and Sarajevo were bad enough but the loss of Kosovo, heartland of the Serbian Orthodox Church, would be even worse. This view was endorsed by my long-standing friend Professor John Erickson, of the University of Edinburgh, author of those great scholarly volumes, *The Road to Stalingrad* and *The Road to Berlin*, which I described in an obituary for the *Independent* and in his encomium from the pulpit of St Mary's Cathedral in

Edinburgh as the most remarkable narrative of war since Thucydides wrote *History of the Peloponnesian War*, his account of the war between Sparta and Athens. Married to Ljubica, a Serb, Erickson knew a great deal about the issue.

Against this background, I eagerly accepted the invitation of Lieutenant Colonel David Allfrey, then the commanding officer, to visit the Royal Scots Dragoon Guards on their next tour of duty in Yugoslavia, this time in Kosovo. I record three of many episodes.

One was walking through the nickel plant, Kosovo's only real engine of economic growth, which had been left a tangled mess of twisted machinery by NATO bombing. Wanton, senseless and counter-productive to any hope of economic re-generation, this was American policy.

The second was visiting the Serbian Orthodox Church bishop, isolated in his monastic surroundings at Gracanica, surely one of the glories of medieval European architecture. His was a woeful tale of persecution by the Albanian majority, who had set fire to so many religious buildings.

My third indelible memory is being taken in a tank, commanded by Major Ben Edwards (later to command the Scots Dragoon Guards with distinction in the Second Gulf War) to an Albanian-run village. Through an interpreter, I was introduced to the headman. A heated discussion gradually developed between him and me. He contended that the British Army should remain for at least 20 years to assist the Albanians against the Serbs. And it became only too clear that what Putnikovich had told me about Albanians having a policy of taking over Kosovo by 'the power of the penis' was no exaggeration. The headman boasted of women giving birth to 12 or more children to Albanian men.

As we parted company, Colonel Allfrey whispered to me, 'I'm delighted that some British politician could tell these people a few home truths.'

I replied, 'I would not have dared enter into a dispute with that fellow and his cronies unless I had known that your loaded tank machine guns were behind me.' I felt the Albanians would happily have slit my throat.

On my return to Westminster, my support for the Serbian case had an icy reception from the Parliamentary Labour Party. Tony Blair had become a great hero to the Albanians and he wallowed in television pictures of him being garlanded with flowers by grateful Albanians. NATO actions in Kosovo were portrayed as being an example of ethical foreign policy. A few months later, Alice Mahon and I flew to Budapest and made the long car journey to Belgrade. I was shocked. Great, solid buildings of the Austro-Hungarian Empire were in a precarious state as a result of NATO bombing. It was difficult enough to repair Bishop's Gate in London; it will be ten times more difficult to repair the city-centre structures of nineteenth-century Belgrade.

My views on Kosovo, if controversial, are shared by some cognoscenti. Sir Brian Barder, a friend at Cambridge (where he was chairman of the university Labour Club) who had become an ambassador and British High Commissioner in Nigeria, wrote to me:

> It is extraordinary that so few pundits and commentators seem to recognize the many parallels between Kosovo and Iraq – use of force without UN authority, so amounting to the crime of aggression; false justification for resort to force (the sham conference at Rambouillet to concoct a pretext for attacking the Serbs); misrepresentation of intelligence about WMD; doomed attempt to side-line or exclude Russia; botched military action and botched management of the aftermath; and, in the case of Kosovo, total failure of the NATO attack on Yugoslavia either to stop the flow of refugees out of Kosovo (it actually only began after the NATO attack was launched) or to force the Serbs out of Kosovo (which was eventually achieved by the secret diplomacy of the US-Russian-Finnish Negotiating Team, set up by President Clinton when the bombing was getting nowhere) or to topple Milosevic (ejected many months later by his own electorate).

I make no apology for trying to discredit some of the perceived wisdom about Kosovo.

*

In 1999, I was chairman of the All-Party Latin-American Group of MPs and was chosen by Madam Speaker Boothroyd and her Committee of Selection to lead the IPU delegation to Peru. I had been to Lima 15 years before on a flying two-day visit with my Argentinean friend Guillermo Makin, an academic at Cambridge, to see President Fernando Belaunde Terry and his prime minister, Manuel Ulloa Elias, to ascertain the facts about the Peruvian Peace Proposals in relation to the Falklands conflict. Forced to have a 48-hour turnaround, I had acquired a compulsive urge to return to this fascinating land.

Three months before going, we had a planning session in London. Either we could spend three days of our six-day visit going to the famous attractions of Cuzco and Machu Picchu or we could go to Iquitos, on the other side of the Andes, and see the challenges facing Amazonian Peru. Since it was a working visit and not a jaunt, I opted for non-tourist Iquitos. Our Peruvian hosts were pleased. Most foreign politicians had made a beeline for Machu Picchu and they wanted to show modern Peru and how it had changed for the better, since my previous visit. I quote from my Outward Delegation report:

Our host, Doctora Martha Hildebrandt, president of the Congress, received us in the Palace of Legislation. A formidable speaker, she made it clear that she regarded herself first and foremost as an academic professor, now, on a temporary basis, performing a political task at the request of President Fujimori. A crony? No. She had not met the president until she was asked by him to take on the job in succession to Dr Martha Chavez, who had come to London as Speaker in 1996. He had seen her on a couple of television programmes.

Later, we had a meeting with the former President of the Congress, Señor Vicotor Joy Way Rojas, the President of the Congressional Commission on Foreign Relations and the secretary of the Peruvian Group of the IPU [Inter-Parliamentary Union] Señor Oswaldo Sandoval Aguirre. They told us that they were agricultural economists before becoming MPs!

After a working lunch, which included members of the PromPeru [the Peruvian Tourist Board] on the Peruvian economy, we were well informed of a creditable growth rate, and the achievement of the Fujimori government in bringing down hyper-inflation to an equilibrium of c. 4 per cent. Time to relax and to visit the gruesome Museum of the Inquisition. What was clear was that the atrocities of the Inquisition have been widely exaggerated, and those who actually died at the hands of the Inquisition can be numbered not in hundreds, but in tens. Dining at the Museum of Congress in the Plaza Bolivar, our hostess proved that she could indulge with relish in fierce political argument. Vehemently, she defended the Fujimori Government's handling of terrorism – Sendero Luminoso (Shining Path) had been among the most fearsome of their genre to emerge on the face of the planet – and on drugs . . .

[W]e will never forget the Mayor of Iquitos. 'The grey warships you see are not to fight Brazil. They are to fight coca leaf merchants. The dogs sniff every piece of luggage. We do our best to fight drugs. But our hands are tied behind our backs, so long as you allow anonymous bank accounts!'

On our return to Lima, we put the mayor's sentiments to the UN Drug Central Agency and to President Alberto Fujimori, in a 50-minute meeting. They could not have been more forceful in urging the developed world to tackle anonymous numbered bank accounts!

There was an outstanding sequel to this visit. Every member of the delegation, on our return, followed up the issue of money laundering with the Treasury and had some impact. Normally, a head of state does not see an IPU delegation. However, I asked my friend, the distinguished Amazonian botanist Professor Ghillean Prance, if he could arrange a meeting with President Fujimori himself, which he did.

At the meeting, one of the delegation members, the irrepressible Lady Flather, who was of Indian extraction, asked a question that the rest of us could not have got away with but the answer to which intrigued us: 'How is it, Mr President, that you, to all intents a Japanese person, could manage to achieve power in a Latin American state across the Pacific?' He answered at great length and movingly, to the effect that Peru needed an outsider at that time in its history to impose law and order, not only on guerrilla groups such as the Sendero Luminoso but also political factions and sectional interests, who found it impossible to reconcile with each other. Whatever happened later – and I tend to believe he was framed – President Fujimori will have his place in South American history.

*

In the year 2000, it was not my turn to lead another IPU delegation to Latin America. The former Conservative minister, Sir Peter Emery, was chosen but, at the last moment, Lady Emery put her foot down and said Peter was not to go for medical reasons (and, alas, was soon to die). The assigned deputy leader, my friend Andrew Bennett, hitherto a super-fit hill walker, also withdrew for medical reasons. So Madam Speaker Boothroyd invited me to lead the delegation. I was not a member of the delegation but was chosen as chairman of the All-Party Latin-America Group. I recall these long-forgotten details to protect myself from charges of ignorance for, had I been involved in the planning stages of the delegation, I would have resisted an itinerary which had us flying from London, with a flight stopover at Miami, to La Paz, the capital of Bolivia. I would have insisted that we started our visit in the southern city of Santa Cruz and acclimatise to reach La Paz at 13,000 feet (the height of the Matterhorn summit) above sea level. The reason that the height hazards of La Paz had impacted on my mind was this – how on earth did it come about that mighty football sides, Argentina and Brazil, both world champions, had been trounced in away matches against Bolivia? The answer was that the venue was La Paz and the less skilful Bolivian side were used to the altitude conditions – the boys from Buenos Aires, Sao Paulo or Rio de Janeiro were struggling and breathless.

My daughter-in-law, Pamela Leslie, a medical doctor, had warned me to insist on four hours' rest on arrival before attempting to fulfil any engagement. Alas, we were met by the excellent British Ambassador to Bolivia, Graham Minter, on the tarmac. 'You have a choice,' he said, 'either you go to the hotel and rest or, since this will be your only opportunity to do so, you come with me to see Lake Titicaca and the dramatic ruins and superb archaeological site of Tiwanaku.' We succumbed. On the way back from the lake, we were held up by three roadblocks of striking workers, presaging the discontent which was to bring Evo Morales to the presidency five years later. Only Minter's charm and fluent Spanish enabled us to run the gauntlet. Delayed, tired and hungry, we eventually returned to our hotel only to find that the British Council in La Paz had laid on a reception and at least the leader of the delegation had to turn up. They had gone to trouble and, like the British Council the world over, performed estimable work.

Exhausted, I returned to the hotel and flopped into bed. In the middle of the night I woke with excruciating pains. Altitude had had its revenge. I really did think my end was nigh. I scribbled a note to my colleagues asking them to tell Kathleen not to try and have my body returned to Britain – from constituency work I knew the dramas, agony and expense of repatriating corpses – but to let it remain in the Andes. Then I staggered down to the hotel desk and produced the medical emergency card which, as leader of the delegation, I had in my pocket. I handed it to the sleepy, night-duty receptionist behind the desk, a diminutive, wizened indigenous Bolivian with a kindly face. I asked him if he could get through to the medical centre which served the diplomatic and ex-patriot community. He went away and, on his return from a back room, I asked him if he had got through. 'No,' he said quietly, 'I phoned my own doctor. He says he will come round if I call him again but only after you have drunk a pot-ful of tea.' And off he shuffled to boil the kettle. Five minutes later he resurfaced with the pot of tea – not, of course, ordinary tea, as I realised after the first mouthful, but coca tea, a substance banned in the UK. Registering my surprise, the kind man smiled and said, 'If it was good enough for the Great Inca, it is good enough for you!' Four hours later, having slept, I came down to join my colleagues at breakfast feeling fine. They had themselves had varied experiences but had had the advantage of being given instructions as to how to operate the oxygen machine, an elderly contraption, in each room, while I had been absent doing my duty at the British Council.

That morning, we were programmed to make a courtesy call on our host, the vice-president, Jorge Quiroga, acting president of Bolivia. In all my life, my jaw has never dropped so sharply as when we went into that room. You see, it was the duty of the leader of a delegation to take with him in his hand baggage the beautiful Wedgewood Westminster plate as a gift to our chief host. Accordingly, I had stored it carefully in the cabin rack above my seat on the plane from London. When we landed at La Paz, a very cavalier, as I supposed American, student roughly handled my bag while extracting his own. He had been sitting comfortably with his girlfriend, seemingly snogging in the front seats of the first-class cabin. I ejaculated, 'For pity's sake, have a bloody care about my bag – it contains a fragile Wedgewood plate for the vice-president of Bolivia!' To my irritation he just grinned and went on his way. Heaven's above, this 'cavalier student' on the Miami–La Paz plane was our host, vice-president and acting president of Congress, Quiroga. He laughed uproariously. 'My wife nudged me,' he said, 'and told me to introduce myself and save you the bother of carrying the plate. But I thought, no, I will wait until the delegation – and the gift – arrive in my office!'

Quiroga was a University of Texas-trained economist, tougher in capitalist outlook than many who came from that stable. After an hour of intense political discussions, he hosted a dinner for us. The delegation thought that, after a mandatory five-year gap, following his vice-presidency, he would be a formidable contender for the presidency in 2007. But I shall not forget sitting next to a senior university professor who forecast precisely what, in the event, occurred – that Bolivia, with significantly the highest indigenous Indian population in Latin America, would elect a president who would oppose the entrenched establishment elite descended from Spaniards and Italians.

On day three, courtesy of the US Embassy, we embarked on a Hercules aircraft to take us 300 miles to Chapare, centre of the illicit coca-leaf growing area. Although we were forbidden to put ourselves at risk by travelling outside the military base at this time of social unrest, we were shown round the startling drugs museum. There was a poignant war memorial to those who had given up their lives in the 15-year struggle against drugs. No one can be in doubt about the seriousness of purpose of the Bolivian government to eradicate the illicit coca from this, the poorest of South American countries. We arrived in Santa Cruz and had discussions with many commercial interests.

Courtesy of the oil company, Chaco, in which BP/Amoco has the majority private-sector stake, the delegation and the British Ambassador flew to a gas exploration site in the Bolivia Chaco. Familiar with North Sea exploration, the delegation had never before seen land exploration in a difficult geological mountain area. Skilled men from as far apart as Northern Ireland and Patagonia, as well as many Bolivians, were co-operating under the watchful discipline of a mighty Texan site manager, Ben Arot. To lay persons, it was an awesome undertaking.

And it was, indeed, the indigenous Evo Morales, rather than Quiroga, who assumed the presidency of Bolivia.

*

Lest the reader think I spent most of the 1990s abroad, domestic concerns also occupied my time. These included the only other occasion in which I became entangled publicly in Irish affairs – and, like so many other of my campaigns, it had its genesis in my constituency work. There came to see me at my Bathgate surgery the ramrod figure, wearing his Brigade of Guards tie, of police Constable John Hamilton of Torphichen. He was secretary of the local branch of the Scots Guards Association. He said that his members were incensed by the treatment of two guardsmen, Jim Fisher and Mark Wright, who had been court-martialed.

I felt a natural empathy with the squaddies. The reactions, Hamilton said, of his members was 'There, but for the grace of God, go we.' In truncated form, the case involved the shooting of a Northern Irish Catholic boy, who was holding a jam jar which in the split second of the moment they thought was a Molotov cocktail, about to be thrown at them. I told Hamilton that I would do my best to put their side of the story. In this campaign

I followed a sensible approach, raising it in the House of Commons, emphasising that I was regurgitating the deep concern of private soldiers and not simply acting on behalf of the generals. This appealed, at any rate, to a few of my Labour colleagues but bluntly the majority of the Parliamentary Labour Party were angry that I seemed to be taking the side of the army against the Irish Catholic civilian population and against an innocent teenage youth. His family were even angrier and denounced me to the Labour leadership. However, I rather treasure the approval of Scots Guards generals Sir Michael Gow and Sir David Scott-Barrett, and of Major Ronnie Wilkie, writing officially on behalf of the Scots Guards Association.

On 16 March 1998, I asked the Secretary of State for Defence, John Reid, if he would make a statement on the procedure relating to the issuing of a challenge current in the first Battalion Scots Guards in September 1992, on how many occasions, since 1 September 1992, such procedures had not been complied with and what revision to procedures has taken place since that date.

Reid, who was the most popular of all Labour Defence Secretaries with the army, replied that he would write a letter to me and put it in the Library of the House of Commons, which meant that it was the authoritative outline of the Government's position. If I quote rather extensively from the letter, it is because it encapsulates a very important point:

Soldiers receive extensive training for operating in Northern Ireland, and particular emphasis is given to the law relating to the use of lethal force. It is impressed upon soldiers that any person may use reasonable force in the prevention of crime, and that the reasonableness of force is dependent upon the particular circumstances. In all situations only the minimum force necessary should be used and lethal force should only be used as a last resort.

The rules for opening fire are contained within the yellow card and issued to all soldiers deployed to Northern Ireland. The yellow card summarised the law and is used as an aide-memoire by soldiers, but it does not provide immunity from prosecution. Whilst on duty in Northern Ireland it is essential that soldiers operate within the law and they are subject to the same criminal law as other citizens of the United Kingdom. Although soldiers receive a great deal of guidance and instruction on the use of lethal force, it is only the individual soldier who can judge when lethal force should be used in particular circumstances; and the individual soldier takes responsibility for that decision in circumstances.

Afterword

I AM OFTEN ASKED, 'Do you miss the House of Commons?'
The answer is 'No', and nor have I set foot in the Palace of
Westminster since I ceased to be an MP in April 2005. The truth
is that I would have greatly missed parliament had it remained
the institution it once was and to which I was first elected. I do
not at all miss parliament as it has become. Perhaps, as I
approach my eighth decade, I seem to be wielding a stick at
the modern world but I do think that the parliament of 1959 to
1964, which I joined in 1962, was of greater service to those who
elected us than the parliament of 2001 to 2005 when I left the
Commons. It is not that the current MPs are less hard working –
on the contrary, they appear to be more hard working at
politicking.

Let me be frank; I am completely out of step with what is
becoming the general trend in all parties, whereby MPs rising to
the top of the greasy pole have little or no experience outside
politics. I believe that the House of Commons benefitted greatly
in earlier times from the presence of those who earned much of
their living outside politics. Now, the career path of too many of
those at the top in politics has been school, university, researcher
to an MP, think tank, safe seat and then a meteoric rise through
the great offices of state. If ever I had won a place in the first 20 of
the ballot for Private Members' Bills, which I never did in spite of
putting my name in the draw on 45 occasions, I would have
introduced a Bill to ban anyone standing for parliament who had
not had, during their working lives, a job unrelated to politics for

five years. And being a housewife *is* a job. As Lord Pter Mandelson warned the Shadow Cabinet on 20 June 2011, the public will never be won over by a party led by 'ex-political assistants, researchers and Trade Union apparatchiks recruited from inside the Westminster bubble'. One thing is for sure and that is, whereas it was possible in 1962 for a constituency Labour Party to adopt a Tam Dalyell, 50 years later in 2012 a Tam Dalyell-type would not stand a cat-in-hell's chance of being selected. The current rules and vetting would see to that. If there are awkward candidates, it is a great disservice to democracy if they should feel the need to dissemble their awkwardness throughout the selection process.

To bolster the case against full-time MPs, I return to the parliament to which I was first elected but, in doing so, I must make a confession. At the age of almost 80, I am still crystal clear about people and events with whom and with which I was involved at the age of 30. I am far less clear about people and events when I was 60. 1962 is etched on my memory but 1992 would be hazy in many areas. It is a common human experience. If it has appeared that I have often been unduly kind about those who were political opponents, it is, I suppose, partly because, as Denis Healey memorably put it in a reference to Margaret Thatcher, 'when we politicians are lucky enough to reach 80 years of age, and older, we are all friends now!' But it is partly that, from the day I became a candidate in the then Tory seat of Roxburgh, Selkirk and Peebles, I was determined not to name call or be gratuitously rude to those who took a different view. Besides, those who live in glasshouses are unwise to throw stones and the House of The Binns most certainly was a glasshouse! If it is interjected that this is a bit rich coming from the man who was ejected from the House of Commons more than any other MP for calling the Prime Minister a liar, I respond that I never resorted to generalised personal abuse. I pinpointed a specific lie told for a specific purpose – self-preservation.

Since I retired in 2005, Kathleen has often said to me, 'How on earth did you manage to remain an MP for 43 years?' Since so many lose their seats, often in middle age, for a host of different reasons, it is a question to which there is an obligation to address. Any convincing answer must contain a number of elements.

First, and above all else, was the love, understanding, forbearance and day-to-day grind and hard work of Kathleen herself. She dealt with constituents, who often phoned late at night. She dealt with many, many constituency cases, not least before the introduction of MPs' secretarial allowances. Crucially, she had excellent relations with local authority officers and successive managers of the Ministry of Labour and National Assistance Board's local offices. In the 1960s and '70s, given the nature of West Lothian people, if they had had to deal with a paid secretary they would have muttered: 'What is Tam Dalyell doing about my case?' If Kathleen, as a local, was dealing with their case, it was rather a different matter. The increase in workload and the introduction of allowances mean that case workers as well as secretaries are now often employed by MPs to deal with their constituency cases. Many of my colleagues had very much the same arrangements with their wives as I had and almost all my colleagues would agree their wives played a crucial role in their political life. When our eldest child, Gordon, was three years old, he said to Kathleen, 'I want a new daddy' – in other words, a daddy he saw a good deal more. Fortunate is the MP whose wife is prepared to bring up the children virtually single-handedly. Perhaps most valuable of all, there were a host of occasions when Kathleen's acute political judgement saved my bacon.

Secondly, my parliamentary longevity owes much to the West Lothian Constituency Labour Party (CLP) which was, over the years, politically serious and of generous disposition. Without their choosing and subsequent support, none of us would have got to Westminster in the first place or remained there without our CLPs and local party members. For my part, I never, ever took the CLP or its executive for granted. I was punctilious about attending and reporting back to the monthly Sunday lunchtime meetings. In 43 years, the number of meetings I missed could be counted on the fingers of two hands and on no occasion was it without agreed absence. Whenever I contemplated voting out of line with Labour Party policy, I would give the CLP as much advance warning as possible. Exemplary good manners can help to anaesthetise vengeful political disagreement.

In the 1962 by-election and over eleven subsequent General Elections, I had only four election agents – Councillor Jimmy Boyle and, from 1966, Archie Fairley, followed for one election by Fred Smart and then Archie's son, Brian Fairley. All four had the priceless advantage of being popular with the party and the wider West Lothian community. For Jimmy Boyle, soon to be convener of West Lothian Council, mine host at the Clachan public house on the Main Street of Whitburn and owner of a printing business, I was very much a young candidate on trial. Years later, he told me that he had agreed with Willie Marshall, the secretary of the Scottish Labour Party, that, if I failed to 'do the business of an MP', they would make sure that I would not be their candidate at the 1964 General Election.

A word about Willie Marshall. He was an ascetic Fife miner who had been injured in a pit accident and was one of a species long gone in the Labour Party – John Anson in Yorkshire, Paul Carmody in Lancashire and Cheshire, Jim Cattermole in the East Midlands and Douglas Garnett in East Anglia were others. They were deeply committed (and poorly paid) officials of the party and persons of great influence. Marshall believed in horses for courses and he would steer the CLP choosing candidates in the direction he thought was to the advantage of the Labour Party nationally – a bit different from the later practice of imposing candidates. This Fife ex-miner told me that I was acceptable as a candidate to him because he surmised that the 'occasional' public school candidate would gather votes in marginal constituencies among floating voters whose support was required to give Labour an election victory. It was Willie Marshall and his successors, Peter Allison and Jimmy McGrandle, who all gave an opportunity to a host of future ministers, such as Tom Clarke, Donald Dewar, George Robertson and, significantly, John Smith, to enter the House of Commons. The regional organisers saw their job as fosterers of talent for the sake of the party. My time in politics owes much to the Fairley family, father and son, who acted as my election agent on nine occasions. Archie was a foundry worker who became a full-time official with the General, Municipal and Boilermakers' Union. Brian, meanwhile, worked with the South of Scotland Electricity Board. Both had the knack, invaluable in an election agent, of getting on with potentially prickly people and getting them to do things when the electoral chips were down – and they were unflappable in any of the many crises that an election can throw up.

The relationship between an MP and the chairman of the CLP is crucial. If they are at odds, not only are electoral chances diminished but there can be deleterious effects on the morale and performance of the MP. Time and again, I sensed that the performance of an MP deteriorated and one wondered why. Often the explanation was 'trouble at t'mill' involving prickly relations with a CLP chairman. Sometimes the basic trouble was that the chairman or another officer of the CLP was casting covetous eyes on the MP's job or, more seriously, differences of opinion on the MP's stance on particular policies. I counted myself exceedingly fortunate in the successive chairmen of the West Lothian/Linlithgow CLP who not only became personal friends but had other significant fish to fry in their lives, rather than having time on their hands to plot to undermine me.

My first chairman, Crawford Morgan, the son of a famous Manchester City international winger, was an insurance agent with Liverpool Victoria. I cannot pretend that he enthused when I was chosen as candidate. As he put it later to me, 'From my point of view, the least unsatisfactory of the six on the leet from which you were chosen.' He nevertheless worked extremely hard for me as the Labour candidate and spoke passionately at meetings and on the motorised loudspeaker during every election. His successor as chairman for the decade of the 1970s was Councillor Ronnie O'Byrne. He was a former army Physical Training Instructor (PTI) and had the pugnacity of the successful army boxer he had been. Fortunately for me, his pugnacity was directed towards the Scottish National Party, whose aims he thought were nonsense. He became a process worker at the ICI Dye Stuffs Division of their Grangemouth plant and a shop steward. Well thought of in the Amalgamated Engineering Union (AEU), he was entrusted by them with a pivotal role in their national pension negotiations, bringing him into contact with AEU heavyweights like Bill (later Sir William) Carron, the union's president, (Sir) John Boyd, Salvation Army general secretary of the AEU, Hugh (later Lord) Scanlon, as well as the serious men of the main board of ICI, none of whom saw the advantage of a Scottish Assembly.

It mattered hugely to me to have a supportive chairman of the CLP. On one occasion, when Labour headquarters wanted to pull me into line on devolution, O'Byrne curtly replied, 'Tam Dalyell is ours. If we think he is wrong to defy party policy, we will deal with him.' He consigned further letters to the wastepaper basket. At the 1979 referendum, one senior official, Jimmy Allison, soon to be general secretary of the Scottish Labour Party, blurted out, 'How can I discipline Tam Dalyell when I cannot persuade my mother, a Labour stalwart of many years and my wife, the Labour Provost of Paisley, to vote "yes"?' Attempts to undermine my position petered out. It mattered that his formidable wife, Mrs Bridget O'Byrne, was fiercely against Scotland 'going it alone' and that his brother-in-law, James McWilliams, a qualified medical attendant at the BP plant in Grangemouth, would come out, day after day, accompanying me round doors at election times in harvesting votes. He would say with a chuckle, 'There is no substitute for shoe leather.' This is still my view in the age of Twitter!

My routine during elections was to start knocking on doors at 9.30 a.m. and going on to 12 noon, starting again at 1 p.m. and going on until either an evening meeting or the onset of darkness. I had one or at most three companions. At many homes, it was a question of just saying, 'I'm Tam Dalyell, the Labour candidate – here in case there are any questions you might have about the General Election.' In most cases, the householder would indicate they had no questions, allowing us to move on quickly. Did this alter political opinion? Not significantly, I suspect. However, what it did do was to give a pervasive feeling that 'Tam Dalyell is not taking our votes for granted and, if the man took the trouble to plod round an area, we will bother to take the trouble to go out on polling day'. Overwhelmingly, even those who had no intention whatsoever of voting Labour were friendly. The main problem was that later on in the day, I was frequently invited into homes for a cup of tea – often extremely welcome – which it would have been impolitic to refuse even on the third or fourth occasion. Besides, I enjoyed talking to constituents. The old cliché that elections are a re-invigoration for politicians is profoundly true. I would not be sure that such activity would be the optimum use of a candidate's time in a city constituency but it was a good use of time in the old West Lothian constituency of 20 and more years ago where the electorate was relatively static and a network of family and neighbours had known each other for generations. There were, of course, occasions when the cup of tea and conversation were provided by electors of a different persuasion as a ploy to delay my activities!

When Ronnie O'Byrne gave up the chairmanship on the understandable grounds that his work for the AEU in their negotiations with ICI in Millbank was immersing him in trade union affairs, he was succeeded by the Bathgate solicitor John Teague. He was full of stratagems to discomfort the SNP and did not have a bee in his bonnet – he had an entire hive of bees in his bonnet. But, again, as MP, I was lucky. Teague was a real friend to me over my unyielding pro-European Economic Community stance, when the EEC was the subject of acute and bitter divisions within the Labour Party family. Through the eyes of his wife, Frances, who was of Spanish descent, he knew the Continent well and was a pro-marketeer by conviction. Teague gave up the chairmanship when his one-man solicitor's business was expanding and was succeeded by Hugh Higgins.

Higgins worked at British Leyland in Bathgate and, on promotion, moved elsewhere. While he was chairman, he was a tremendous support during a time of delicate and deep-seated industrial troubles. He was followed by Councillor Donald Stavert, son of a distinguished provost of the papermaking town of Penicuik in Midlothian. With Crawford Morgan, I had been dealing with an older generation brought up by Manny Shinwell,

MP for West Lothian 1922–24 and 1928–31; with O'Byrne and Teague, I had been dealing with comrades of my own generation; but with Stavert, I was dealing with someone 20 years younger. To my surprise and relief, the relationship soon became excellent. Stavert was a hands-on leader of the council and helped to lay the foundations for a situation where, in 2006, West Lothian Council could be chosen as 'UK Council of the Year'. Stavert worked in close harness with the CLP secretary, Bill Gilby, probably as efficiently organised a secretary as any CLP ever had. Both moved to London – Stavert to a full-time post with Lewisham Council and Gilby as personal assistant to Lord Tom Sawyer, and my friend Rodney Bickerstaffe, General Secretary of National Union of Public Employees and later chairman of the Labour Party nationally. Gilby was to hold positions at the epicentre of the Trades Union Congress with his wife, Sheena Cameron, becoming a pioneering London headmistress.

When Stavert left for London, Neil Findlay from Fauldhouse stepped in to replace him. He was 40 years younger than I was. I admired his idealism and the work that he had undertaken for his community in opposing the dumping of toxic waste from all over Scotland on to the nearby moorland. One of the tectonic plates of politics has shifted in that many of those who participate in politics are actually devoting more time and energy to single-issue campaigns. However, in Neil's case, once he was elected a councillor, his campaigning extended over a wide field and not just to his constituents. Neil gave up the chairmanship to concentrate on his studies to qualify as a lecturer. I am delighted that in May 2011 he was elected to the Scottish Parliament.

He was succeeded by Rachel Squire, an NHS trade union official, who had come to Scotland from Birmingham. She was a very able (and extremely nice) lady who, after a short period in office, allowed her name to go forward for the Dunfermline West constituency as a parliamentary candidate. To her surprise, in spite of but maybe because of fierce local rivalries, she was chosen as the Labour candidate. Had it not been for tragic ill health, resulting in her premature death, Rachel would have been a leading member of the Parliamentary Labour Party. The most moving speech that I ever heard Gordon Brown make was, in his capacity as MP for Dunfermline East, his encomium at Rachel's funeral.

Reluctantly, Allister Mackie agreed to step into the breach. Allister was the man who had dared to take on Robert Maxwell on behalf of the print unions. A printer to trade, he was the moving spirit in founding the short-lived but gallant *Scottish Daily News* and resisted pressure from Maxwell, who had threatened to ruin him in the courts. Son of a father and mother who had both been provosts of Kilmarnock, Allister was a superb Burns scholar, president of the Jolly Beggars Burns Club in Bathgate and a really marvellous reciter of the Bard. He was the first chairman with whom I had a deep policy difference of opinion – on devolution. Allister fervently believed in a Scottish Parliament – I didn't. But we were united, not only in personal friendship, but by a support for the Common Market and vehement opposition to Blair's wars. When, in 2001, Blairite operators put out feelers to West Lothian CLP that they hoped I would retire, Allister would have none of it. After a lifetime devoted to the broader Labour movement, Allister tore up his party card in disgust, mainly on account of foreign wars and Prime Minister Blair's treatment of the party. Allister Mackie is a deeply committed, courageous and proud socialist, who believes there is still much that needs to be changed. I respected him for his strongly held views and appreciated his respecting mine and my right to voice them on the matters over which we disagreed.

My last chairman was Tom Conn – as he said, 'not the most appropriate surname for a politician' but a serious official of the Assessor's Office in Edinburgh and 'straight as a die'. Tom somehow kept the party together, both in the period when Labour was heading for defeat and after 2005. Without the likes of Tom Conn, the party would have imploded.

*

Naming individual Labour members is invidious. If the reader feels that I have paraded my supporters in detail, I do not apologise. The simple fact is that, without their selfless help –

particularly, but not only, at election time – I would not have remained a Member of Parliament for 43 years. The scalp that the SNP particularly and understandably coveted above all others was mine. My opponent at seven General Elections was their leader William Wolfe. In October 1974, the SNP were astonished to win seats such as Clackmannan and return 11 MPs. There was consternation that their leader was not to be numbered among the victors, though he did come within 2,690 of doing so.

The fact that they did not win was due to the efforts of members of the West Lothian Constituency Labour Party, who worked their butts off at one or more of the 12 parliamentary elections in West Lothian, and without whose efforts I would not have been sent to the House of Commons or remained there so long. At the risk of being invidious, I name some to demonstrate the broad nature of support, so crucial to a healthy democracy. If I have inadvertently left out any names, I don't know that I can plead age – maybe there were just so many that did so much for me.

ARMADALE

Adjacent to high-grade coking coal, grew with the nineteenth-century foundry industry. It was the Atlas Foundry which provided most of the heavy armour for the dreadnoughts at the Battle of Jutland 1916.

Tony and Jan Clayson; Billy Cunningham; Jack Cunningham; Margaret Dundas; George Ewart; Frank Fagan; Willie Ferrier; Charlie King; Kate McCallum; Stan McKeown; Archie McMillan; Danny Main; Crawford Morgan; Jonathan Rowney; Jessie Sharp; William Watson

BATHGATE

The birthplace of Sir James Young Simpson, who developed anaesthetics and pioneered the use of chloroform. Chosen site for the truck and tractor division of BMC which was to become the biggest concentration of machine tools under one roof in Europe in the 1970s. Already the centre of notable industries: North

British (Balbardie) Steelworks owned and run as a family business by the Menzies family; Telegraph Condenser Company (TCC) which became Plessey employing 1500 women; agricultural centre for the important West Lothian farming community, with its creamery and agricultural machinery.

Peter Bell; James Boyle; Jim and May Brunton; John and Betty Burns; Joe Campbell; Peter Cameron; Harry Cartmill; Nancy Collom; Hugh Dugan; Pat Dugan; Stefan and Betty Haluch; Michael Heron; John King; Charles Mackenzie; Allister and Pat Mackie; Bill McBride; Joe McCann; Peter and Paula McGuire; Mary McIntyre; Ray McLaughlan; Ruth McLaughlin; June McNab; John Marshall; Pat Mulligan; Gerry O'Donnell; Liam O'Donnell; Charles Savage; Ian Scobie; Fred and Heather Smart; Matt and Millie Sommerville; John Teague; Mary Tierney; Adam Walker; Margaret Williamson

BLACKBURN

A traditional coal mining community that expanded to meet the housing needs of the motor industry, it recently became world famous as the hometown of the singer Susan Boyle, who was catapulted to fame by the TV programme Britain's Got Talent. *Her talent was nurtured at social functions in the community where it was the custom for those known to have a good voice to be called upon 'to oblige the company with a song'.*

Willie Connolly; Rob Curran; Bobby Farquhar; Jim Hamilton; Willie Hanlon; Tony and Kate Murphy; John O'Hara; May Rodger; Willie Russell; David Stenhouse; John Wardrop; Hugh Whelan

BLACKRIDGE

A mining and whinstone-quarrying community, it provided a significant element of the solid stone for eighteenth-century Edinburgh New Town.

Jimmy Barras; Sandy and Nessie Currie and family; Willie Drummond; Norman Sinnett

Bo'ness

Lying at the east end of the Antonine Wall, it was the third largest port in Scotland in medieval times, known for its whaling, saltpans, pit props and ship building. This mining, ship-breaking, chandling, pottery and textile-manufacturing community became a home for many who earn their living in the huge adjacent petro-chemical complex at Grangemouth.

John Allison; Ian and Christine Ballantine; Bob Baptie; Diane Barry; Alec Buchanan; Emerson Cook; John Dickson; Bill Gilby; Harry Graham; Mary Greenhorn; Peter Hempstead; Tommy Ledgerwood; George Mackenzie; John Mann; Archie and Jean Meikle; David Paterson; Sandy Phillips; Willie Rodger; George Savage; Charlie and Margaret Sneddon; Willie and Betty Sneddon; Janet Spowart; John and Carol Spowart; Marion Spowart; Eddie Tooey

Bridgend

Along with the contiguous village of Philpstoun, this small shale mining community mainly worked in the nearby Whitequarries shale mine that left the distinctive red shale bings. Much of the material was used as motorway foundation, while some of the bings have been landscaped with trees and shrubs planted on them.

John Christie; Peter and Anne McNee; Ena Murray

Broxburn and Uphall

The centre of the shale oil industry was based here. From the shale high-grade engine oils and by-products, such as industrial wax, were extracted. Historically the area was associated with James 'Paraffin' Young (1822–83) who discovered that the low-temperature distillation of shale yields the maximum amount of paraffin.

Broxburn, over the years, became a centre of diversified industries, ranging from the manufacture of potato crisps and meat products to the heavy electrical engineering industry of Parsons-Peebles and Bell's whisky bottling plant.

Neilly and Martha Boyle; George Brown; Jimmy Coyne; Michael
Coyne; George Crawford; Joe and Pauline Cumming; Alex
Davidson; Joe Dunnigan; John Freeman; Elsie Hamilton; Gavin
Howieson; David and Beatrice Lewis; Jim and Rena Lynch;
Henry and Mamie McCormick; Eddie McKechnie; Graeme
Morrice; Ron Scott; Donald Stavert, Jim Strachan

East Whitburn

This mining community served the Whitrigg Colliery.

Willie McMillan; Alec Sangster; Les and Pat Williams

Fauldhouse

*A close-knit mining community, they were greatly offended when the first pit
closure ordered by Emmanuel Shinwell (MP for Linlithgowshire, as it then
was, 1922–24 and 1928–31), when he became Minister of Mines in 1947,
was the Fauldhouse pit. The highest village in the county, it gets the worst of
the weather but it was chosen by the Forestry Commission for one of their
major planting programmes.*

Ellen Barclay; Mary Boyle; John and Agnes Cairns; Geraldine
Drysdale; Bob Heaney; Robert and Nula Lee; Tommy and Jessie
Lee; Maurice O'Donnell; Frank Owen; Neil Scott; Annie Som-
merville; Pat Thomas; Peter Walker

Kirkliston

*The home of a distillery and malt producer, as well as the renowned Drambuie
plant., it was historically dubbed 'Cheesetown' because it provided lodgings for
many of the workers who built the Forth Railway Bridge and they would take
quantities of cheese each day to sustain them during an uninterruptible 10-hour
shift work on the bridge. In recent years, Kirkliston has become a dormitory
town for Edinburgh.*

Denis Chiappa; Alan Knowles; Jimmy Todd

LINLITHGOW

Historically Linlithgowshire's county town, it was the birthplace of Mary Queen of Scots. Lying halfway between the great castles of Edinburgh and Stirling, Scots monarchs and their courts would hastily decamp to Linlithgow in times of disease or when general filth required the 'airing of the palaces'. Its air and water were good and much valued and the town had many wells which are still commemorated in its street names.

Linlithgow has benefited from being one of three major stops on the Edinburgh–Glasgow railway line and, by 2020, its population had reached 15,000. It is one of the centres for the important farming community in West Lothian.

Jimmy and Willie Alexander; John Barton; Ian Grant; Simon Mason; Alex Merker; Irving and Mary Nichol; Sanny and Susie Provan; Douglas Roxburgh; Sydney and Hetty Smyth; Jim and Helen Spankie; Bill and Maggie Stuart

LIVINGSTON STATION

Originally, the village that grew up around the station which was built in 1849 and ceased to operate in 1948. Formerly, it was a shale-mining community. Later, it was the village around which the New Town of Livingston, the biggest of Scotland's New Towns was established in the 1960s. The New Town of Livingston was built on excellent farmland, partly because the attractiveness of the site would bring high-profile industries but mainly because of its location in the centre of Lowland Scotland which had been a thoroughfare for centuries. The Antonine Wall, seen as a barrier, also provided communication along its length – the Union Canal; the railway; the M8 and the M9; and the airport at Turnhouse.

Bob Dowds; Peter Easton; Joe Forsythe; John Hart; David Jarman; Hugh Owens; Willie Pender; Maureen Ryce; Les Stirling

SOUTH QUEENSFERRY

The town sits at the south ends of the Forth Road Bridge and that marvel of nineteenth-century engineering, Sir William Arrol's Forth Railway Bridge with its three cantilevers. It has been the traditional crossing point of the Firth of Forth since time immemorial. Until 1964, ferries set out from a pier opposite the Hawes Inn immortalised by Robert Louis Stevenson. South Queensferry was chosen in 1962 by Bill Hewlett and David Packard as the location of the largest Hewlett Packard manufacturing unit in Europe.

John Armstrong; Jimmy Bonnar; 'Granny' Morton; Bill Nelson; Richard Perry; Walter and Kathleen Stone; Paul Taylor; Gordon Thomson

STONEYBURN

A village surrounded by dairy farming, this mining community was involved in both coal on the north side and shale on the south side.

Agnes Cherry; Tina Haggerty; Michael Hart; Norrie Munro

WHITBURN

This is the site of the shaft of the Polkemmet Colliery, the second largest in Scotland, which provided the bulk of the coal used by the Ravenscraig steel complex at Motherwell. Large numbers of women worked at the Levi Strauss jeans factory from the 1960s until the 1990s. The community provided a successful outcome for the experiment of grafting Glasgow overspill on to an existing community. It boasts an outstanding prize-winning brass band.

Helen Beck; Alec and Nancy Bell; John Boyle; Willie Docherty; Arche Fairley; Elizabeth Fairley; Brian Fairley; Lawrence Fitzpatrick; Michael Fitzpatrick; Danny Flannigan; Mary Flannigan; Bert Gamble; Willie Griffiths; Hugh Higgins; Carol Houghton; Jim Jolly; Janet Kelly; Robert McCarron; Pat McLaughlan; George Paul; Bill Schroeder; Jim and Christine Swan; Paul Telfer; Martin Tierney

Winchburgh

This had been an ancient settlement for over a thousand years before becoming a Shale mining community. It is surrounded by distinctive red shale bings.

Bill Cannon; Tommy Devlin; John Finnegan; Bill Hadden; Bob McLean; James McWilliams; Stewart McWilliams; Tony and Norma Murphy; Ron O'Byrne; Ronnie and Bridgie O'Byrne

Index